An Affair of Chances

Ian McGeoch

An Affair of Chances

A Submariner's Odyssey 1939–44

Imperial War Museum

Published by the Imperial War Museum, Lambeth Road, London SE1 6HZ

Copyright © Ian McGeoch 1991

Foreword © Lord Lewin 1991

Preface © Trustees of the Imperial War Museum 1991

Dust jacket illustration by Jeremy Sancha

Designed by Herbert Spencer

Printed and bound in Great Britain by Butler & Tanner Ltd, Frome and London

Distributed by Leo Cooper (Pen & Sword Books Limited)
through Airlife Publications Limited, 101 Longden Road, Shrewsbury S73 9EB

Photographs: Wright and Logan, 41; R Bannar-Martin, 67; Royal Navy Submarine Museum, 110; Bibliothek für Zeitgeschichte, 111; E Luff, 161; Weidenfeld and Nicolson Ltd, 167; G Dodrumez, 187; H Bigou, 191, 198; C Villalongue, 194, 196, 198.

Extracts from *Periscope View* by G W G Simpson and *Mariners* by James Casing by permission of Macmillan Publishers Ltd; from *Ultra and Mediterranean Strategy* by Ralph Bennett by permission of Hamish Hamilton Ltd; from *The War at Sea* by Stephen Roskill by permission of the Controller of Her Majesty's Stationery Office; from *The Second World War* by Winston Churchill by permission of Curtis Brown Ltd on behalf of the Estate of Sir Winston Churchill, © Winston S Churchill; and from *Seedie's List of Submarine Awards for World War II* by permission of Ripley Registers.

Maps by Julia Mills

Frontispiece: The author in 1938

British Library Cataloguing in Publication Data
McGeoch, Ian 1914–
    An affair of chances: a submariner's odyssey, 1939–44.
    1. Great Britain. World War 2, Naval operations
    I. Title
    940.548141

ISBN 0 901627 66 6

Contents

In memory of those who did not grow old

Foreword

As an erstwhile destroyer man I have always had the greatest admiration and respect for submariners. Operating as they do in craft that are designed to sink, albeit in a controlled manner, they demand and achieve a degree of professional competence from all hands seldom reached in the surface ships of the Royal Navy.

When Ian McGeoch was commanding HMS *Splendid* in the Mediterranean, patrolling to intercept the Axis supply convoys to North Africa, I was serving in a destroyer with the same mission. The difference in our experiences is profound. While we slipped out of our forward base to catch the enemy at night and were often back in harbour at dawn before the Luftwaffe was active, the submarines patrolled for weeks at a time, playing the waiting game in conditions that favoured the submarine hunters. But whereas, at that time, our success rate was meagre, throughout the whole of the war in the Mediterranean our submarines made a major contribution to the Allied armies' ultimate victory in North Africa by strangling the enemy's supply line – but at a price.

The *Splendid*'s five patrols before being sunk were probably about par for the course in the Med – forty of our submarines were lost in this theatre. Ian McGeoch was unlucky to meet an efficient and experienced German destoyer. You have to be alert when reading this modestly written account to discover that in this period at the turn of 1942–43 the *Splendid* was highly successful, sinking more tanker and supply ship tonnage than any other submarine. The heavy responsibility borne by the submarine captain emerges clearly as does the character of this particular commander. It took great moral courage to take the decision to abandon ship and thus save the lives of the majority of his crew, it required a special sense of purpose to have escape as his own personal first priority and it required great determination to pursue this aim to its final realisation.

This book is an exciting excerpt from the long career of a distinguished officer highly regarded for his thoughtful contribution to the profession of naval warfare. I very much hope there is more to come.

Terence Lewin

Admiral of the Fleet

Preface

It is a particular pleasure to write the preface to this, the eleventh volume in our series of personal reminiscences, because the author is an old friend of the Imperial War Museum and indeed served as a Trustee from 1977 to 1987. Anyone who knows Ian McGeoch will not, I think, be too surprised by the story he tells here, for his resilient and resourceful character is still apparent beneath his natural wit and charm. It is nonetheless a very remarkable story, reminding us once again that many who displayed courage in the face of battle during the Second World War went on to demonstrate amazing fortitude in captivity and extraordinary initiative in escape. There is no doubt that this account will take its place as one of the classic escape stories from the Second World War.

Although we can only publish a few of the first-hand accounts we receive, the Museum's Department of Documents exists to collect and preserve personal narratives, letters, diaries, and private papers relating to war and conflict in the twentieth century. It is a large collection, much used by scholars and researchers from all over the world, and we are always keen to add to it. I hope that readers of this book will be encouraged to think of the Imperial War Museum as the appropriate home for their own family archive of wartime material. We will always be pleased to hear from you.

The production of these volumes is the result of much hard work by our tried and tested team of Mrs Jan Mihell and Dr Christopher Dowling. It is the sixth volume in this series on which they have both worked, although Dr Dowling has worked on all eleven. This is a rare achievement and the Museum stands in their debt.

Alan Borg, Director General   January 1991
Imperial War Museum

Author's Note

It is fair to ask first why this book has been written, let alone published; and secondly, why it should appear only now, half a century after the events which it describes took place. As to the first question many people, over the years, on hearing some part of the story have asked to be told the whole of it; but the age has long since gone when households spent the winter evenings grouped round the fireside listening to sagas being recounted by an elder. If the tale were to be passed on, in these days, it had to be made into a book, or even a TV script. Settling for the former, the next question was when?

By 1970, when I retired from active service in the Royal Navy, I had been encouraged by Mr Derek Priestley, then managing director of Peter Davies Ltd, to put on paper my experiences in the world war which was by then receding, ever more rapidly as it seemed, into the distant past. So I began to assemble the material – the letters, photographs, my official reports of war patrols, documents relating to my escape after being a prisoner of war – stimulated by periodical reunions with survivors of the submarine crew which I had had the honour and good fortune to command. I had already, with my wife and three of our children, visited at their homes in France those members of the Resistance who had risked certain imprisonment and quite possibly torture and execution by affording me shelter and guidance during my journey across occupied France.

During the early post-war years, also, I had been able to meet most of the people whom I mention in this book as key players in my submarine patrols or escape from Italy. Every one of them had a story to tell that would have made a riveting book in itself. In September 1943 both Ken Burridge and Tom Roworth had managed to evade the German roundup of Allied POWs and regain their freedom, Ken finding his way down through Italy to the Allied lines, and Tom taking sanctuary in the Vatican; within a few months Ken was serving once again in a submarine while Tom was fighting with the Italian partisans. Robert Balkwill, despite an injured pelvis, succeeded twice in escaping but was recaptured and ended the war in a POW camp in Germany. This was the fate of Gordon Hardy and Eddie Luff, also. Having reached the Pyrenees with the aid of the Resistance, their party was ambushed by a German patrol and they were recaptured. Maurice de Milleville, who was with the same group, was lucky enough to slip through the net into Spain and freedom.

Of the ratings who survived from the submarine all were finally held in German POW camps although one or two were on the run for a bit at various times. Tragically, our most efficient and respected Chief Petty Officer torpedoman, Sam Dixon, was killed in a strafing raid by Allied Mustangs near Halberstadt while being transported from one POW camp to another; and in 1954 Meg Todd-Naylor, having been appointed MBE for her selfless welfare work in Geneva, died in a road accident there – a grievous loss to the British community as well as personally to me.

For more than ten years after my retirement I was not single-minded enough to write a book. I believed that the advent of nuclear weapons had rendered indispensable the continued application of philosophical rigour and scientific method to strategic studies and operations analysis. Hence I engaged in academic work on various aspects of national security, first at Edinburgh University under the supervision of Professor John Erickson, and then independently. I found myself, also, editing *The Naval Review* and after that, *Naval Forces*, activities which were as time-consuming as they were congenial. But in 1977 I had the good fortune to be appointed a Trustee of the Imperial War Museum. When in due course I sought the support of its Director General, Dr Alan Borg, and his staff for my book project this was generously given and the Museum became my publisher.

It was not an ideal grounding for authorship in the public domain to have joined at the age of eighteen what was still known as 'the Silent Service'. Nor did training as a staff officer, whose métier demands accuracy, brevity and clarity above all, conduce to the development of a lively, colourful, open literary style, but rather to that 'taut and nervous prose' for which Sir Arthur Conan Doyle praised *Bradshaw's Railway Guide*. Sensible of this problem I wrote for all that I was worth. Whoever said that 'old men forget'? My recall seemed to be total. When, therefore, to paraphrase one Irishman writing of another, I 'marched on the Imperial War Museum at the head of 130,000 words', my editors faced a tough task. Dr Christopher Dowling and Mrs Jan

Mihell stood proxy, to change the metaphor, for the 'divinity that shapes our ends, rough hew them how we will'. With diligence and tact they have pruned reminiscence where it trailed into irrelevance and reflection where it slowed the pace, while eliminating as far as possible the infelicities of expression to which a prentice hand is prone. To them and to all who have helped to produce this book may I here record my warmest thanks, as also to Robert Balkwill, Rawdon Bannar-Martin, Frank Macvie and my brother A J McGeoch for their constructive comments on my drafts.

I wish to acknowledge, also, with grateful thanks the help given me by Commander Richard Compton-Hall and Mr Gus Britton of the Royal Navy Submarine Museum; and Mr R M Coppock of the Ministry of Defence, Foreign Documents Section.

Finally, may I make honourable mention of my wife, our children and grandchildren who, with other well-wishers, have continued hopefully to enquire when my book was going to appear, and give them all the answer – here it is!

' … consider the vast influence of accident in war, before you are engaged in it. As it continues, it generally becomes an affair of chances, chances from which neither side is exempt, and whose event we must risk in the dark.'

Thucydides, *The Peloponnesian War*

Prologue

'Captain in the control room!'

The voice of the control room messenger penetrated my consciousness as I lay, fully clothed, on my bunk next to the gangway. In a moment or two I was standing by the chart table hearing the officer of the watch's report.

'Turbine HE,[1] sir, bearing zero-eight-zero. I can't see anything on the bearing yet. It's up-sun and the sun's still pretty low.' I considered the situation. The time was soon after 8.00 am on 21 April 1943. I had dived HM Submarine *Splendid* at first light about two hours previously and set course at slowest speed – so as to conserve battery power – towards the southern entrance to the Bay of Naples, called the Bocca Piccolo.

'HE increasing and drawing slowly left.' The voice of the asdic operator had taken on a slight edge. I stationed myself at the attack periscope. The drill was automatic – always take a quick all-round look in low power with the attack periscope before raising the much more conspicuous but higher powered search periscope.

'Up periscope!'

The watchkeeper moved the appropriate lever and with a quiet sighing hiss the long brass tube came quickly up from its housing. I crouched, ready to grab the handles as the eyepiece came level.

'Thirty feet, sir,' said the officer of the watch.

'Thank you, Robert. Keep that.'

I flipped the handles down. With about three feet to go I motioned to the panel watchkeeper. He stopped the periscope while I aligned it so as to be looking along the bearing of the HE when the top glass broke the surface.

It was dark in the control room. Electric bulbs not only use precious

---

[1] Hydrophone Effect – the noise made by the revolving propellers of a ship received as sound travelling through the water.

battery power but generate heat. Eyes fully adapted could read depth-gauges, compass and attack instruments illuminated by shielded lights; the 'blowing panel', with its vertical banks of levers and wheel valves, and the chart table with its automatic course-plotter, also had their own carefully shielded lighting. The air was dank and smelt of diesel oil. It was slightly chilly. In April the Tyrrhenian Sea was still cold.

'Up!'

Stoker Dinsdale knew his stuff. Gently he raised the periscope further. I straightened up with it, eyes glued to the unyielding eyepieces, seeing at first nothing, then a lightening of nothing. Suddenly, strong sunlight filled the field of view.

'Well!'[1] I said, and the rising periscope was instantly stopped while I swung it swiftly round, scanning the bright blue, barely-ruffled Mediterranean. There was nothing in sight. As I completed the 360 degree 'look' I flipped up the periscope handles.

'Down!'

I moved forward and stood by the search periscope, thinking. The visibility was good. Asdic[2] conditions must also be good to enable the target to be heard when it was still hull down. Of course, if it was a U-boat it could be within three or four miles. But the HE was turbine, not diesel, so it wasn't a U-boat.

'HE increasing ... bearing Green three-zero,' came the next report from the asdic office.

'Up! Twenty-eight feet please, Robert.'

As the big periscope rose I slewed it round to my right and, looking up at the graduated bearing ring, set the index line on the periscope tube at Green[3] 30 degrees. Vic Davis, the control room artificer, was wiping surplus grease off the index line with cotton waste and examining it with a torch. I glanced at the big round 100-foot depth-gauges at which the planesmen were gazing intently. The needles showed 28 feet.

'Up!'

Dinsdale eased the periscope up until abruptly its top glass broke through the surface. Again the bright daylight in my eyes contrasted with the dimness of the control room.

'Well!'

The periscope stopped. I was standing fully upright now. At 28 feet on the depth gauge there would be four feet of the high-power periscope

---

[1] Seaman's term for 'stop' (hauling and veering).
[2] Asdic was the acoustic detection device now called sonar.
[3] Green for starboard side.

above the surface of the sea; and even at our slow speed – about two and a half knots – there would be a feather of disturbed water. In the near-calm conditions prevailing that day an alert lookout with good binoculars might sight this periscope at a range of two or three miles. I suppose that I looked on the bearing for a few seconds only.

'Down!' I snapped up the handles. 'Diving stations! It's a destroyer, Robert.'

'Diving stations!' The order was rapidly passed. Officers and men came quickly and quietly into the control room, taking over from the watch keepers as necessary. Robert Balkwill, who was the first lieutenant, was already at his station having been officer of the watch. 'Buster' Burridge, the torpedo officer, was now at the 'fruit machine' – the somewhat complex-looking torpedo fire-control instrument. At the chart table was Gordon Hardy, the navigator, busying himself with one of the special attack-plotting diagrams which Chatham Dockyard's drawing office had produced for me. 'Good-time Charlie' Laidlaw, our recently joined engineer officer, stood at the after end of the control room. It was 8.25, less than two minutes since I had ordered diving stations.

'Stand by to start the attack.' I was at the search periscope again.

'Up!' This time I set the bearing on Green 25 degrees.

'Ship's head?'

'Zero-five-zero, sir,' from the helmsman.

I brought the periscope round a degree or two until the hairline cut through the middle of the enemy destroyer.

'The bearing is ... that! Start the attack!'

'Down!'

'Bearing Green two-eight,' intoned the control room artificer as the periscope came down.

'I'm fifteen degrees on his port bow, Buster. What's his course?'

'Two-six-three, sir.'

'HE increasing, sir, two hundred revs,' from the asdic office – a different voice now. Petty Officer South, the expert, had taken over.

'Give him twenty knots, Buster. Bring One, Two, Three and Four Tubes to the ready – depth setting eight feet. Where are we, Pilot?' I moved over to the chart table and looked at the chart. The submarine's track had been neatly plotted. Cross-bearings of the island of Capri and the mainland at Point Campanella had fixed our position at 8.00 am six miles south of the Bocca Piccolo.

I now had all the data I needed for carrying out the attack, with one exception. It was good practice to plot the movements of the target as accurately as possible, in the first place as a check on the asdic operator's propeller revolution count and, secondly, because one's estimate of the speed of an enemy vessel by 'revs per minute of the propellers per knot of speed' could well be wrong. But, in order to develop a valid plot quickly, as least one reliable target range was essential. To obtain this, the height above the waterline of some clearly visible part of the target had to be set on the periscope – masthead height was best, otherwise the funnel tops. This could be gauged if one knew the type of ship one was attacking, even if not its actual identity. Large destroyers tended to be about 90 feet from masthead to waterline.

I remained by the search periscope. My mind, totally concentrated on the attack, was working fast, taking in data continuously and processing it according to knowledge and experience. During our previous five war patrols we had been in action many times, often successfully. Despite having been depth-charged after some of our attacks we had suffered no damage. My sole concern was always to find worthwhile targets. Our army, now supported by the Americans, was fighting desperately to clear the Axis forces out of North Africa. Our job was to cut off their supplies. They were using destroyers both as convoy escorts and for rushing troops and fuel across. I must therefore sink the one now coming into range – provided I could approach within a mile of her. The proviso was vital. We knew that the air-driven torpedoes with which we were armed left a highly visible bubble track on the surface. This could be seen as much as a mile away in a calm sea, giving time for the target to 'comb the tracks' by turning either towards or away and thus avoid the torpedoes. All this was in my mind as I stood by the periscope. It was four minutes since the previous 'look'.

'Up!'

This time, before the periscope was fully raised, I set 48 feet on the rangefinder (the waterline to top of funnel height of a typical British destroyer).

'HE still increasing ... bearing Green two-zero.' Petty Officer South's voice was confident.

I set the periscope on that bearing and signalled with my hand to raise it further. The brightness of the sun made it hard to discern the target. But in a moment or two I had it clearly in the middle of my field of view. By turning the rangefinder knob I brought the funnel tops down to the waterline.

'Range is ... that!' I waited a second or two while Vic Davis, using his torch, read off the scale and reported the result loudly, so that

Buster Burridge could hear and apply it on his fruit machine.

'Down!' I ordered. 'Port twenty. Thirty feet. Half ahead starboard, slow ahead port.'

The orders were repeated back.

'One to Four Tubes ready, sir. Depth set eight feet.'

'Very good. Course for a hundred track?[1] What's the range?' I looked over Buster's shoulder at the situation display on the fruit machine. It seemed straightforward enough. 'If she's outside a mile I won't fire,' I said.

'Course for a hundred track zero-zero-three, sir. Range three thousand three hundred.'

'Steady on north. Slow ahead together.'

'What's the DA,[2] Sub? How far off track am I?'

'DA fifteen, sir, three thousand one hundred.' This was young Burridge's third patrol with us. Straight from training class, he was doing well.

'What d'you make target speed, Gordon?'

'Eighteen knots, sir.' The navigator was good too. The tense silence in the control room was broken only by the faint clicking of the helmsman's gyrocompass repeater.

'That range I took may have been wrong. It's definitely not a *Navigatori* although she's got two funnels. She looks just like one of ours – any of the 'A' to 'I' classes. Camouflaged. Probably built in Britain for the Yugoslavs – there were one or two produced by Yarrow and Thorneycroft for export. No doubt the Italians took this one over when they invaded ... keep twenty knots set, Sub.'

'Course north, sir,' from the helmsman.

'Very good.'

I stepped to the attack periscope and motioned for it to be raised. As it came up I looked at the clock.

It was 8.38 am. Thirteen minutes since I started the attack. At 20 knots the target would have covered just over 8,000 yards. She could be less than 3,000 yards away now. I must be very careful with the periscope.

'Thirty feet, sir.'

'Up slowly.' As I gripped the handles and lined up the periscope I could hear Petty Officer South calling out, 'HE loud and increasing.' The top glass of the 'stick' broke surface and my eyes took in the

---

[1] The torpedo approach angle most difficult for the target to avoid, being 100 degrees from its course.
[2] Director Angle. The amount to 'aim off' ahead of the target.

brightness. All was clear on the bearing. But as I swung quickly round there came into view the most chilling and horrifying sight which a submarine captain can ever see – the sharp bow and high, glistening-white bow wave of a hostile destroyer coming straight towards him at close range.

'Down! Flood Q! Full ahead together! Ninety feet! Damn! Damn! Damn! Must have seen the periscope.' The boat took up a steep bow-down angle as Q tank (used only for going deep in an emergency) flooded.

'Stop flooding Q.' Robert, as first lieutenant, was in charge of the trim of the submarine. 'Stand by to blow Q ... Blow Q,' he ordered. Vic Davis at the blowing panel opened up the compressed air. Robert had judged it nicely. The coxswain on the after planes and the second coxswain on the fore planes had no difficulty in levelling the boat off with 90 feet on the gauges.

'Slow ahead together. Vent Q inboard.' It was my decision whether or not to let the compressed air with which Q tank was now filled vent itself back into the submarine or alternatively to vent it outboard, which inevitably resulted in a huge air bubble rushing to the surface of the sea and confirming our presence to the foe. The penalty for venting inboard was a prolonged deafening blast accompanied by a pressure on the ear drums as the high-pressure air escaped through the open valve into the boat. Shouting to be heard, I ordered, 'Shut bowcaps! Shut off for depth-charging! Starboard twenty!' Mercifully the screech from Q vent soon ceased.

'HE very loud. Bearing steady.' Petty Officer South's voice was urgent. It was just three minutes since that last brief look through the low power periscope.

SwishswishswishswishSWISHSWISHSWISHSWISHswishswish ...

Everyone could hear the fast revving propellers of the angry destroyer passing over us. Forty-eight men cooped up in a steel tube 90 feet below the surface held their breath and waited – was this going to be it? The seconds hand on the control room clock circled steadily. The more imaginative of us visualised the depth-charges tumbling down through the water above.

Then came the explosions.

Thrum-m-p! ... thrump-m-p! ... thrump-m-p! The boat shivered a little, dust and small flakes of paint flew out here and there. I looked at Robert and he caught my eye as we waited for the next one. A destroyer's depth-charge pattern could be as many as ten ... Thrump-m-p! Not so near this time. Not ten, but fifteen charges went off around us in that first attack. We were very lucky to get away with it.

I realised that the boat was still swinging to starboard.

'Ship's head?' I asked.

'One-seven-five and still swinging, sir.'

'Steady on two-three-zero.'

'Steady on two-three-zero, sir,' came the helmsman's calm repeat.

I had instinctively selected the course to steer. It was the reverse of our approach course towards the Bocca Piccolo. This would ensure keeping in deep water, with plenty of sea-room and less chance of running into a defensive minefield. All was quiet again in the control room.

'We'd better go deep, Robert,' I said. 'Make it three hundred feet.'

'Three hundred feet, coxswain,' said Robert.

'Shut off shallow gauges.'

I went over to the chart table.

'Well, Pilot, that's blown it. We'll have to get the hell out of this area till the dust settles. Just what I did *not* want to happen – alerting the locals before we've had a decent target. It would have been useless firing at that bloody destroyer outside a mile – he'd have seen the tracks for sure. What's the depth here?'

Gordon lifted the attack diagram and we pored over the navigation chart.

'I make us here, sir. That's just over five hundred fathom.'

'Right. We may have to dodge a bit. But I'll try to keep south-westerly.'

I moved back into the middle of the control room. Robert was gazing intently at the deep-diving gauge between the planesmen. Its luminous scale was marked down to 500 feet. The needle was still creeping round – 240, 250, 260, 270 . . .

'I'm afraid he'll hear that ballast pump,' said Robert, 'but it can't be helped.' The swishswishswish of the destroyer's propellers had died away.

'He's transmitting on asdic, sir,' came the somewhat strained voice of Petty Officer South in the asdic cabinet. 'He seems to be searching. He may have lost contact. I'm having trouble training our set, sir. That depth-charge – the one that was near – must've done it in.'

'Slow right down as soon as you can, Robert. He's probably pinging on the mush left by the depth-charge. Any sign of a layer?'[1]

'No, sir,' said Robert. The gauge was now hovering around 300

---

[1] A layer of sea water of differing density and temperature can help a submarine to avoid detection by sonar.

feet. 'But I'll try to hold her at slow one. Stop starboard.'

As the order was repeated back there came to our ears the short regular metallic 'ping ... ping ... ping' of the enemy destroyer's asdic as it probed the depths, seeking the echoing 'pings' which would indicate that the target had been located. This was no time to reflect upon the sudden change of fortune, the drama being enacted when the hunter became, in an instant of unwisdom exploited by trained alertness, the hunted. But what had become all too clear to me was that we were up against it. The warship above was being well handled. We were only a few miles from the crucially important naval base and shipping port of Naples. The single destroyer would soon, no doubt, be reinforced by additional anti-submarine forces, including aircraft.

Worse still, it was as yet early in the day. It would be ten hours or more before darkness might enable us, with luck, to come cautiously to the surface and sneak away, as we had done several times before. A submarine is, above all, a weapon of surprise. To disclose its position by carrying out a successful attack is the risk it must always be prepared to take. To be detected following an abortive attack is disheartening, and may be fatal. But to have been located as the *Splendid* had been – when I had already decided not to attack – was an unmitigated setback.

Ping ... swishswishswish ... ping ... swishswishswish ... ping ... swishswishswish.

He had got us. Another pattern of depth-charges was no doubt on its way – but to be lethal it would have had to be fired soon enough to allow for our movement through the water during the time taken by the charges to reach our depth, and they would have to be set to explode at that depth or very near it.

Thrum-m-p! It seemed to be further away than the last lot.

Thrum-m-p! Then thirteen more.

As the sound of the destroyer's propellers died away there were smiles in the control room. Someone wisecracked *sotto voce*, 'It seems to be clearing up. Anyone for tennis?' The engineer officer returned from a tour of inspection.

'Any damage, Chief?' I asked.

'All right so far, sir. Except for the asdic set. It's still u/s.'

'The asdic conditions are so good it doesn't seem to matter. We can hear his bloody props and his bloody pingings quite well enough without it.'

On such occasions in the past, the enemy had been a good deal less persistent. Usually, within half an hour or so of our going 'deep and quiet', the opposition had given up. Somehow this time it was different.

Ping … ping … ping …

'He seems to be in contact again, sir,' said Petty Officer South calmly. I thought so too. Fortunately Robert had got the boat well-trimmed. We were in 'silent routine', proceeding at slow revolutions on the port shaft only. There was no option but to await the next attack and hope that, once again, it would be wide of the mark. To have 'grouped up' the submarine's batteries and set off at high speed would have been useless. The noise of our propellers would have confirmed beyond doubt the enemy's asdic detection, without enabling us to move out of range of a vessel which could hold contact with us no matter how fast we were to go. True, high speed would allow us to manoeuvre sharply in an attempt to throw off the enemy's aim. But against that was the overriding need to conserve battery power. After all, it was just possible that the destroyer might run out of depth-charges, and so far we had not heard any other vessel joining the hunt. However, such musings were soon cut short.

Ping … swishswishswish … ping … swishswish … ping … swish-swishswish …

He was coming in again. Something about the combination of asdic and propeller beat worried me. I sensed, I think, that the destroyer was not only in contact but coming straight towards us. My reaction was sharp.

'Hold your hats on! Full ahead together! Starboard thirty! We'll try to get out from under this lot.'

Thrum-m-p! … Thrum-m-p! … Thrum-m-p! … Thrum-m-p! … Thrum-m-p! … It was as if a gigantic sea-terrier had grabbed the submarine by the scruff of the neck and shaken it with intent to kill. The boat whipped as if it were made of flesh and blood rather than the toughest steel. Surprisingly, not all the lights went out – probably owing to their flexible mountings. But as the last of the dozen or more depth-charges exploded – further away – the submarine's stern went down. In the control room everyone grabbed what came to hand and held on. From aft in the engine room came the clattering of steel plates as the walkways between the diesels slipped into the bilge. I looked at the 500 foot depth gauge. Already the needle had passed 450 feet. With an angle of 20 degrees or more the stern must already be well below 500 feet. Reports from aft were of flooding and fire in the motor room. The one remaining shaft was already turning full ahead. The sea bottom was 3,000 feet below. The needle on the depth gauge came up against the stop. There was now no quick way of telling what depth the sinking submarine had reached. I knew that at 600 feet or so the hull would inevitably be crushed in by the pressure, which would then exceed twenty atmospheres. I had to get the boat up at once.

'Blow all main ballast!'

Vic Davis opened up the valves with lightning speed. Luckily, all the compressed air bottles were fully charged as we had not used any, other than the small amount needed to blow Q tank, since diving early in the morning. But there was no means of knowing what effect, if any, the blowing was having. The steep angle down by the stern remained. Again, forty-eight men cooped up in a steel tube held their breath – and waited. I do not recall that my past life flashed through my mind, but I do remember fear. I have little doubt that all of us during those crucial seconds felt the boat struggling to survive and experienced fear and the imminence of death. Suddenly the needle on the 500 foot gauge flicked off the stop and began to register. I had no hesitation in deciding what had to be done.

'Stand by to abandon ship.'

Men moved in an orderly fashion, some taking life-belts and putting them on. In the control room Bob Auckland, our signalman, who always followed me up the conning tower to the bridge on surfacing, stood by as best he could to bring the conning tower ladder down from its stowage and open the lower hatch into the tower. The coxswain, who had already reported the after planes jammed at 'hard-a-rise', and the second coxswain, eyes glued to the 500 foot gauge, were ready to open and vent their 100 foot gauges.

But things were happening much too quickly. The massive volume of compressed air blown into the main ballast tanks had eventually overcome the enormous sea pressure and driven some of the water out. The boat came up at an ever-increasing pace as more and more water was forced from the tanks until suddenly she levelled off with a mighty thump and I knew that we were on the surface. Indeed, the thousand-ton submarine must have leapt out of the water like a salmon.

In moments of crisis one acts according to notions formed before-hand. I had several times expressed to people in the boat my firm opinion that whereas HM submarines were, in the last analysis, expendable, their crews were not. To have delayed even momentarily giving the order to abandon ship would have unnecessarily imperilled my crew. In view of the damage sustained aft, with one motor out of action and no telemotor (hydraulic) pressure available to operate the hydroplanes and vent valves, it would have been impossible to regain control of the submarine. Furthermore, having come to the surface unable to manoeuvre, we were at risk of being rammed by the enemy destroyer. There was nothing for it.

'Abandon ship!' I ordered.

At once ready hands opened the lower conning tower hatch and the gun tower hatch in the wardroom. Men disappeared up the ladder. I found myself standing alone in the control room with Robert. Next to getting the crew out, what was burning in my mind was to make absolutely certain that the boat would disappear forever below the surface before the enemy could board and capture it. The rate at which water was coming in through the damaged after hatch, while potentially lethal with the sea-pressure at 300 feet or more, would be readily controllable at or near the surface.

'Come on Robert, we'll have to open main vents by hand.'

That done, I followed Robert up the ladder into the conning tower. As I climbed a body fell down past me. Then I was on the bridge. Standing, dazed for a moment by the brightness and looking out from between the periscope standards, I saw the enemy destroyer. She was lying stopped or nearly so, still firing with main and secondary armament. She was less than a mile away, beam on, and there could be no question about her British build. As to her present ownership, flying at her gaff was the unmistakable naval ensign of the German Reich. This was a complete shock. In none of the intelligence reports which I had seen was there any mention of a German destroyer operating against us in these waters, let alone an ex-British one.

Satisfied that I was the last to leave the *Splendid* I went over the side and joined Robert Balkwill in the sea. As the boat was still moving ahead, the rest of the crew were already some distance away, in two or three groups.

'We might as well make for Capri,' said Robert as we trod water.

'Why not, it's only about four miles,' I replied. 'I've always wanted to go there ... Do you realise that that bloody destroyer's a kraut, by the way?'

'No wonder he was so bloody good,' said Robert.

We were wearing only shorts and shirts, and had kicked off the sandals we often wore at sea. In a minute or two the destroyer ceased fire and began to pick up the survivors. There was time to begin the mental process of adjustment to the new situation. Undoubtedly one was in a state of shock – physical, emotional and psychological.

Neither of us was seriously wounded (I had in fact received a tiny shell splinter in my right eye, but was not yet aware of it) and we did not realise that the destroyer's gunfire had killed or mortally wounded many of our crew as they emerged from the submarine and jumped into the water, as well as injuring several who managed to stay afloat, helping each other until picked up. Out of the forty-eight of us in the submarine, eighteen did not survive her destruction.

Emotionally, my overriding feeling as we began to swim slowly towards Capri was one of fury mixed with chagrin and self-criticism. Why had our intelligence failed to alert me that I might encounter a British-built destroyer operating under German colours? Such a combination was both confusing and formidable. Trying to identify the vessel had been my downfall. In the adverse conditions prevailing I ought not to have taken the risk of tangling with her but made certain of remaining undetected until the hoped-for southbound convoy appeared. These were disturbing thoughts. But to counter them ran a strong undercurrent of relief at being alive.

1 · 'Pilot', 'Jimmy' and 'Perisher'

When war came on 3 September 1939 I was a junior lieutenant, Royal Navy, aged twenty-five, and third hand of HM Submarine *Clyde*. I had joined her in Malta fresh from the submarine officers' training class two years previously and become her navigating, signals and gunnery officer. The Spanish Civil War being still in progress, the Home and Mediterranean Fleets were virtually at war stations. From then on crisis had followed Hitler-induced crisis. By mid-August 1939 we had found ourselves, in company with a few more submarines and some destroyers in reserve, the only warships still in Malta. Without a depot ship, living conditions in the sweltering heat were most uncomfortable. Then came a signal ordering us to sail for Gibraltar forthwith. It was welcome indeed.

My captain was the small, spare, nut-brown, twinkling Commander 'Willie' (WE) Banks.[1] Immediately on our arrival at Gibraltar he had reported to the Flag Officer, North Atlantic, and returned with the news that we were to prepare to operate in the South Atlantic against German raiders. 'Pilot,' he had said, 'see that we have all the necessary charts and Sailing Directions, and that they are corrected up to date.' This task had kept me hard at it for the next couple of days. Everyone else in the boat was flat out too, with final preparations for a war patrol. Buff envelopes of varying sizes began to arrive on board, hand delivered, each containing a smaller envelope marked SECRET, the receipt of which had to be acknowledged by signal. In most cases the content was an order to open one or other of the sealed envelopes which had been held (and accounted for periodically by me) in the ship's safe. One of them had within it a printed sheet giving the latitude and longitude of points on the 'searched channel' (the route to be kept mine-free) in the approach to Freetown, Sierra Leone. And when the

---

[1] Captain W E Banks CBE DSC.

Clyde sailed from Gibraltar after dark on 1 September, Freetown was her destination.

Shortly before noon on our third day out we were nearing the Canary Islands and could see away to the south-west the cotton-wool cloud that marked the peak of Tenerife. I was on the bridge preparing to take sun sights, when the chief petty officer telegraphist climbed the conning tower ladder and emerged, looking somewhat less glum than he usually did. In his hand was a pink signal form which he gave to the officer of the watch. 'We are now at war with Germany, sir,' he said 'I've informed the captain.' After so many months, indeed years, of increasing tension the actual advent of war was anti-climactic. Up the voice-pipe came the routine request, 'Permission to ditch gash, sir?' from the control room watch keeper, followed a moment or two later, permission having been granted, by the 'chef's' assistant with a bucket of spud-peelings. Suddenly, there came from Signalman Bailey, perched aloft on the periscope standards as lookout and almost forgotten, the cry, 'Green three-oh, sir! Smoke!'

The officer of the watch was our newly-joined fourth hand, Sub-lieutenant Frank McVie. Quickly he scanned the horizon to starboard with his binoculars. 'I've got it,' he shouted, then yelled down the voice-pipe, 'Captain, sir! Smoke on the starboard bow.'

A moment or two later Willie Banks appeared out of the conning tower hatch, clad only in a towel and his binoculars. He had been having a shower when told we were at war and decided that he would have time to complete his ablutions and get dressed before meeting the enemy. But suppose we had already encountered one of the German commerce raiders that we had been sent to hunt down? Action could not be delayed. At this point Signalman Bailey's next report came down to us from aloft.

'Masts and funnels, sir. Trawlers maybe.'

And so they proved to be – Spanish and neutral. On we went towards Freetown. I took the sun's meridian altitude and disappeared below to the control room to work out our noon position. When war broke out the *Clyde* had been, I calculated, some forty miles off the coast of Morocco in the latitude of Agadir – a name which I had last encountered when studying modern history at school. The German gunboat *Panther*, I recalled, had been sent to register her government's claims to a 'place in the sun', in other words more colonies in Africa. And now Germany was at it again. Would she never learn?

During the next four months, in the course of four patrols based upon Freetown, the *Clyde*, operating on the surface almost continually,

Officers and men of HM Submarine *Clyde* at Dakar, December 1939.

quartered the South Atlantic without result. Our only dive, apart from the daily 'trim dive' to check the ballasting and keep the crew on their toes, was a reconnaissance of the harbour of Fernando Po, an island off the Cameroon coast. A German merchant ship, which could have been converted to a raider, had been reported there. So she was, but moored with rusty cables and with no sign of life on board. On our extremely boring return passage to Freetown the opportunity was taken to dive under the equator where it intersected the meridian of Greenwich. 'Are you quite certain, Pilot, that we're now in position zero-zero?' Willie asked. By this time I had had plenty of navigational practice and was able to assure him that we were indeed there.

Having no submarine depot ship at Freetown, we sometimes used to berth on HMS *Albatross*, a small seaplane carrier which was supporting some Walrus flying boats whose task was reconnaissance and anti-submarine patrol. We much appreciated the use of her amenities and the hospitality of her wardroom and messdecks. I am glad to say that at least one of the Walrus pilots, Lieutenant David Kyrke, survived the war and became a rear-admiral. The King's West African Rifles, stationed nearby, also looked after us. My host on one occasion was a subaltern who in peacetime had been an assistant district com-missioner in the Colonial Service. His experiences in the course of exercising British rule over an area about the size of Wales, mostly bush, were to me quite fascinating – it was like being read to from

27

Lieutenant W E Banks, 1938.

Blackwood's Magazine. The native soldiery, I noted, were extremely smart and cheerful.

As to the war itself, only at sea was there any action. On the very first day of hostilities U30 had sunk the liner *Athenia* and since then minefields had been laid, German aircraft had attacked the Home Fleet at sea and in harbour, our own submarines had operated vigorously in the Heligoland Bight, and as far afield as the Indian Ocean Hitler's 'pocket battleships' were preying on our shipping. We now know that on 10 October the *Clyde* was within 1,500 miles of the *Graf Spee* and on 22 October SS *Trevanion* had managed to make a distress signal before being sunk by a raider, identity uncertain. But her position, on the route between Freetown and the Cape of Good Hope, was 2,000 miles from us. Late in November came the sad news that the P&O liner *Rawalpindi*, converted to an armed merchant cruiser, had been sunk by a German heavy ship between Iceland and the Faroes. I felt this loss personally as my wife and small son, with her parents and their housekeeper, had taken passage home from Malta in that very liner the previous August.

Then came some excitement. We had sailed from Freetown early in December, heading for a position midway between Africa and South

America. To the west of us were the cruiser *Neptune* and four destroyers. The net was closing in on the *Graf Spee*. At noon on 12 December we sighted a large oil tanker heading south-east. Could it be a supply ship for the German raiders? We prepared for action. Alas, the ship turned out, on close examination by a boarding party, to be Norwegian. As we had reached the limit of our patrol line we turned and headed for Dakar, where we arrived on 15 December and entered the dry dock. Two days later we learned that the *Graf Spee*, after being forced to take sanctuary in Montevideo, had put to sea and then scuttled herself. We were able to celebrate this news appropriately in company with the aircraft carrier *Hermes* which, forming Force X with the French cruisers *Foch* and *Dupleix*, had just arrived back in harbour.

The crew of the *Clyde* were accommodated ashore in a hotel and I spent my second wedding anniversary (Christmas Eve) playing the drums in a Dakar night club, supporting Lieutenant Jimmie Dundas of the *Hermes*, who was an excellent jazz pianist. Soon after Christmas, having undocked, the *Clyde* was ordered to sail from Dakar and join a convoy homeward-bound from Freetown. Apart from being buffeted by winter gales in the North Atlantic, when watchkeeping on the open bridge of the submarine was most disagreeable, the passage home was uneventful and in mid-February 1940 we arrived in Portsmouth in cheerful mood, to be blissfully reunited with wives, families and sweethearts.

My wife's parents had returned to Malta, where my father-in-law was Rector of Holy Trinity church, Sliema; and, for the second time, was made an honorary chaplain to the forces. My own parents lived in Glasgow. Happily, Ursula Lambert, to whom my wife is related, and her husband Denis were kind enough to invite Somers and me, with eight-month-old Angus, to stay at their fruit farm in Essex *pro tem*. Denis, having his commission as Lieutenant RNR, was serving at sea, so that our families (there were two small Lambert girls) could keep each other company. However, my leave was soon over. My next appointment was to be first lieutenant[1] of the small elderly submarine H43, then based at Devonport. As her task was to act as 'clockwork mouse' for the benefit of anti-submarine vessels it looked as if I would be back in harbour often enough to justify moving Somers and Angus down west. So I took a furnished flat in Plymouth and we were soon installed there.

My new captain was Lieutenant George Colvin, a slightly built, pale, bearded figure, highly intelligent, precise, with an ironic turn of phrase. He and his brother Ian were sons of the celebrated journalist Ian D Colvin. Ian junior had been a reporter in Berlin for the *News Chronicle* and, according to George, had on a number of occasions informed Winston Churchill in detail of the nature of Nazi tyranny inside Germany. When I met Ian Colvin after the war he had lost a beloved brother and I a warm friend and respected commanding officer. George, by then captain of the *Tigris*, a fine new submarine, had sailed from Malta on 18 February 1943 for a patrol to the south of Naples. He had not returned. It was later established that the *Tigris* had been depth-charged and sunk in a position only about forty miles from where my own submarine was to suffer the same fate.

Shortly after I joined the H43 she was sent, in company with an armed trawler, to patrol just outside the territorial waters of the Irish Free State, hoping to catch any U-boat which might have been receiving fuel or stores, or even just sheltering, in Irish waters. This kind of ploy had been successful in 1915 when the trawler *Taranaki* had enabled the submarine C34 to sink a U-boat in the North Sea. We had no such luck and it was not until after the fall of France that we had another operational task.

[1] First lieutenant was second-in-command and known as 'Jimmy the One' or 'Jimmy'.

The author and his wife in Malta on their wedding day, 24 December 1937. Among the guard of honour is David Wanklyn (second from right).

Just before dark on 6 July, four weeks after the 'miracle' of Dunkirk, we sailed from Devonport with Second Lieutenant Hubert Nicolle of the Guernsey Militia embarked. Our orders were to land him on the island of Guernsey, where he would carry out a reconnaissance preparatory to a commando raid which was being planned. The navigator of the H43 was Ted Leitch, a sub-lieutenant RNR who in peacetime had been chief officer (with a master's ticket) of an ocean liner. With great skill he brought the submarine, which had been proceeding dived all day, to the spot which George Colvin and Nicolle had selected for surfacing. As the boat edged closer to the land in the moonless darkness I had the fore-hatch opened so that we could get up from below the 'folbot', made of a rubber skin on wooden frames, which Nicolle had brought with him. He told us that it had been purchased in Gamages the day before he had left London for Devonport. At first the sea was calm and Nicolle, accompanied by Ted Leitch who was to bring the folbot back, set off for a tiny bay called Le Jaonnet at the southern end of Guernsey. By the time the folbot reached the shore an onshore breeze had sprung up, making disembarkation difficult. But we did not realise this. Lying less than a mile off what was now the enemy coast, the waiting was tense. A dog barked. We peered intently into the darkness and listened. Two hours passed. There was nothing we could do. Then, just when George Colvin was about to give up hope of seeing him again, Ted Leitch appeared alongside, soaked to the skin and utterly exhausted in a half-swamped folbot. Looking for the submarine in pitch darkness and an increasingly loppy sea, he had missed us initially and had had to turn back. But Nicolle was safely ashore.

Three days later, having returned to Devonport and collected two more intrepid Guernseymen, Second Lieutenants Desmond Mulholland and Philip Martel, we set off for Guernsey again. The weather forecast was slightly less favourable this time, but it would still be moonless during the landing operation. Like Hubert Nicolle, these two had decided to land in civilian clothes and take their chance of being treated as spies. They were a brave little team. For them, unlike the rest of us in Britain, the German invasion was a fact, not just a threat, and they were determined to help throw the Germans out at whatever cost.

Ted Leitch once again demonstrated his meticulous skill in navigating the submarine, deeply submerged most of the way, to within a mile or two of the desired surfacing position. When eventually we came up, it was to find a breeze blowing directly onshore so that conditions for boatwork were marginal. It was the intention that the two would be landed at the same spot as Nicolle and it had been arranged that he would meet the newcomers, brief them, then return to the submarine with Leitch. As a folbot carried only two people it had been decided to utilise the submarine's Berthon boat. This was a dinghy made of canvas stretched over wooden frames, designed to fold flat so that it could be stowed inside the casing which surmounted the submarine's cigar-shaped pressure hull. No one on board, from the captain downward, had ever seen a Berthon boat in use, so I had organised a trial preparation and launch during the afternoon before we sailed from Devonport.

This was just as well, but we could have done with much more practice before launching the Berthon in the pitch darkness a mile or so off the enemy coast. Thorpe, the second coxswain, was a good man but he was in his late forties, having been a village postman in the West Country for several years before being recalled to the colours. His first task, with the help of another hand, was to lift one of the large steel plates which formed the casing doors, in order to get at the Berthon. Just as the two of them had succeeded in raising the heavy plate head-high, the submarine lurched in the seaway and caused them to let go, whereupon there was the most shattering and resounding clang.

In the silence that followed everyone held their breath, gazed shorewards towards the steep dark cliffs and listened. A minute or two passed with no signs of alarm. Not even the dog which had barked so persistently the last time gave tongue. Our practice paid off, despite the bad start, and before long the Berthon boat, rowed by the two soldiers and steered by Ted Leitch, was on its way inshore. We on board the H43 could only watch and wait, wait and watch, for any signs of hostile activity. What followed is best described in Ted Leitch's narrative, submitted in due course as a part of George Colvin's official report:

On approaching the beach the swell was seen to be breaking heavily directly on to the beach. A 30lb boat's anchor was let go on a warp and the boat controlled in to the beach using the anchor to keep her head to the swell. Even so the boat swamped and capsized. Second Lieutenant Nicolle was waiting for the boat and he helped drag it clear of the water and bail it out. He also briefed Martel and Mulholland about the conditions on the island and the disposition of German troops. In fact there was a machine-gun post covering the Bay less than half a mile away.

The boat was then launched to take Nicolle and Leitch back to the submarine, but again it swamped when only a few yards offshore, sinking in about four feet of water. With considerable difficulty the boat was dragged ashore once more and bailed out; Martel and Mulholland, who were by then halfway up the cliff, returning to help. Without their help the boat could not have been relaunched.

This second attempt was successful though a considerable amount of water was shipped in the process and as the boat had been damaged it began to sink slowly. The return journey was made with Leitch pulling and Nicolle bailing, arriving alongside the submarine with very little buoyancy left.

'At 0218,' according to the report, 'the submarine began the return journey, securing alongside in Devonport Dockyard at 0630 the following morning, the 12th July.' Both George Colvin and Ted Leitch were mentioned in despatches for their part in Operation 'Anger'. Fortunately, Nicolle (who was landed again in Guernsey the following September) and both Mulholland and Martel, despite eventually being captured, had all been able to obtain Guernsey Militia uniforms and were treated as POWs. After the war all three were awarded the MC.

On 16 July 1940 – the day that Hitler issued his directive for Operation 'Sea Lion', the invasion of England – I received a new appointment: I was to be first lieutenant of the almost new 'T' class submarine *Triumph* which was in Chatham Dockyard being repaired after striking a mine in the North Sea. It seemed to be an opportunity not to be missed to have my wife and son with me. So we installed ourselves in the Queen's Head, a most welcoming hostelry in Old Brompton near the dockyard gate. We thus found ourselves at what one might term the epicentre of the Battle of Britain, just as it was about to begin. I can remember one particular Sunday afternoon when, with our engineer officer, Denis Wright, and his wife we went for a picnic on Bluebell Hill near Chatham. It was a perfect summer's day and we watched the intertwining vapour trials of the raiding bombers, their escorting fighters and our own 'few' fearlessly attacking them – with every so often the angry drone of powering aero-engines punctuated by the staccato burst of machine gun or cannon fire. And once or twice we saw, floating slowly down, the small white canopy of a parachute and felt thankful for a survivor of the fatal mêlée, whether he be 'one of ours' or 'one of theirs'.

We had been able to leave Angus at Winds Point, a lovely house superbly (and safely) situated in the Malvern Hills belonging to the Cadbury family, to whom Somers is related. Early in August, Somers and I went up to see Angus, and I left her there for a few days while I returned to Chatham. We had been very lucky because in our absence a stray bomb, jettisoned at night by a German aircraft *in extremis*, had fallen upon the Queen's Head and destroyed our bedroom. I was able to find lodgings for us in Gillingham. My new captain, who arrived at about this time to take command of the *Triumph* now that she was almost ready for sea again, was Lieutenant Commander WJW ('Sammy') Woods.[1] He was a man of exceptional ability and distinguished presence, whose leadership combined firmness with consideration for the well-being of his subordinates.

One day in mid-August Sammy had left the submarine office in the dockyard to go to lunch in the barracks when there was an air raid warning followed shortly by the crump-crump-crump of a stick of bombs falling somewhere near the east gate of the dockyard. Warnings were so frequent at that time, with most of the air activity being dog-fights at high altitude, that in the dockyard we went on working. But suddenly Sammy appeared, looking serious, and said, 'Ian, I think that

[1] Admiral Sir Wilfred Woods GCB DSO ADC.

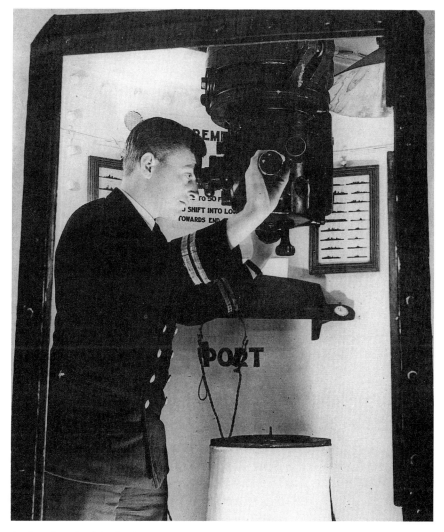

A submarine attack teacher in use.

you ought to go and see if Somers is all right. That last stick must have been pretty near your place.' I grabbed the bicycle that I normally used at that time for getting round the dockyard and pedalled like hell for the east gate. Out in the street, turning right, I sweated up the long hill. Soon I saw first one blitzed house and a little further on another and so on. How many bombs in a stick, I wondered, as I drove the bike up the hill. Six, as it turned out; and it was the fifth which had hit the house next door to ours, where Somers had been crouching behind a sofa. She had emerged covered with dust, picking her way through piles of plaster and broken glass, severely shaken but uninjured.

By mid-September the *Triumph* was on her way to the Clyde to complete her post-repair trials and work up her new crew in readiness for further operations. As we approached the Holy Loch, all ready to berth alongside the depot ship HMS *Forth*, I recalled the many wonderful days I had spent as a boy sailing in these superb waters, amongst the heather-clad hillsides and rugged peaks of Argyll. During the next hectic weeks Sammy Woods put boat and crew through their paces, culminating in two days of rigorous inspection, one in harbour and the next at sea, by the flotilla staff. All went well and a few days' leave was granted before we once again sailed on patrol.

Then, out of the blue, came my appointment to the submarine commanding officers' qualifying course (COQC), known generally as the 'perisher' (periscope course). Within a day or two I was relieved as first lieutenant by Richard Gatehouse. I learned later that after some fruitless patrolling off Norway the *Triumph* sailed for the Mediterranean, where Sammy Woods sank an Italian U-boat, a gunboat and seven supply ships totalling 15,637 tons, as well as damaging the cruiser *Bolzano* and two more freighters, before handing the command over to Lieutenant John Huddert in December 1941. Sad to say, the boat did not return from her next patrol. The cause of her loss remains a mystery.

The first part of the perisher took place at HMS *Dolphin*, Fort Blockhouse, Gosport, the *alma mater* of the British submarine service. Here there was an 'attack teacher' of First World War vintage. It consisted essentially of a periscope mounted in the lower part of a small building, one side of which could be opened to permit the use of a trolley mounted on rails extending some yards. On top of the trolley was a small waterline model of a German warship, the angle of presentation of which could be altered to conform with the relative movement of submarine and target according to the manoeuvres ordered by the officer at the periscope. The speed of approach of the trolley could also be altered, to simulate target speeds from slow to fast.

In charge of the perisher at this time was Lieutenant Commander (later Commander) HP de C ('Pat') Steel. He was a vigorous, highly competent submarine captain who had had the grievous misfortune during the first week of the war, when in command of HM Submarine *Triton*, to torpedo a flotilla mate, the *Oxley*. No blame whatsoever attached to Pat Steel, but he had almost reached the age limit for operational submarine command in war so that his appointment as perisher teacher was ideal in the circumstances.

There were six of us on the course and we were all equally eager to have done with the attack teacher and begin our practice attacks at the periscope of a real submarine. The 7th Submarine Flotilla, with the 35-year-old, coal-burning, converted merchant ship *Cyclops* as depot ship, was stationed at Rothesay, Isle of Bute. The submarines, which now included the H43, were small and elderly, being used mainly for training. But the *Oberon*, in which we perishers went to sea, was large and middle-aged. Her captain, Lieutenant Commander EF ('Bertie') Pizey,[1] had already carried out successful war patrols in the *Triton* and was soon to be given command of the submarine minelayer *Porpoise*, being promoted a few months later to commander.

It was now November, the days were short and the weather for the most part vile. One of us perishers would be detailed each day to be duty captain, and would have to manoeuvre the *Oberon* away from her berth on the *Cyclops*, which was uncomfortably near the shoreline, and take the boat through the narrow and tortuous Kyles of Bute into the exercise area in Inchmarnock Water, while Bertie stood at the back of the bridge biting his nails with anxiety, ready to intervene instantly if the 'makee learn' captain of the day should give a wrong order. Down below in the wardroom the rest of us would have the usual submarine breakfast of cereal, herrings in tomato sauce (or eggs and bacon if we were lucky), bread with tinned marmalade and sweet tea. In due course one would hear the order, 'Diving stations!' shouted through the boat, followed shortly by the raucous, grating, urgent clamour of the klaxon. The rumbling of the diesel engines would stop abruptly and the main vents would snap open, allowing the air to escape from the main ballast tanks and let the water in; then the boat would take up a slight angle as she slipped quietly below the surface. I always found the sudden silence and – if there was a sea running – the cessation of rolling and pitching, most soothing.

Throughout the day and sometimes in the dark, after surfacing, the *Oberon* would be pitted against the target ship *Cutty Sark* (a destroyer-like little vessel, in peacetime the Duke of Westminster's yacht) by the aspiring commanding officers with varying success. At the end of six weeks, during which our skill in attacking had begun to develop and we had shown that we could handle the submarine safely, the great day came when Pat Steel summoned us in turn to his tiny cabin in the *Oberon* to tell us our fate. You either pass or fail the perisher. If I recall correctly, my course all passed. Better still as far as I was concerned, I was to take over command, immediately, of the H43.

---

[1] Captain E W Pizey CBE DSO.

2 · Tennis balls for Mabel

Hugo Newton, whom I was to relieve as captain of H43, I knew of old. He had been 'Jimmy' of one of the boats in the 1st Flotilla in Malta before the war. Eager to assume my first command I sought him out and we agreed to meet in the wardroom of the *Cyclops* as soon as the bar opened, to initiate the turnover. Over a few gins I listened to a monologue from Hugo, sardonic as ever, on the abysmal nature of the submarine CO's task in war.

'Just think of it, Ian,' he said in his husky voice, smilingly determined to dampen my enthusiasm. 'First of all you have to get your boat properly manned, with no defects, and well worked up; then you have to get to your patrol area without being bombed by friendly aircraft or torpedoed by a U-boat; you have to make a landfall without navigational aids and you'll be lucky if you don't hit a mine; you wait around for days – maybe weeks – on the enemy's doorstep, waiting for a target; then one rough day, just when it's getting dark, along comes the big one, heavily escorted and going like the clappers; you try to get in a snap attack with a destroyer coming straight at you; you have to go deep and by the time you can get another look the target's zigged away; you fire a salvo but it's hopeless; you stick around for a few days, hoping to get another chance, but instead of that you get jumped by an aircraft – an enemy one this time – and you're lucky to get your boat back to harbour ...' 'But surely, Hugo,' I broke in at last, 'you wouldn't be anything but a submarine CO, would you?' 'No,' said Hugo, 'but when you think of all the things that can go wrong it's a bloody miracle any submarine ever gets in a successful attack ... Have another gin and I'll tell you about H43.' 'Thank you, tell me the worst.' 'You won't believe this, Ian,' said Hugo, still smiling, 'but you can't dive the boat safely below periscope depth – there's a leak in the duct keel.' He looked at his watch. 'I must be off. I'm taking Jill to the flicks this afternoon. I've told Sluggie and the staff about the keel. Best of luck. See you tomorrow morning first thing, so that we can complete the turnover.' And he departed to catch a boat ashore.

Captain Sluggie Edwards and his flotilla staff were unsympathetic when I complained that the H43 was unfit to dive below periscope depth. I was sailed for Londonderry forthwith, there to act as clockwork mouse once again. My 'clients', for the most part, were the big deep-sea trawlers which the Admiralty had taken over and equipped with asdic submarine detection gear, depth-charges and naval radio. They were of deep draught and I had to be very careful when exercising with them to stay at a safe depth. It turned out that Hugo Newton, with his customary pessimism, had slightly exaggerated the nature of the leak in the keel. But it was there all right and I thought it prudent not to carry out any practice attacks on the trawlers until the defect was repaired. Thanks to the energetic and efficient captain in charge at Londonderry, Philip ('Ruckers') Ruck-Keene,[1] the H43 soon found herself in dock at Belfast.

Not long after being repaired, the boat was ordered to Campbeltown, near the tip of the Mull of Kintyre. No sooner had I arrived there than I was ordered to turn over command to the flotilla spare commanding officer and proceed at once to Sheerness to assume command of the H34, which had just finished a maintenance period, and take her to Tobermory in Mull. But first I had to put the boat through engine and steering trials in the confined and mine-strewn waters of the Thames estuary. That done, the H34 was ordered to join the tail end of an East coast convoy. Off Great Yarmouth we ran into dense fog and the convoy had to anchor. This was a salutary experience, but we arrived in due course at Methil in the Firth of Forth. From here we sailed with a group of ocean-going ships bound through the Pentland Firth to join an Atlantic convoy. One of them suddenly decided that the H34, tagging along astern, must be a U-boat and turned to ram. We did not have VHF (voice) radio in those days, which was perhaps just as well. Nearing Tobermory in the Minches at night, we ran into fog again and I was glad to bring the boat safely into harbour.

It had turned into a glorious sunny spring morning and I was about to clean myself up, preparatory to making my 'number' upon the redoubtable, indeed formidable, Commodore (Vice-Admiral retired) Gilbert ('Monkey') Stephenson. Monkey had set up the anti-submarine training base through which, month after month, newly commissioned escort vessels were to pass throughout the war, to emerge as highly

[1] Vice Admiral P Ruck-Keene CB DSO.

HM Submarine H43, the author's first command.

efficient warships ready to take on the U-boats. Coming alongside my new command was a motor launch with a familiar figure in the stern sheets. It was Lieutenant CP ('Pat') Norman,[1] another flotilla mate from pre-war Malta days. 'Good morning, Ian,' he shouted up, 'I've come to relieve you!' Grinning broadly as he came aboard, Pat announced that he had some more news for me. My wife, it transpired, had discovered that the H34 was on the way to Tobermory and, using her initiative, had somehow managed to get there. Pat very soon found himself in command of his first submarine, while I was reunited with Somers in the Western Isles Hotel. There was just time to catch the ferry back to Oban, from where a kind businessman gave us a lift in his Jaguar to Glasgow. We were in our Rothesay boarding house that night.

My orders had been to 'await appointment'. On 26 March we celebrated, in a mild way, my twenty-seventh birthday. As I recall,

[1] Captain C P Norman CBE DSO DSC.

the local cinema was showing *Ninotchka*, in which Greta Garbo played the part of a woman commissar in a Soviet Union trade mission to Paris. It was very funny and stylish and just what we needed to take our minds off the parting which we knew was imminent – wartime partings were hell. A week or so later, after a false start during which Somers had managed to get me intercepted at Central Station in Glasgow so that we could have a few more days together, I was summoned to the submarine command's headquarters at Northways, a requisitioned block of flats at Swiss Cottage in London. When I reported to Captain Gibson, the chief of staff, he told me that I was being sent out to Malta as spare commanding officer for the submarine force being established there, and should proceed at once to Gosport to await the departure of a submarine which was about to sail for the Mediterranean. 'But first,' he said, 'the admiral would like to see you.'

In the submarine service Max Horton[1] was a legend. His First World War exploits in command of submarines, in the Baltic particularly, had inspired us. But he had a reputation for ruthlessness in pursuit of efficiency. When I met him that day for the first and only time, the great man was sitting at a broad clear desk, with his back to the light. His greeting was genial. With a smile on his rather round but strong and weather-beaten face, he said, 'Captain Gibson tells me that you're going to Malta.' 'Yes, sir,' I replied 'but I don't feel too confident at the moment. I haven't been able to get in a single practice attack since I did my perisher.' 'Why?' he asked, leaning forward and clasping his hands together in front of him. I told him as briefly as I could. 'You'll be all right', he said. 'Commander Simpson[2] ought to be able to arrange some attacks for you before you meet the enemy. Good luck. By the way,' he went on, opening a drawer in his desk and producing a box of tennis balls, 'would you mind taking these to Mabel Strickland? You know her, I expect?'

I certainly knew *of* the formidable Miss Strickland – The Honourable Mabel. No one who had lived in Malta before the war could have failed to do so. *The Times of Malta*, under her editorship, had flourished Britain's imperial splendour with patriotic fervour. 'Of course, sir,' I said, 'I shall be glad to do so.' Taking the box of Slazengers I departed. After finding out as much as I could from various staff officers about the progress of the war in general and submarine matters in particular, I set off for Fort Blockhouse.

Amongst the submarines lying in the Gosport base was the *Urge*,

[1] Admiral Sir Max Horton GCB DSO.
[2] Rear Admiral G W G Simpson CB CBE.

newly built by Vickers-Armstrong of Barrow-in-Furness and destined to join others of her class in the Mediterranean. I was to take passage in her. Her captain was not due back from leave for a few more days, so I was able to relax in the mess, exchanging views with various friends. After dinner one night the talk turned to the recent action in which the entire Mediterranean Fleet, under Admiral AB Cunningham, had engaged a part of the Italian fleet and succeeded in sinking three heavy cruisers. The Battle of Matapan, as it had been dubbed by a quite naturally enthusiastic press, had seemed to most of us a notable victory. But Lieutenant Arthur Pitt, invariably a sceptic and highly perceptive, put a more realistic point of view. 'You fools,' he said, 'don't you realise that Cunningham's been bulldozed? While he's been chasing around after the Eyeties the Huns have been getting more and more troops across to North Africa.' This, I think, was news to the rest of us. But it was true. Following the arrival in Sicily of the German Fliegerkorps X, with its Ju 88s, Cunningham had lost control of the central Mediterranean. No wonder he was keen at last to have a submarine force under his command.

I had not previously met Lieutenant EP Tomkinson, the captain of the *Urge*. Tall and robust, with a long head and a friendly expression, 'Tommo' was one of the best officers of his seniority. He was also a navy golfer. When I introduced myself in the wardroom he said, 'Good. I'm glad you're coming with us. We could do with an extra watch keeper.' The next day, 15 April, we sailed – at the gentlemanly hour of 2.00 pm. This gave us time to have a good lunch, the last decent meal we could expect for ten days or so. As far as I was concerned, it proved to have been too good a lunch. I had remained on the bridge with Tommo as we set course on the surface out through the forts guarding Spithead. The weather was fine and I was enjoying a last look at England. The fresh air was clearing my head of the fumes of pre-lunch pink gins. Pre-lunch, I thought, suddenly. Pre-lunch. Didn't I have those tennis balls with me in the anteroom so as not to forget them? I could see the box now, resting on the mantleshelf where I had put it. 'Tommo,' I said, 'Max Horton gave me some tennis balls to take to Mabel Strickland. Well, I've left them behind in the anteroom at Blockhouse.' Tommo let his binoculars fall on to his chest. 'Too bad,' he said, drawing a hand expressively across his throat, 'but I hope you don't expect me to go back for them.' I didn't. War, after all, is war.

*   *   *

By April 1941 the Germans had established their main u-boat base at Lorient on the French Atlantic coast, from where the *Unterseebooten* sallied forth across the Bay of Biscay to attack the Allied convoys. In consequence our own submarines on passage south to Gibraltar, *en route* to the Mediterranean, ran a risk of being mistaken for u-boats by patrolling aircraft of the RAF's Coastal Command. In order to protect our own boats a system had been evolved known as the 'moving haven'. This was a notional rectangle, 100 miles long and 20 miles wide, which moved along in relation to one of our submarines at the speed of advance which it had been ordered to maintain, submerged by day and on the surface at night. Within such a haven no submarine was to be attacked by our forces. The scheme worked tolerably well, though one of our boats is known, for certain, to have been sunk by friendly aircraft, and several were attacked and badly shaken up.

Naturally, we in the *Urge* were as alert as we could be, hoping to encounter a u-boat and determined that, if we were lucky enough to do so, we would detect or sight him before he heard or saw us. In the event, it was a large, grey-painted oil tanker which crossed our path around midday on 18 April. Tommo ordered diving stations and prepared to attack. We had not received any report of enemy ships in the area. The tanker was steering east, bound probably for Brest. Quite recently the Admiralty had been permitted by the British government to extend the 'sink at sight' zone. Allied and neutral shipping should not be anywhere near us. 'She must be a blockade runner,' said Tommo. 'We'll sink her.' It was a simple attack. 'Stand by One and Two Tubes,' ordered Tommo, and a little later, 'Fire One! . . . Fire Two!' As each torpedo left the tube we could feel a slight shudder in the boat, followed by the report, 'Torpedo running, sir' from the senior asdic operator. In the control room there was silence as we watched the seconds hand of the control room clock. A minute went by, then another twenty seconds. The running range to the target was about a mile. Had we missed? . . . 'Tonk'. We all heard it. 'Damn!' roared Tommo, 'the bloody fish hasn't gone off!' and he rapped out a string of orders to position the boat for another attack. Grim-faced, he slowed the boat down and ordered, 'Up periscope!' Then, 'It's all right, boys,' shouted Tommo with glee. 'Stop the attack. She's sinking by the stern. I can see the water going down the funnel.' The torpedo hadn't been a dud after all. None of us in the control room had ever heard a torpedo hitting a ship and had assumed that it would make a pretty loud bang. But we had not allowed for the fact that sound waves are often bent when they travel through water.

In the circumstances there could be no question of surfacing to take survivors aboard. Had we done so, in broad daylight, the *Urge* would have been in jeopardy from attack by both friendly and enemy aircraft. We could only hope that the tanker had made a distress signal and that her crew would either reach the shore in their lifeboats or be picked up. From the records we know that the vessel was indeed a blockade runner – the Italian tanker *Franco Martelli* of 10,535 tons (large for those days), coming from Pernambuco with diesel fuel for the U-boats.

The *Urge*'s company were in very good spirits when, after a brief stay in Gibraltar to embark replacement torpedoes, fuel and fresh provisions (alas, there were no tennis balls to be had), we arrived in Malta. The boat was sorely needed. Britain was still alone in resisting the armed might of Hitler's Germany and Mussolini's Italy, and it was essential to engage their forces. At Churchill's insistence the British army in North Africa had been reinforced and set the task of driving the Italians out of that region, so that control of the Mediterranean sea route could be regained and the Suez Canal – the jugular vein of the British Empire – secured. The German reaction had been prompt and effective. Hitler moved Fliegerkorps X, which had taken part in the Norway campaign with success and had specialised in attacks on ships, to Sicily – about 150 bombers and dive bombers plus 50 fighters – augmenting the Italian force already there of 45 bombers and 75 fighters. To oppose this concentration of air power we still had fewer than 50 fighters in Malta. It was not surprising that the battleships, aircraft carrier, cruisers and destroyers of the Mediterranean fleet were powerless to intercept the Axis convoys conveying Rommel's Afrika Korps across the Sicilian Channel. Nor, at that stage, had any of the Royal Navy's torpedo-armed Swordfish or the RAF's Blenheim bombers been deployed to Malta. It was up to the submarines to do the job.

Like the surface fleet, our main submarine forces had to be based remote from the threat of heavy air attack. The 8th Flotilla, with its depot ship *Maidstone*, was in Gibraltar, a thousand miles away to the west of Malta; and the 1st Flotilla, with its depot ship *Medway*, in Alexandria, a thousand miles to the east. By the end of April, when the *Urge* reached Malta, seven of these small (650 ton) U-class boats had already arrived from the United Kingdom to form the Malta submarine force. Thanks to the prodigious initiative, resource and determination of a few people, notably Commander GWG ('Shrimp') Simpson, a comprehensive submarine maintenance base had been improvised on Manoel Island in the harbour known as Marsamxett, by utilising the Lazaretto, in which people arriving in Malta had been quarantined in the days of bubonic plague. Since 10 January, when the already damaged aircraft carrier *Illustrious* had been the Luftwaffe's main target in the Grand Harbour, air raids had averaged three every twenty-four hours. Miraculously, none of the submarines had been hit and care had been taken to conceal from the air the fact that Lazaretto was their base.

Within an hour of the *Urge* securing alongside, the air raid sirens sounded and we all went down into rock shelters, leaving only damage control parties in the submarines. That evening I walked the half mile or so up to Bishop's House in Sliema to see my in-laws. The Farries had no idea that I might turn up in Malta. They were as delighted to have news of their daughter and grandson as I was to see them safe and in good heart. My father-in-law was just old enough to have been an honorary chaplain to the forces in the First World War and was glad to be serving in the same capacity again; my mother-in-law, in addition to teaching some of the younger children of British residents, was helping with the censorship of mail. Already, quite apart from the bombing, they were suffering considerable privations. We talked about how it would all end. There was no despondency. But, equally, there were no illusions about the key role which Malta was now playing in the battle for North Africa, and hence its influence upon the outcome of the war. That an invasion of Malta might be attempted by the Axis forces was a real possibility.

My next social activity was one which in prospect I relished not at all. I had to call on the Hon Mabel Strickland and confess to having left behind in the wardroom at Fort Blockhouse, Gosport, the dozen tennis balls entrusted to me by Admiral Sir Max Horton to bring to her. It was still possible to buy roses in Valletta, so I sent some to Mabel with my compliments and a note conveying Max's good wishes, ending by apologising most sincerely for failing to deliver the tennis balls. Mabel's response was to invite me to lunch at the Union Club, adding, 'I hope you don't mind but I've asked Dickie Mountbatten also.' I did not mind! But I wondered whether Mountbatten would.

The lunch was good, all things considered, and, surprisingly, was not interrupted by an air raid. It was fascinating for me to hear the war being discussed by two people so well placed to know what was going on. Arthur Pitt's assertion four weeks earlier that the Battle of Matapan resulted from the Italian fleet being used by the Germans to prevent the Mediterranean Fleet from interfering with the transport of Rommel's force to North Africa was wrong. What the Italian fleet had

Lazaretto submarine base, Malta, *c*. 1941.

been spurred by the Germans into attempting was to interdict the flow of British and Commonwealth troops and their supplies into Greece. Now, a month or so later, we had been driven out of Greece by the Germans and the navy was suffering heavy losses during the evacuation. Mountbatten's 5th Destroyer Flotilla was, for the time being, mined in to Malta. The German assault on Crete had not yet begun. It seemed that, owing to the preoccupation of the RAF with the air defence of the United Kingdom and the bombing offensive against German cities, the navy and the army in the Mediterranean were woefully deprived of air support.

I had been in the Mediterranean Fleet as a midshipman when Mountbatten commanded the destroyer *Daring*. To me, he was an outstandingly able and professional naval officer. As a radio communications specialist he had demonstrated his enquiring mind, technical grasp and flair for putting his ideas across, both to his subordinates and to his seniors – although it must be said that he was more successful with the former than the latter. As a young destroyer

47

captain he not only handled his ship with the requisite dash but set a high standard in reporting by radio, during fleet exercises, the position and movements of the 'enemy' forces. He had realised that it was the failure in 'enemy reporting' which, more than any other cause, had led to the indecisive result of the Battle of Jutland, and he did much to raise the navy's standards in this respect.

As soon as lunch was over, Dickie departed, saying that he must get back to his ship. 'Of course,' said Mabel, as I took my leave a little later, 'you must realise that Dickie is first and foremost a Prussian prince.' Had I then been better informed I might have ventured to correct Mabel – not Prussian but Hessian. Less than three weeks later, Mountbatten's celebrated ship, the *Kelly*, was sunk by dive-bombers south of Crete after successfully bombarding Maleme airfield, which had enabled our forces to retake it.

Back at Lazaretto I tried, without much success, to find something useful to do. Lieutenant-Commander Bob Tanner, the Staff Officer (Operations), had commanded submarines before the war but had had to retire owing to bad eyesight. He had the precise mind and habits and unruffled temperament of the perfect staff officer, leavened by a quirky sense of humour. By keeping paperwork to the absolute minimum he managed single-handed to order the comings and goings, and the activities on patrol, of the eight or ten submarines based on Malta under the well-judged direction of Shrimp Simpson. The administration of the base was in the hands of Lieutenant-Commander Hubert Marsham, another former submarine CO; he was assisted by an ex-lower deck lieutenant, one 'Pop' Giddings, a remarkable character who did much to mitigate the dangers and hardships which the submarine crews had to endure between patrols. The maintenance of the boats themselves was master-minded by Commander 'Sam' MacGregor, who had a small but highly competent team of artificers with the resources of the dockyard to call upon – although, as it was the main target of the enemy bombers, these assets were rapidly diminishing. One day in the mess, Sam recounted how he had been trying to obtain a certain spare part, urgently needed for a submarine due to sail shortly on patrol. Despairing of getting through on the telephone in the middle of an air raid, he had cycled the nine miles round to the dockyard and sought out the appropriate store. But the storekeeper insisted that he did not have the required spare in stock. This did not satisfy Sam, who ferreted round and eventually found the item. Furious, he cursed the offending storeman. 'But, Senu,' the man, deeply hurt, explained, 'I was keeping that one for an emergency.'

It was at this time, mid-May 1941, that an astonishing event crowded out all other news. One evening, when I was having a drink with Wingrave and Greta Tench, friends of my in-laws, we heard that Hitler's deputy, Rudolf Hess, had arrived in Scotland by parachute. 'Gravy' Tench was a leading civilian in Malta who had been appointed by the Governor as head of censorship and organiser of food rationing; with us were two remarkable characters whom I met from time to time in the Tenchs' most hospitable house at St Julian's Bay, namely Andrew Cohen'[1] the Deputy Civil Administrator, and Francis Gerard, a novelist who, in the rank of major, was the government's information officer. Stimulated by the entrancing Greta, and Gravy's Scotch, speculation on the purport of Hess's unexpected call upon the Duke of Hamilton ranged widely. Andrew imitated Churchill growling 'Peasch! What short of people dush he think we ah?' while Francis was Hitler ordering Hess to tell His Majesty King George that he could keep his Empire if he would sack his Prime Minister.

I soon realised that, as spare commanding officer and hence liable to be given a command at short notice, there really was no worthwhile job that I could do, and I began to feel more and more depressed. All the cos seemed to be fit and doing their stuff. Tommo, on his first Mediterranean patrol in the *Urge*, had sunk a supply ship of 4,856 tons off the Tunisian coast; Wanklyn, on his seventh in the *Upholder*, had one morning sunk a supply ship of the same size near the Straits of Messina and that same evening intercepted an Italian troop convoy heading for Tripoli, consisting of four large liners very heavily escorted, and sunk the *Conte Rosso* of 17,870 tons; Dick Cayley in the *Utmost* had sunk two and damaged two good-sized supply ships; Johnnie Wraith had recently relieved Dudley Norman[2] in command of the *Upright*, after the latter had sunk the cruiser *Armando Diaz* in a snap attack on the surface at night; Tony Collett in the *Unique* had sunk a supply ship; two other boats, the *Usk* and the *Undaunted*, which were on patrol when we arrived in Malta in the *Urge* had failed to return and were considered to have been lost.

There remained the *Ursula*, commanded by Lieutenant AJ Mackenzie. She was a boat whose name had already, early in the war, made the headlines by carrying out what had appeared to be a successful attack on the cruiser *Nürnberg* in the Heligoland Bight (in fact she had sunk an escort). On a later patrol she had sunk a supply ship off the Danish coast; since coming to Malta the previous January she had

---

[1] Later Sir Andrew Cohen KCVO KCMG OBE LLD. Governor of Uganda, 1952–57.
[2] Captain E D Norman DSO DSC.

sunk another supply ship, but had had no further success. Shrimp had decided that Mackenzie needed a stand-off, and so at long last, as it seemed to me, (it was by now late May) I was to have command of a front-line submarine – even if only for one patrol.

Raring to go, I went to see Bob Tanner about my patrol orders. These were simple enough. I was to proceed, on the surface by night and dived by day, to a position some 35 miles north of Tripoli and then patrol westward for about 80 miles until I was off the port of Zuara, 'where you might see something to your advantage', as he put it.[1] I had already asked Shrimp if he could arrange at least one practice attack for me before I went on patrol, as I had not done a single one since my perisher six months before. He said that as Dick Cayley would be sailing shortly after me, in the *Utmost*, he might be prepared to act as target for me, and we left it at that. In the event it was mutually agreed that in view of the recent mining of the entrance to Grand Harbour (one of Mountbatten's destroyers, the *Jervis*, had struck a mine there) it would be more prudent if we remained firmly in the swept channel until we were well clear.

What happened was this. The passage south towards Tripoli was uneventful but, having dived at dawn and begun to patrol eastward, I had to surface so that a defective muffler valve could be repaired. This took about an hour. Luckily the visibility was very poor so that we did not feel too exposed to air attack, and we counted on hearing any approaching vessel in time to take evasive action. It would be at least a year before any of our submarines was equipped with radar, or radar search-receivers, and we had no reason to believe that the Axis forces deployed against us had these devices either. Early the following morning, off Zuara, we saw the lighthouse there come on, presumably to enable an approaching vessel to fix its position. Assuming that Bob Tanner's hot tip was about to pay off, I positioned the *Ursula* to the westward, so as to get the target silhouetted against the dawn light while the boat would be less easy to see from the escorts. I had hoped to carry out the attack on the surface, but by the time the target – a large supply ship with a destroyer on either bow – was sighted steering straight for Zuara, dawn had broken, so I had to dive the *Ursula* and carry out the attack submerged. Lieutenant Mike Lumby,[2] the Jimmy, was most efficient, as were his crew, and everything seemed to be

---

[1] One was not encouraged to enquire too closely into the source of 'operational intelligence' and tended to suspect that one of our cloak and dagger men was at work. Hence I assumed that there was a supply ship bound for Zuara.
[2] Captain M G R Lumby DSO DSC.

going according to plan. But alas, as I put up the periscope for a final look before firing, I saw that the target had altered course more than 90 degrees to port and was now going away from me, heading for Tripoli. I fired torpedoes but with little hope of a hit, given the most unfavourable 'track angle', and there was no result – not even a 'tonk'. I have never felt more frustrated, as much, if not more, for the officers and men of the *Ursula*, to whom I could only apologise. But they took it in their stride, having already experienced both success and failure, learning in the process neither to be too elated by the one nor too cast down by the other.

Shortly after returning from my abortive patrol in the *Ursula* I found myself in the military hospital at Imtarfa near Mdina, the lovely honey-coloured, battlemented, quiet, ancient capital of Malta. Our medical officer, Surgeon Lieutenant-Commander Critien, had diagnosed a stomach ulcer. A course of treatment was begun. A few days later I developed double pneumonia, a much more serious matter. However, the appropriate drugs soon took care of it, although it was a month before I recovered fully. I remember being required to blow hard into a rubber bag in order to exercise my lungs. Outside my window was an air raid siren to which I became so accustomed that I could sleep through it. The wards were light, airy and sunlit, with brisk, considerate, tireless ward sisters and Maltese VADs, all attentive and mostly rather pretty. My dear mother-in-law, Gladys Farrie, was able to visit me once or twice, in spite of the difficulties in moving around Malta. Someone provided me with a copy of *War and Peace*. Hitler had launched his attack on Russia a week or two earlier and I was fascinated to hear on the BBC News, which was relayed to the wards, the very place-names – Minsk, Vitebsk, Smolensk and the river-crossings, Dvina and Berezina – about which I was reading in Tolstoy's masterpiece.

It was mid-August by the time I was allowed to return to duty at the submarine base, although even then I was not passed as fully fit for sea service. All I could do was to recuperate while trying to keep up my spirits and picking up as much information as I could from the COs in from patrol. To this end I prevailed one day upon Tony Collett, who had acquired a pony and trap, to lend it to me, and I invited David Wanklyn to come for a drive. It was a sunny afternoon and not too hot as we clip-clopped along the rocky road leading off Manoel Island, turned left along the waterfront past the head of Msida Creek, where in peacetime the submarine flotilla with its depot ship had lain; then right up the gentle slop towards Birchicara and back to Sliema.

We talked of the pre-war days – 'Wanks' had been one of those who, with their swords, had formed an arch over Somers and me as we emerged, just married, from Holy Trinity church; I had performed a like service at his wedding a few months later. David's VC had not yet been gazetted but he had already established himself as an 'ace'. After some general chat I broached the question that was burning in my mind. 'Given that we've all learned or relearned about how to conduct a war patrol, how do you actually achieve your successful attacks?' I asked. 'I know that you didn't get your eye in for a bit.' [Shrimp had actually considered relieving Wanklyn, after several missed attacks.] 'What's the secret?' 'Oh, I really don't know,' Wanks replied, 'I think that maybe we were always being trained in attacks on high speed targets, like destroyers and the occasional cruiser, and it has taken us time to get used to tackling these relatively slow supply ships.' I had to be content with that.

In his modesty of bearing and quiet though unfailing efficiency, David Wanklyn contrasted sharply with other, more flamboyant and in the end far less successful, COs. The loss of Wanklyn and the *Upholder* in April 1942, on what would have been his last patrol before taking the boat back to the United Kingdom, was truly most tragic.

While I had been on the sick list, the Malta submarines had been organised into the 10th Flotilla, with Shrimp Simpson, newly promoted to captain, still in command, although remaining under the operational control of Captain SM ('Sammie') Raw[1] commanding the 1st Flotilla at Alexandria under the Commander-in-Chief, Mediterranean. Since June, when the Germans had redeployed Fliegerkorps X to the Russian front, the scale of air attack on Malta had much diminished, and it had become feasible to operate a cruiser/destroyer force from there for short periods, with some dramatic successes. All these forces – submarine, air and surface – operating against the North Africa supply route, were being directed by the Vice-Admiral, Malta, Vice-Admiral WTR Ford. In the Mediterranean as a whole, our submarines had sunk, during the first five months of 1941, 76 Axis supply ships of a total tonnage of 253,534, the lion's share of the bag falling to the eight to ten U-class boats which now formed the 10th Flotilla. But the losses were heavy. Besides 'Podger' Darling's *Usk*, mined off Cape Bon in April, and Livesay's *Undaunted*, depth-charged off Zuara in May, Galloway's *Union* had been depth-charged off Pantellaria, and both Abdy's P32 and Whiteway-Wilkinson's P33 had been mined towards

[1] Rear Admiral SM Raw CB.

the end of August off Tripoli. One more addition to the flotilla, Teddy Woodward's *Unbeaten*, was still going strong. My place as spare CO had been taken by Lieutenant AR ('Baldy') Hezlet,[1] who had relieved Tony Collett in the *Unique* and promptly scored a major success by sinking the *Esperia* (11,700 tons), one of four liners in a heavily escorted troop convoy.

By the end of September the Mediterranean submarines had sunk another 49 supply ships, totalling 151,744 tons; once again the 10th Flotilla had the highest score, which now included several U-boats, a destroyer and damage to a cruiser. The COs in the flotilla all seemed to be at the top of their form and remarkably healthy, whereas my stomach ulcer was still grumbling and I had lost all confidence in being able to carry out a successful attack. I therefore suggested to Shrimp Simpson that I had better go back to the United Kingdom and requalify as a perisher. He agreed. As luck would have it, Baldy Hezlet was about to be appointed in command of the *Ursula*, to take her back to be refitted. He would then assume command of one of the new submarines now nearing completion. So I offered to serve as his Jimmy for the passage home. He and I had been midshipmen together in the battleship *Royal Oak* and had similar views on most service matters, while tending to laugh a good deal at the various absurdities of life. So I was signed on to replace Mike Lumby, who had left the *Ursula* to fly home for his perisher.

We sailed from Malta early in December and had an uneventful passage home, lengthened somewhat by being diverted to patrol off Brest where the German battlecruisers had been stationed since March, posing a serious threat to the Atlantic convoys. This meant that we spent Christmas Day at sea, with 60 feet on the depth gauge most of the time. We had a carol service in the fore-ends of the submarine, packed in between the reload torpedoes. The words of half-a-dozen carols, cooperatively remembered, had been typed out and duplicated in the wireless office, while David Spring-Rice, sub-lieutenant RNVR, provided the tunes on his clarinet. The captain read from *The Book of Common Prayer*:

> O Eternal Lord God, who alone spreadest out the heavens, and rulest the raging of the sea; who hast compassed the waters with bounds until day and night come to an end; Be pleased to receive into thy Almighty and most gracious protection the persons of us thy servants, and the Fleet in which we serve. Preserve us from the

---

[1] Vice Admiral Sir Arthur Hezlet KBE CB DSO DSC.

dangers of the sea, and from the violence of the enemy; that we may be a safeguard unto our most gracious Sovereign Lord, King George, and his Dominions, and a security for such as pass on the seas upon their lawful occasions; that the inhabitants of our Island may in peace and quietness serve thee our God; and that we may return in safety to enjoy the blessings of the land, with the fruits of our labours, and with a thankful remembrance of thy mercies to praise and glorify thy Holy Name; through Jesus Christ our Lord.

Amen

It had never seemed to be more apposite.

The reunion with Somers and eighteen-month-old Angus was all that we had been looking forward to since that dreary day when I had left them behind in Rothesay the previous April. After a short spell in hospital – the Royal Masonic in Hammersmith, where I was very well looked after – I was appointed to the depot ship of the 3rd Submarine Flotilla, HMS *Forth*, in the Holy Loch. Once again my appointment was as spare CO, but this time I was able to be of some use. The Commander (Submarines), Ronnie Mills,[1] collared me on arrival to run the attack teacher for the benefit of COs who wished to train their 'attack teams' and for aspiring Jimmies in advance of doing their perisher. The teacher was a primitive structure, similar to that already described in HMS *Dolphin*; but I was able to devise and have made in the *Forth*'s work-shops a means of representing escorts which moved – or appeared to move – in conjunction with the main target.

In due course I was attached to a COQC being run by Commander HF ('Boggie') Bone,[2] who had lately been captain of the *Tigris*, in which he had sunk two armed trawlers, three supply ships and a U-boat during patrols in the Bay of Biscay and off northern Norway. I found his advice and encouragement most helpful, so that when the signal came early in June appointing me to command the 'S' class submarine P228, now completing in HM Dockyard, Chatham, I felt fully confident at last of my ability to carry out successful attacks on the enemy.

---

[1] Captain R G Mills DSO DSC.
[2] Captain H F Bone CBE DSO DSC.

3 · In time for 'Torch'

July 1942. Chatham Dockyard. I knew my way to the fitting-out basin, where the *Triumph* had lain when I joined her as first lieutenant two years previously. Another, somewhat smaller, submarine was now in her berth, firmly secured fore and aft by wire ropes looped over bollards on the dockside and distanced from the dock walls by large catamarans of heavy timber. A cat's cradle of assorted air hoses and electric cables connected the boat with shore services; men in grimy brown boiler suits – shipwrights, joiners, engine-fitters, electrical fitters and copper-smiths – were coming and going across heavy wooden gangways. Others were working on wooden stages slung from parts of the sub-marine's structure already in place, and the flash of welding torches could be seen even in the summer sunshine as the superstructure or casing of the boat was secured like a carapace over the cigar-shaped hull. Nowhere, so far, had the red lead paint on casing or conning tower yet been covered with grey; and the identity of the boat was not anywhere revealed. But this, I was sure, was my new command, the P228.

The submarine, I noted, was floating high in the water, so the main battery had not yet been put aboard. I walked into the submarine office building and found, in the room which I had myself once occupied, an extremely young-looking, fair-haired, smiling two-striper, who introduced himself as Bannar-Martin, the first lieutenant. He told me that the coxswain, Petty Officer Castle, and several key ratings had joined; the remainder were expected to arrive in time for storing the boat. The ship's company were accommodated in the naval barracks and had no complaints. Two more officers had yet to be appointed. After a quick look at the outline programme for completion and trials, we went next door to the engineer's office. Here a small older man in shirt-sleeves looked up from a table on which were spread engineering drawings, saw the two stripes on my uniform and said, 'Good morning, sir, welcome to your new boat.' My eye had taken in the thin gold stripe, trimmed with purple, of a warrant engineer on the jacket hanging by the door. 'Good morning,' I replied, 'you must be the Chief, Mr McMillan.' 'That's right, sir,' he said, 'and this is Saunders, our Chief ERA – he and I saw the boat launched, back in January.' He nodded towards the blue-shirted, curly-haired young man beside him. 'I expect you'd like to know how we are getting on, sir.' For the next couple of hours 'Chiefy' McMillan, in his pleasing West Country (not, as one might have expected, Scots) voice, told me all there was to know about the submarine which, until my arrival, he had quite rightly regarded as 'his' and which was now 'ours'.

The P228 had been laid down on 7 March 1941, the first of the wartime 'S' class submarines to be built in Chatham Dockyard. The earlier boats of the 'S' class included eight built at Chatham, beginning with the *Swordfish*, which had been completed in 1931. Being of medium size, but with a good armament and excellent all-round operational qualities, the 'S' class had borne the brunt of Britain's submarine offensive in the North Sea and Channel since the outbreak of war. But they had suffered severe losses from enemy mines and anti-submarine forces in these confined and shallow waters. Of the Chatham boats, six had been sunk by the end of February 1941, and with two more of the class also lost, this made eight out of the total of 12 built to that design.

The wartime 'S' boats were, however, more strongly built than the earlier ones, with welded rather than riveted hulls, giving them a maximum operational diving depth of 350 feet compared with 300; they were also several feet longer and had more powerful diesel engines, hence they were about a knot faster, being capable of over 14 knots on the surface and eight knots or so submerged. But what pleased me particularly was the news that our boat was to have, besides the six bow torpedo tubes of the earlier boats in her class, a seventh tube mounted aft outside the pressure hull and pointing astern.

We were to be the first boat, also, to have a 20mm Oerlikon anti-aircraft gun, which would be mounted on a platform at the after end of the bridge structure, as well as the 3-inch gun forward of it.

According to the Chief, fitting out and preliminary trials were to be completed by 8 August, as per programme. But the detailed work which remained to be done looked to me, as we studied the bar chart covering most of one wall in the office, most formidable. During the next few days I made my 'number' on the various dockyard officers who were directly concerned with fitting out submarines. It was evident that the dockyard was doing its best. The young constructor officer responsible for the P228 was most helpful. Perhaps because he was a 'hostilities only' member of the Royal Corps of Naval Constructors he was not afraid to comply with certain requests I made for alterations which could be done without causing delay in completion. The first of these was to remove some of the plating at the after end of the bridge structure so as to reduce the silhouette of the submarine and thus improve the chances of carrying out a night surface attack unseen. I asked him, also, to dismantle the bridge steering wheel and its associated rod gearing. I explained that when at sea in wartime the submarine was always steered from the control room; to have the helmsman on the bridge would be one more person to get down through the conning tower hatch when the submarine had to dive, which was nearly always in a hurry. So bridge steering was used only when entering or leaving harbour.

I took the view that the best way to make sure of reliable communication between the bridge and control room when attacking on the surface at night, when it really could make the difference between success or failure, was to use control room steering at all times, which must include going in and out of harbour. My cooperative constructor saw the point and ordered his fitters to remove the steering wheel and its gearing from the P228's bridge. Chiefy McMillan viewed this process with some concern. He foresaw the disapproval of higher authority being visited not only on me, but on himself as the engineer officer, when it was discovered that we had accepted the boat from its builders minus steering wheel; wisely, he ensured that the redundant steering wheel and its gearing were kept on board for the time being.

Our excellent constructor was also able to help by getting reproduced for us a special plotting chart which I had designed for use with an electrically driven plotting table – the latest submarines were all being equipped with this. I had cut out part of an antiquated Admiralty chart publication known as a mooring board, used by the navigating officers and signalmen of Jellicoe's battleships, and stuck it on the back of an old navigation chart, then added a suitable speed-time-distance scale. The resultant submarine plotting chart was eventually copied by the Admiralty and published (without any acknowledgement to me, I may say) for general use in submarines.

I had been able to find a comfortable bedroom and sitting room for Somers, Angus and me in the Queen's Head, Old Brompton. This was the pub which we had stayed in while I was standing by the *Triumph* in 1940, when the Battle of Britain was going on overhead and a bomb had fallen on our bedroom – luckily when we were away. The damage had been repaired and we were very happy to be back there. It was summer and with the window open Angus could hear all sorts of sounds and voices drifting in. One day he heard the tramp of marching feet, saw below him a fine body of men (Royal Marines, as it happened) and piped in a firm treble, 'Get into step, you ruddy soldiers!' Apart from occasional sneak raids the bombing had ceased, thanks to our mastery of the air over Britain coupled with (or perhaps because of) the preoccupation of the Luftwaffe with the campaign in Russia. But Somers and I knew that we would not have very long together. Every moment was precious.

The P228's programme of tests and trials went on according to plan. The main engines, Admiralty designed diesels which had been built in the dockyard, performed well; the main motors, which would drive the boat when she was submerged, were installed and ran perfectly; the main battery was embarked, cell by cell, and connected up; the telemotor system for operating the numerous valves, the hydroplanes and the steering gear; the high pressure and low pressure air systems; the gyro compass, wireless telegraphy equipment and periscopes; the torpedo control system and so on; everything was brought forward in the correct sequence, installed and tested. Then came the very special test known as the 'basin dive'. It was the first time that the submarine had been fully submerged. The depth of water in the fitting-out basin was just enough for this, leaving the conning tower exposed. No water came in.

By now two more officers had joined, Sub-lieutenant Terence Martin, who was to be third hand and navigator, and Sub-lieutenant Robert Balkwill RNVR, who was to be fourth hand and armament officer. Terence was a keen young warrior who had already volunteered to serve in 'X' craft (midget submarines) and was awaiting his appointment for training. As to Robert, it was his first submarine, but in civilian life he had completed his articles with a firm of solicitors and I had no doubt of his capacity to learn on the job. The full ship's company had now joined and the first lieutenant, with the coxswain, was very busy organising them into their various watches and stations. Stores of all kinds, spare parts, torpedoes and gun ammunition had to be embarked. It was hard work for all. The efficient and timely completion of the myriad tasks depended critically upon the cooperation of my crew with the many individuals who manned the dockyard and the naval, victualling and armament stores.

This was forthcoming, and by 8 August the P228, resplendent in

HM Submarine P228 (later *Splendid*) leaving Chatham, August 1942.

her final coat of grey with her number painted on the conning tower, was ready to be formally commissioned. This involved none of the ceremonial, witnessed by families and friends, followed by hospitality on board and parties elsewhere, which marks the commissioning of one of HM ships in peacetime. I held a short meeting with senior dockyard officers in the submarine office to get their agreement to complete the few items which still had to be done; then the chief engineering officer on the staff of the Admiral (Submarines) inspected the boat, pronounced her satisfactory and that was that. We had laid on a few drinks in the submarine's wardroom for the little group to whom we owed her successful completion. Having alerted the Mayor of Chatham to our imminent departure, we had received from him the somewhat equivocal message: 'Goodbye and best wishes. We hope that you have better luck than the last Chatham boat.' This was the *Sterlet*, which had been sunk in the Skagerrak in April 1940.

The day after the formal commissioning I took the P228 out of the dockyard basin, down the Medway and into the Thames estuary for engine and steering trials. Only minor adjustments were needed. I then made the necessary signals to various authorities of my intention to sail for Portsmouth five days later on passage to the Holy Loch for acceptance trials and working up. There was time for forty-eight hours' leave for those of the ship's company who requested it. Not all did. I took Somers and Angus back to the Manor Farm, travelling by a combination of taxi, rail and bus. Denis was at sea but Ursula Lambert was welcoming as ever, and I felt so thankful that Somers, who was now seven months pregnant, would be in safe and happy surroundings with Angus while I was away which, this time, might be for a year at least.

Early on the morning of 19 August the P228, 'being in all respects ready for sea slipped and proceeded'. By late in the afternoon we were off Beachy Head. Suddenly the sky seemed to be full of aircraft – friendly as it turned out – and the horizon in the direction of France became dotted with small vessels, which the fighters were protecting. No one had told me, quite naturally I suppose as I really had no need to know, that a large-scale raid on Dieppe was taking place that day. What we could see were the surviving landing craft, with a few escorts, returning to Newhaven. As we heard in due course, the raid was a near disaster, with heavy casualties among the Canadian army and the commandos. But many lessons were learnt which contributed to the success of the Normandy landings two years later.

It had been a tribute to Britain's control of the Channel coast and the air space above it that the P228 had been able to make the passage to Portsmouth safely, unescorted. But for the rest of the way to the Clyde we were given an escort. During our short stay in the submarine base at Gosport, Terence Martin had departed to join 'X' craft. His relief was Lieutenant Gordon Hardy RNVR, a barrister-at-law by profession, fresh from the submarine training class.

How agreeable it was, in bringing my smart new submarine alongside the depot ship *Forth*, in the Holy Loch, to sound off on the bo'sun's call in salute to my former captain, 'Tinsides' Ionides, and then be piped aboard the depot ship, to be greeted by the tall, strong, friendly figure of Ronnie Mills, the Commander (Submarines) for whom I had been working two months before. A happy turn of events, also, despite the agonies of war, to find myself with my own command in those superbly scenic waters where, in peacetime, I had loved to sail. But there was little time for such reflections. We were soon at sea again with flotilla staff officers on board, carrying out our acceptance trials. The first of these was to test the steering gear. On the way to the allocated area Number One made sure that the engineer commander who had to witness the trial was given the best breakfast that we could lay on. It was a fine morning and after his second cup of coffee he appeared on the bridge. I greeted him and said that in a few minutes we would be in the area and could start the steering trial. 'Right, captain,' he said, 'we'll start with the bridge steering position.' At this point there was what is known as 'a deathly 'ush'. That is to say, one could hear the muffled exhaust of the diesels rumbling away and the swish-swish of the sea along the saddle tanks – but no word spoken. After a long pause the very senior commander, who had been staring at the space where the steering wheel had been in all the submarines he had ever been aboard, said coldly, 'Where is it? The steering wheel, where is it? What have you done with it?'

I began to explain my views on the undesirability of bridge steering wheels in submarines in wartime, but the commander cut me short. 'Captain,' he said, 'I am not in the slightest bit interested in your views. I have no intention of accepting this submarine on behalf of their Lordships if it hasn't got a bridge steering wheel. What *have* you done with it, by the way?' I mentally thanked God for Chiefy McMillan's wisdom and replied, 'It's on board, sir. We kept it just in case our initiative was not approved.' 'Just as well,' said the commander, 'because you're going to have to put it back PDQ. Meantime we'll get on with the trial, using control room steering. When you're ready to put the rudder hard over to starboard let me know and we'll take it from there.'

We then carried out a satisfactory full-power trial on main engines and in the afternoon returned to harbour. By next day the Chief and his team had reinstalled the bridge steering wheel. They had worked all night, bless them. Fortunately the wheel functioned to the commander's satisfaction when tried, so our programme of acceptance trials was not delayed.

The next thing was the 'deep dive', and this produced a thrill. Having reached the deep-water area between Arran and the Mull of Kintyre, I dived the submarine carefully to periscope depth; then, when the trim was right and no leaks had been reported, I began to take her down by stages to 350 feet. As we reached that depth the stern suddenly went down and the boat took up an angle of about 20 degrees. I ordered the main ballast tanks to be blown and we came to the surface. An investigation by Chiefy McMillan and the first lieutenant revealed no cause for the occurrence. I tried a second time. Once again, having reached 350 feet on the depth gauges, the stern went quickly down. This was most disconcerting, but there was no report of water coming in anywhere so, rather than blow the main ballast tanks, I speeded up the main motors and the boat was easily brought under control. It was generally agreed, although never proved, that an air lock in the telemotor (hydraulic) system had resulted in a valve which should have been shut remaining open and allowing water to enter an after trimming tank. At any rate no structural fault had been revealed and the P228 was formally accepted from her builders by me, representing the Lords Commissioners of the Admiralty. That night her bridge steering wheel was again removed, this time never to be replaced.

The P228, I and my crew were aware, was destined for the Mediterranean; we knew that only our submarines and aircraft were capable of sinking the supply ships on which Rommel was totally dependent in the desert war. His Afrika Korps had run out of steam less than 60 miles from Cairo. If we could cut his supply line decisively our army could beat him. To me, it was the prospect of operating directly in support of our land and air forces which was the greatest incentive to complete our work-up without delay and get into the battle. Fortunately, with the efficient support of the flotilla staff of experienced officers and senior ratings, all went well: the torpedo firings at Arrochar, on the Loch Long range; the noise trials in Loch Goil; the torpedo attack practice in Inchmarnock water; and the opportunity to fire our guns.

By now I had fully regained my confidence in being able to attack a target successfully with torpedoes; and I had been able to train my crew to a satisfactory pitch of efficiency. By the last week in September we had passed both the harbour inspection and the sea inspection by the flotilla work-up staff, and been pronounced ready for operational employment. Officers and men were given a few days' leave. All that we could say to our nearest and dearest was that our submarine was about to sail on operations and they would not be hearing from us for many weeks – even months. In the case of Somers and myself I could not even say that I might be seeing her parents in Malta. The few days at the farm with Somers and Angus in the Lambert household was as happy as, in the circumstances, it could be. Much of Essex is fairly flat and low-lying. But Danbury is on some higher ground between Maldon and Chelmsford; indeed, its parish church, with a fine spire, can be seen for many miles around. Brigadier Sir Bernard (later Lord) Fergusson of Ballantrae told a delightful story of an army exercise in 1940 when his regular brigade, representing an invading force, encountered the Home Guard defenders, commanded by Colonel (retired) Sir Carne Rasch Bt, squire of Danbury. In the post-exercise discussion, Sir Bernard asked Sir Carne why he had selected a particular defensive position on Danbury Common which had proved so effective. 'Oh, that's what we did when the Danes came,' replied Sir Carne. But the square head, piercing blue eyes and bushily moustachioed face, which one could easily imagine under a burnished and horned helm, testified on the contrary to what the Danes had done, despite local resistance.

The peaceful days, with walks in the autumnal countryside, tea in the nursery and evenings in the drawing room with a log fire, went much too quickly. Somers and I had been parted so often, with little idea of when or where we should be together again, that to be so on this occasion was no more than usually dreary. And the ease of mind in having Ursula and (when he was on leave) Denis Lambert in support of my little family was a blessing beyond words. As I passed through Glasgow on my way back to Holy Loch, I was able to call in and see my parents. They seemed to be in good spirits. Then it was down the Clyde to Gourock and across by launch to Holy Loch and so aboard the depot ship. On 3 October we sailed with orders to proceed direct, diving by day, on the surface at night, to Gibraltar. We would have an escort down the Irish Sea and take our departure from the Bishop Rock, off the Scilly Islands.

Our passage across the Bay of Biscay began uneventfully. The ship's company soon settled down to the routine of two hours on watch and four off, with diving stations at first light and evening twilight – the most dangerous times to be on the surface but necessary in order to take the starsights on which our ocean navigation depended. Only Chiefy McMillan, the boat's 'chef' Able Seaman 'Fred' Freeman and myself were excluded from the regular watch-keeping routine. From a captain's point of view, it was most heartening to feel the crew begin to develop into more than just an efficient team – our passage from Chatham to the Clyde, followed by the packed programme of acceptance trials and work-up, had left little time for us to get to know each other as individuals. Now it was no longer 'Strudwick' or 'Payne' in the stokers' mess but 'Vic' or 'Whacker'; and the lanky figure inserting himself with some difficulty into the tiny wireless office was 'Lofty' Goodhall, while the electrical artificer, whose name was Clarke, had inevitably become 'Nobby'.

I did not have a cabin in the P228 so I spent my time when awake mostly in the wardroom, reading. PG Wodehouse was a favourite with an occasional dip into Herbert Read's wartime anthology, *The Knapsack*. From time to time I would wander into the control room to see whether I agreed with the Pilot's view of where we had got to and perhaps bring the boat to periscope depth to take a look at the weather. Now and then I would walk through the boat with Number One and the Chief to see that everything was ship-shape. Rawdon Bannar-Martin, who by this time answered in the wardroom to 'Banger', had performed admirably ever since joining the boat before she was commissioned. He looked even younger than his twenty-three years and had a sense of fun which did not always appeal to the third and fourth hands, Robert Balkwill and Gordon Hardy, who though junior in naval seniority were older than he was and prone to affect a certain *gravitas* when Banger chose to fool about. Robert was unemphatic in manner – reserved perhaps – reflective and sceptical, and his personality complemented that of Gordon, who tended to be excitable and outspoken, particularly against himself. 'What a — I've been!' he would say after some minor mistake, using an Anglo-Saxon expletive seldom seen in print. But both men were extremely good and stimulating company, who learned fast and pulled their weight, and we laughed a good deal from time to time.

The P228's first brush with the enemy turned out to be a non-event. We had been at sea for about a week and were within 50 miles or so of Cape Finisterre, when a signal from the Admiralty informed us that an inward-bound blockade runner was in the area and that one of our cruisers was trying to intercept her. As we were now out of range of our own anti-submarine aircraft based in the United Kingdom, I decided to surface and set up a patrol. It was good to be running on the surface again, zig-zagging to confuse any U-boat whose path we might cross and enjoying the fresh air drawn through the conning tower into the control room to dissipate the clammy, over-utilised and stale air, redolent of diesel oil and cooking smells, which was our normal environment by day. On the bridge, with an officer of the watch and two lookouts, I strained every nerve to be the first to sight the blockade runner which we all felt was to be our first target. But it was the lookout on top of the periscope standards who shouted, 'Green five-zero! Smoke!'

'Diving stations!' I ordered down the voice-pipe, followed by 'Starboard twenty' and further conning orders to bring the smoke right ahead. It was vital for the submarine to present the smallest possible silhouette and by holding that course for a few minutes it would become apparent whether the vessel which was producing the smoke was moving right or left; once I knew this I could make sure that I did not lose contact. It would probably be necessary, unless the course of the target was going to bring her within two or three miles of me and permit me to carry out a dived attack, to shadow her until it was dark and then attack on the surface at night.

I felt sure that if the vessel was not a trawler she must be a German blockade runner. Our own and Allied shipping was routed hundreds of miles away, out in the Atlantic. Tankers apart, the blockade runners were medium-sized, modern freighters and assumed to be diesel-engined, not coalfired (they had nowhere to go for coal). Perhaps I should have had doubts, therefore, when we began to overhaul the target quite quickly and I could see that it was, indeed, a coal-burning merchant ship. She was slow, too. At our best speed, a little over 14 knots, we soon approached to within a mile or so. Then I saw that the vessel had stopped and was lowering a boat. I stopped also. I recalled our own use of Q-ships, which would lure a U-boat to come close by simulating panic stations and lowering a boat, then suddenly run up the White Ensign and open a withering fire with guns which had been concealed behind dummy upperworks.

The SS *Gaiska*, as our quarry turned out to be, was neither a blockade runner nor a Q-ship, but an innocent little Portuguese tramp steamer which had sailed two days previously from Oporto bound for Dublin with a cargo which probably included port wine for the German embassy there. No doubt the U-boat command had been warned not to attack her – but the signal from Flag Officer North Atlantic reporting her sailing was not received by us until next day. Fortunately her crew, in taking to the lifeboat, had had the presence of mind to bring with them some cases of port and sherry, which were quickly exchanged for cigarettes.

This episode, trivial as it was, served to knit the P228's crew even more closely together. The prospect of sinking a blockade runner, the excitement of the chase and the not entirely fruitless outcome, amusing in itself, raised morale, even if we had not found an enemy. I was glad of such activity because I had obtained permission, exceptionally, to omit from our programme the working-up patrol in some area of relatively low operational priority which usually preceded the deployment of a newly-commissioned submarine into the front line.

Hardly had we set course once again for Gibraltar when we received a signal telling us that a blockade runner bound outward, the *Burgenland*, had taken refuge temporarily in the Spanish port of Ferrol. We were ordered, together with a sister ship of ours, the P217, and the older submarine *Proteus*, on passage homeward from the Mediterranean, to form a patrol line off Ferrol in order to intercept the *Burgenland* when she sailed. As the P228 was near enough to enable me to be there at least twenty-four hours before either of our patrol mates I decided to enter the great haven of El Ferrol, dived by daylight, in order to take a good look at the *Burgenland*, even though there could be absolutely no question of torpedoing her in a neutral harbour. I regarded the operation as having some military value, mainly as a further substitute for the working-up patrol.

It proved not too difficult to bring the submarine to a point within a couple of miles of a ship in Ferrol harbour, which looked like the *Burgenland*, as far as we could glean her particulars from Talbot-Booth.[1] The temptation to torpedo her was considerable, but to have yielded to it might well have brought Spain into the war against us, which Hitler had so far failed to do. Unfortunately, while withdrawing to seaward down the long narrow approach to Ferrol, I met the returning fishing fleet and had to dive deep to avoid them. The largest scale chart which I had of the area was inadequate for precise position fixing and while I was executing the manoeuvre the submarine touched the bottom. This was not clever, as the streamlined dome surrounding the asdic oscillator was damaged and could only be repaired in dock.

That evening the P228 took up her station, which was the northernmost of the three boats in the patrol line, to seaward of Ferrol outside Spanish territorial waters. We closed a fully lighted ship which left the harbour and came in our direction, just in case it should be the *Burgenland* trying a *ruse de guerre*. But it was not her.

Two or three days later we were ordered to proceed to Gibraltar, the blockade runner having sailed.[2] Although we were forced to dive by one of our own aircraft when nearing Gibraltar we arrived there safely on 16 October to join the 8th Submarine Flotilla, commanded by Captain GBH Fawkes[3] in the depot ship *Maidstone*. Receipt of our recognition signal by the port war signal station at Europa Point on the famous Rock was followed immediately by the transmission of a signal addressed, 'P228 from s8. Personal for Commanding Officer from Captain Fawkes', informing me of the safe and timely arrival on 8 October of Alexander. This was glad news indeed and a great relief to me. I had known, before sailing from Holy Loch, that Somers was to be taken into Fulmer Chase, a private house in Buckinghamshire which had been turned into a maternity home for the wives of junior officers. By the time that I turned in that night in my comfortable cabin on board the *Maidstone*, McGeoch Mark II's health had been guaranteed, together with that of his mother, in repeated libations and, as the phrase has it, I was 'feeling no pain'.

I had not met 'Barney' Fawkes before. His style of leadership differed

[1] Author of *Merchant Ships* (London, 1942).
[2] The P217 had radioed a report of the *Burgenland*'s departure but she had avoided further attack (P217's was aborted by a torpedo failure) and reached Japan in January. On her return passage a year later she was sunk in the South Atlantic by the US Navy.
[3] Rear Admiral G B H Fawkes CB CVO CBE.

Lieutenant Rawdon Bannar-Martin, 1941.

from that of Shrimp Simpson in being more conventional and less (openly, at any rate) sceptical of the navy's higher leadership, steeped as it still was in the ethos of the battleship era. Shrimp had seemed to thrive on running the 10th Submarine Flotilla, which was in the very forefront of the battle, on a shoe-string. With a handful of staff officers he improvised a submarine base in bomb-shattered and beleaguered Malta. Barney, by contrast, appeared to be weighed down by the responsibility of running his flotilla despite being aided by a large and competent staff with a fully manned and equipped modern depot ship berthed in a major dockyard where the only danger was the occasional sneak air raid. I formed the impression that whereas Barney hankered after eventual promotion to flag rank and was anxious not to prejudice his chances by speaking out of turn, Shrimp had no such ambition and said bluntly, on all occasions, whatever he thought had to be said.

Nevertheless, I found Barney a friendly and considerate officer to serve under and the atmosphere in the *Maidstone* was welcoming.

The Staff Officer (Operations) was Lieutenant-Commander Joe Cowell, whose younger brother Louis had served with me in the *Clyde*, where he had relieved Tom Craven-Phillips as engineer officer. Joe was invariably cheerful and supportive. His own experience had included torpedoing the German torpedo-boat *Luchs* off Norway in the *Swordfish*, and bringing back to Alexandria, when in command of the *Thrasher*, 78 British troops who had remained hidden in Crete since the end of the fighting there. I managed to convince him that although P228 was newly commissioned and had not done a work-up patrol before leaving the United Kingdom, she did not need one, and could be sent into the fray after the necessary repairs, maintenance and replenishment had been carried out.

Soon after our arrival in Gibraltar we heard the announcement of the British army's successful offensive at El Alamein. The rejoicing was tremendous. By this time, despite the emphasis on security, I had become aware that a formidable Allied operation called 'Torch' was about to be launched. The airfield just inland of the Rock was packed with aircraft. The harbour was full of ships. Everywhere there was bustle. When I received my patrol orders on 30 October I found that the P228 had been given the equivalent of a walking-on part in Act I of the forthcoming drama, with the possibility of a more important role later.

On sailing next day we were to proceed to a patrol billet off Toulon. This station would have been vacated by Ernie Turner's[1] P217, which should have departed by then for Algiers, having embarked clandestinely the wife of a French general (Madame Beaufre) and several of General Giraud's staff officers. My orders were to observe and report the French fleet if it should sally forth to oppose the Allied landings in what was still French North Africa. Should the French remain in harbour during the critical period of Operation 'Torch', the P228 would be released to 'proceed to the Naples area via the Gulf of Genoa, keeping one full salvo of torpedoes for use there as the three Littorio battleships were known to be in Naples.'

We sailed as directed soon after dark on 31 October and proceeded eastward into the Mediterranean on the surface. It was standard practice for a submarine on leaving harbour to take the first opportunity to submerge in order to make sure not only that all the possible sources of entry into the hull of water under pressure had been properly shut off – this was particularly important after having been in dock –

[1] Captain E J D Turner OBE DSO DSC.

but also that the right amount of water had been put in the various trimming tanks to compensate for any changes of weight that may have taken place, such as embarkation of stores, torpedoes, fuel and fresh water since arrival in harbour. A trim dive was not practicable in the immediate vicinity of Gibraltar, owing to the probable presence of U-boats, for one of which we might have been mistaken by our own forces.

When at dawn we had reached a point some 80 miles east of Gibraltar I dived the submarine with due care. I was satisfied that the first lieutenant, whose job it was to work out the trim and see that it was correctly 'put on' before leaving harbour, had got his sums right. However, it quickly became apparent, in a somewhat alarming fashion, that the after hydroplanes (which are used to control the angle up or down of the submarine) were seriously defective. After rapid but thorough checks Chiefy McMillan established that only by docking the boat could the defect be located precisely and remedied. In consequence I had to surface forthwith and head back for Gibraltar, hoping that the emergency secret signal which I had to make to the authorities there giving my expected time of arrival and the reason for my return would be received, understood, approved and disseminated in time to save P228 from another assault by friendly aircraft.

By 3 November we were once again in the dry dock. Captain Fawkes and his 8th Flotilla staff could not have been more efficient and understanding. Even the Commander (Submarines) in the depot ship, 'Bertie' Pizey, a man not known for his tolerance of errant COs, accepted as 'just one of those things' the considerable extra labour involved in fitting the P228's unscheduled requirements into his already most intricate programme of submarine movements. Having made all the preparations which I could for the coming war patrol I decided to take as much exercise as possible.

Accordingly, on the afternoon of 6 November I walked up the Rock by the steepening path above Europa Point as far as the wartime defences permitted, and stood gazing seaward. It was a view which I had frequently enjoyed, not only for its scenic beauty with the scarcely-ruffled blue sea of the Straits stretching away to east and west and the dimly-discernible snow-capped mountains of Morocco to the south, but for its historic significance for Britain and the navy. I had not been conscious until that moment of playing a part in some great campaign which one day would find its place in the history books. But as I looked, first eastward to the Mediterranean, where fierce and bloody battles were in progress in the desert, then west towards the Atlantic, where the u-boat war still raged, I suddenly noticed that beneath the red ball of the sun as it set in the autumnal haze the horizon was dotted with ships. As I strained my eyes I realised that a vast convoy was approaching, with that deceptive lack of obvious motion characteristic of distant vessels. It was indeed the leading assault convoy of Operation 'Torch', carrying the troops who would land at Algiers and Oran at daybreak two days later. Soon the Straits appeared to be completely filled with shipping – the assorted transports, nearly fifty of them, in their columns on a broad front and their escorts stationed all around. As darkness fell the armada would be passing Gibraltar, to be faithfully reported by the enemy's agents on Spanish soil as yet another major operation for the relief of Malta. The deception had been complete.

At 6.00 pm on 7 November the P228 sailed from Gibraltar to patrol off Toulon in support of Operation 'Torch', as previously ordered. I arrived in my billet on 12 November, saw nothing at all and two days later was ordered to patrol off Naples. The next day, having crossed 8 degrees East (the longitude of Monte Carlo) I came under the operational control of Captain (s) 10 in Malta. In his signal he ordered me to proceed coastwise via Genoa, reporting when I had passed through the Corsica-Capraia strait for the benefit of the *Sturgeon* and *Tribune* which were to follow.

Our first encounter with the enemy came in the mid-morning of 16 November when we had reached a position about 25 miles south-west of the main Italian naval base of La Spezia. Robert Balkwill, who was on watch, called me into the control room to look at an object which he had sighted. It was a sunny day with enough breeze to create small waves. What I saw when I looked through the search periscope in high power was a white (or so it seemed with the sunlight on it) bridge structure, which at first I took to be that of an oil tanker hull down on the horizon. Then I realised that what I was looking at was the conning tower of a German 500-ton u-boat, painted light grey. 'Down periscope! Diving stations! Port thirty! Group up! Full ahead starboard! Half ahead port! Bring all tubes to the ready!' Round we went, hellbent on getting in a shot at so vital a target. I had not expected to see a u-boat on the surface in broad daylight in the relatively confined waters of the Mediterranean where we ourselves almost invariably remained submerged by day. Having turned through 180 degrees and slowed down I looked again at the target. From the angle of its conning tower, which was all that I could see of it, the u-boat had already gone past the bearing at which, given the range of 5,000 yards or so, I could have a reasonable chance of scoring a hit. Then it altered course towards us and offered the prospect of a successful attack. Off went my first salvo of the patrol – six torpedoes fired individually and spread so as to allow for considerable error in my estimations of the target's course and speed.

Two minutes – as we know from Remembrance Day – can seem a long time, but our torpedoes would have had at least that time to run before hitting the target if they were going to do so. The minutes ticked by as I stood in the control room. When, after twelve minutes or so, we heard the faint explosions of the six torpedoes as they hit the sea bottom eight miles away, all I could think of saying to those within earshot was, 'Sorry, chaps. That was a U-boat, that was – and still is. But at least we know we can fire a full salvo in action conditions without breaking surface – and the fish ran correctly.' At once I got to work with Gordon to analyse the attack. We soon came to the conclusion that I had considerably underestimated the U-boat's speed as being 12 knots, when it was probably doing at least 15 knots, the German boats being much faster on the surface than our own submarines.

Petty Officer Dixon, our calm and utterly reliable torpedo expert, lost no time in reloading the torpedo tubes, but we knew that we must not expend another salvo before we had reached our billet off Naples, and then only on the Italian battleships if they should come within range. So it was with some satisfaction that, on the afternoon of the same day, we came upon an auxiliary schooner of some 300 tons. After stalking her thoroughly with the search periscope in high power I came to the conclusion that she was some kind of naval patrol vessel. I thought that, with luck, she might have on board charts which would show where the Italians had laid mines and especially if they had done so in the Corsica-Capraia channel, through which we would have to pass that night. Provided that the vessel did not turn out to be a Q-ship, a surprise gun attack, followed by boarding and then sinking with a demolition charge, seemed to be called for.

The P228 surfaced about a thousand yards from the schooner and at once opened fire, achieving some hits, at which the crew of the vessel lost no time in lowering a boat and piling into it. We ceased fire and I laid the submarine alongside, so that a boarding party consisting of Robert Balkwill, Petty Officer Electrician Oram and Leading Signalman Auckland could leap across to what was now our prize. Meanwhile we kept a keen lookout for aircraft or any other sign of the enemy. In less than five minutes the boarding party had returned with various trophies. By far the most important was a bagful of confidential books and documents found by Robert in the master's cabin in a safe in which he had obligingly left the key. Petty Officer Oram had over his arm what appeared to be the master's shoregoing suit, complete with condom in the vest pocket; while our signalman had taken possession of the schooner's Italian ensign.

It had been my intention to use a demolition charge to sink the vessel – although I had no wish whatever to destroy such a fine little ship – but Oram reported that there was some ammunition in her hold, so I decided to haul off and let the gun's crew have some practice. It took 35 rounds in all, of which about 20 hit, before she sank. Submerged and heading southwards again, we spread out on the wardroom table the secret and confidential material which Robert had collected. There were twenty-two items in all, including an envelope containing Italian recognition signals for vessels under 1,000 tons. There was also a handbook of instructions for the cos of anti-aircraft and anti-submarine vessels. We thought this might come in handy. But of the positions of minefields there was no word. It appeared from the nature of most of the documents, which were concerned with aircraft recognition, that the *Sao Paolo*, as the schooner was called, was being used as a picket to provide early warning of the approach from seaward of Allied aircraft. But the equipment with which she was provided for this purpose was pathetically (and hearteningly, from our point of view) ancient, consisting as it did of a rather outsized ear-trumpet. Nevertheless, even if one felt rather as one did as a boy when one had shot a 'cheeper', the *Sao Paolo* had enabled us to break our duck, although not, alas, by sinking a U-boat as Mike Lumby had done the previous August on his working-up patrol in the P213.

Having passed safely between Corsica and Capraia and signalled Captain (s) 10 to that effect, we arrived in our patrol billet some 15 miles south-west of the Bay of Naples on 18 November. Bearing in mind the directive to keep a full salvo of torpedoes for the Italian battlefleet, I had the mortification of having to let pass first an armed merchant cruiser and then, what hurt even more, an Italian submarine. This was ambling along on a steady course towards Naples, emitting a cloud of black smoke which indicated that something was seriously wrong with its engines. I consoled myself and my crew with the opinion that to put my telescope to my blind eye and ignore my orders *à la* Nelson at Copenhagen would not have been justifiable. That evening yet another U-boat passed by, although it was too dark to identify it. This was a bit much. It seemed to me that the wave of

U-boats returning to base indicated acceptance by the Axis of the Allied landings in North Africa as a *fait accompli*, in which case the prospect of a sortie by the Italian battlefleet would have ceased to be a strong possibility. I decided to attack the next enemy submarine that came along.

It had to be assumed that the approaches to so important a naval base as Naples would be scanned by RDF (as radar was called then) so that when we were on the surface at night charging the battery it would prudent to keep more than 15 miles to seaward of the flanking islands of Capri and Ischia. To be sure of finding targets it was essential to close to within a few miles of the arrival point, the position of which we had already plotted. During daylight on 20 November we stole slowly inshore, just keeping clear of a sweep of anti-submarine schooners which came out in our direction and then went back. It happened that moonrise was early that night. This enabled me to remain submerged a bit later than usual, so as to be as near as practicable to the enemy's arrival point. As we crept quietly along, Gordon and I sat at the wardroom table trying out with matches the tactics of carrying out an attack on a target which could be heard but not seen except at the last moment. Robert, I seem to remember, was making characteristically sardonic remarks, when the cry came, 'Captain in the control room!' followed by 'Diving stations!' Banger was wasting no time. 'Diesel HE, sir. Must be another U-boat.'

It was. 'If I miss this one,' I said to the control room in general as I grasped the handles of the search periscope, 'I'm a Dutchman.' I did miss, and was thereafter called 'Jan' by my crew, although I did not know this until many years later. Why I had missed I found it difficult to determine. The U-boat had appeared in my periscope view, crossing the path of moonlight as I had hoped. I had fired a full salvo of six torpedoes, all of which were heard to run properly, and I had spread the salvo over two targets' lengths, which should have covered substantial errors in the estimation – admittedly difficult in the circumstances – of the U-boat's course and speed. It was probably the speed that I had again under-estimated. We were not yet fully versed in the technique of attack using only the bearings of a target which could be obtained by listening on the asdic, supplemented by a count of the beat of its propellers to give the revolutions per minute (RPM) and hence an approximation of its speed.

It was necessary to withdraw forty miles or so from the land (since our position would be revealed to the enemy's radio direction finders) before transmitting the obligatory report to Captain (s) 10 that I had expended more torpedoes to no effect. I could well imagine the comments of the redoubtable Captain Simpson when he received my signal. Although the supply of submarine torpedoes was by now adequate, it had not always been so. Indeed, during their early operations from Malta in 1941 it had been necessary for our submarines to husband very carefully the stock of torpedoes, which had led to many missed attacks arising from firing only two torpedoes at supply ships when it could be shown theoretically that by firing three in a salvo the chances of scoring at least one hit were doubled. It had always been policy, however, to fire a full salvo (in our case six) torpedoes in any attack on a u-boat, so vital was it to sink as many of them as possible.

Moodily munching my unappetising breakfast of flaccid tinned bacon afloat in a mess of tomato pulp, I could not help being aware that the high morale engendered in the P228's crew by our boarding and then sinking the *Sao Paolo* had by now evaporated. It cannot be denied that the captain of a submarine on war patrol has a task more exacting than that of the captain of a surface warship. For the latter seldom, if ever, finds himself operating alone and unsupported in waters wholly under enemy control, and if he should encounter the enemy the officers and men around him can see as much of the action as he can and help him to fight it. I still had one torpedo left with which, if Fate were kind to me, I might redeem myself and enable my ship's company to hold their heads high amongst their flotilla mates when we returned to harbour. So I continued hopefully on the course which I had set at dawn, when with the battery well charged we had dived and headed for the main entrance to Naples Bay – the Bocca Grande.

From various indications I knew that the asdic conditions were more than usually good, particularly because it was dead calm, and I decided to keep the submarine deep. Not long after I had swallowed my seldom varied lunch of cold corned beef and pickles I was summoned to the control room. I waited for the P228 to come to periscope depth. The big search periscope revealed two merchant ships and a destroyer.

We ran in at full speed towards the convoy at right angles to its bearing in order to close the range as much as possible. With only one torpedo we had to get within a thousand yards to have a decent chance of hitting the target. After ten minutes at our best submerged speed I slowed the boat down and came to periscope depth for another look. I had calculated I might be able to torpedo the escorting destroyer and then surface to engage at least one of the supply ships with gunfire. I now saw that there was another destroyer over on the far side of the convoy. However, the nearer destroyer looked a good big modern one and a worthwhile target. Provided that she did not detect us on her asdic, which in the control room we could hear pinging away, we could sidle across her bows and fire our stern torpedo at her from a most advantageous position. The sea being still glassy calm it was necessary to use the periscope with the utmost care. We remained unseen and undetected as the smart-looking Italian destroyer steamed unconcernedly past and I was able to draw a bead just abaft its single fat funnel. A fairly loud bang indicated that we had at last scored a hit.

It was several minutes before the inevitable counter-attack developed – ten depth-charges in quick succession, too far off to worry about. In the meantime Chiefy McMillan had reported, 'Shut off for depth-charging, sir. Boat in silent routine,' adding in a *sotto voce* which could be heard throughout the now noiseless control room, 'If I were you, sir, I'd tur-r-n ar-r-se on and crawl away.' This succinct saying, embodying as it did the essence of prudent evasive tactics following an attack which had disclosed the submarine's position, became something of a catch-phrase in the wardroom. Certainly on this occasion it proved to be sound advice. Apart from single depth-charges going off at intervals for an hour or two, no doubt to act as a deterrent against any further attack upon the damaged destroyer, we had no more trouble.

That night the P228 received the order from Captain (s) 10 to leave patrol and return to Gibraltar. We set off on a course to pass well south of Sardinia, hoping that we would not sight any more targets as, with no torpedoes left and not much gun ammunition, we could do very little about them.

Not long after we had surfaced at the end of a completely uneventful day on passage across the Tyrrhenian Sea, we sighted a small convoy and began to shadow it. Having determined its composition, course and speed, and transmitted an 'enemy report' to Captain (s) 10, we were about to continue on our way to Gibraltar when an aircraft, which in the bright moonlight we could easily recognise as a Wellington by its conspicuous tail-fin, began to attack the convoy. As we watched, line after line of tracer fire leapt up from the escorting warships towards the Wellington, which soon departed apparently unscathed. The attack had been successful and left one of the merchant ships stopped. About half an hour later, as we approached, it seemed to have been abandoned and we decided to sink it by gunfire.

Remembering some sage advice which I had once read in an official publication called *Submarine Experience* compiled after the First World War, I manoeuvred the P228 into a position from which Robert Balkwill and his gun's crew could fire at point blank range into the target from ahead. She eventually sank[1] but not before we had used up all our 3-inch ammunition, including the starshell which was carried to illuminate targets. As we altered course to the westward and began to increase speed, the boat began to roll and Banger, seeking to relax with a cup of coffee in the wardroom, was disconcerted by a periodical thump somewhere beneath the table. He discovered one remaining round of 3-inch starshell which had been overlooked. This was duly secured and held in readiness in case we should encounter the enemy yet again.

During the middle watch, Gordon sighted an object in the moon's path which he reported as a submarine. Acting on my standing instructions for such circumstances he gave the order to dive. Shortly after he arrived in the control room and shut the 'lower lid'[2], men in the fore-ends of the boat reported a noise 'just like the refrigerating machine'. Some minutes later two explosions were heard and it was concluded that the P228 had been attacked either by an E-boat or a U-boat.

Apart from sighting in the distance another small convoy, which appeared to be unescorted and in any case was heading towards Italy, the remainder of our passage back to Gibraltar was uneventful. As we entered harbour on 28 November, three weeks after setting out on our first war patrol, we displayed the Italian flag taken from the schooner *Sao Paolo*. This was frowned upon, as it would only have been correct to do so if the submarine itself had been a captured Italian one being brought in under the White Ensign. I had decided that the P228 would not follow the practice of flying the Jolly Roger. I had three reasons for wishing to break with what had become a custom in the submarine service when returning from a successful patrol. In the first place, I was strongly averse to making claims of sinkings which so often turned out to be damage only or even a miss. Secondly, I felt that the White Ensign was enough of itself – if submarines could fly a piratical flag after being in action why not other HM ships? Surely it was no more piratical to sink an enemy destroyer by torpedo from a submarine than, say, by gunfire from a cruiser. Thirdly, I had no

---

[1] This was the *Luigi Favorita* (3,576 tons).
[2] The lower of the two hatches in the conning tower.

wish to emphasise in any way the 'private navy' aspect of the submarine service. In my view we were as much part of the fleet as any surface ship.

Captain Fawkes and his staff welcomed the P228 warmly and the many helpers in the depot ship rallied round to assist in preparing the boat for her next patrol. There were few defects to be rectified but much routine maintenance to be done. Captain and crew also needed rest and recreation.

I was certainly thankful that I had not flown the Jolly Roger when coming into Gibraltar because next day I was required to present myself in my best uniform to the Flag Officer, North Atlantic, Vice-Admiral Sir GFB Edward-Collins. He listened to my much condensed report of my first war patrol and then said, 'Thank you, McGeoch, better luck next time,' making it clear that the interview was at an end. He may have been thinking, when I told him that I had missed not just one but two U-boats, of Oscar Wilde's Lady Bracknell: 'To lose one parent, Mr Worthing, may be regarded as a misfortune; to lose both looks like carelessness.' But I am more inclined to think, now that I know what happened to the destroyer which I hit, the *Velite*,[1] that he already knew from secret intelligence to which I was not privy that she had only been damaged and had been towed into harbour. If so, 'better luck next time' was not unreasonable comment.

Be that as it may, my officers and fellow COs, when told this story in the wardroom bar of the *Maidstone*, thought it hilarious, as I did. 'Better luck next time' became something of a watchword.

[1] I know now, also, that the escort of the convoy which I attacked included a third destroyer. Perhaps it was just as well that I did not see it.

4 · The P228 gets a name

The P228 sailed from Gibraltar on 8 December for her second war patrol, this time in the Sicilian Channel, the area between Sicily and Tunisia. When east of 8 degrees East, we were once again to be under the operational control of Captain (s) 10 at Malta, joining the twenty-five or so other boats with which he had been directed to support the Allied landings in North Africa. Since I had left the Mediterranean in the *Ursula* the previous December, a period of reintensified German bombing in the first few months of 1942 had succeeded in denying us, between May and August of that year, the use of Malta as a submarine base. As Shrimp Simpson[1] wrote:

> The number of civilian death tells the story; in the last ten days of December 1941 there were more than fifty deaths; in January 1942, eighty people died, while in February there were some 200 deaths from nearly 1,000 tons of bombs dropped on the island. March and April were, however, the real months of horror. In March 1942 over 2,000 tons of bombs were dropped on Malta while in April over 6,700 tons of bombs rained down on the inhabitants – a 'Coventry' size raid every day for over a month. The people of Malta endured during this bombing, and for most of the rest of the year, a state of semi-starvation – often receiving below 1,000 calories daily or less than one-third of the normal ration, without any firm prospect of likely improvement. Three hundred thousand men, women and children were always hungry. Their towns and ancient buildings were seriously wrecked, their businesses ruined, their whole future suspect and insecure and their native country wide open to invasion. Yet never for a moment did they flinch, although the more intelligent may have been doubtful

---

[1] Rear Admiral GWG Simpson, *Periscope View* (London, 1972) p. 186.

of the outcome. It was the discipline of the people in these circumstances that remains to me the miracle of Malta.

Several submarines had been sunk or severely damaged while in harbour, and the survivors – the P31, P34, P35, *Una* and *Urge* – had left Malta between 26 April and 10 May. Sadly, the *Urge* did not arrive at her destination, Alexandria. It seems most probable that she was destroyed on 29 April by Italian anti-shipping aircraft while attacking a supply ship by gunfire. Her captain, Tommo Tomkinson, whom I knew so well and whose activities I had followed closely, should in my view have been awarded the Victoria Cross – preferably before he was lost. In the course of seventeen patrols in command of the *Urge* Tommo had accounted for 26,000 tons of supply shipping sunk and a further 37,000 tons damaged; he had sunk the cruiser *Bande Nere* and put a torpedo into the battleship *Vittorio Veneto* so that she was out of action for two critical months. Like Wanklyn,[1] Tomkinson was indeed 'a verray parfit gentil knight', who sacrificed his life fighting to preserve Christendom from the forces of evil.

The strategic situation which governed the operation of our submarines in December 1942 was described by Shrimp Simpson in the following terms:

> Once Admiral Cunningham judged the threat to the 'Torch' landings to be both improbable and unimportant he immediately switched his central Mediterranean submarines to their normal and still vital duties of preventing supplies reaching North Africa, and signalled me to redispose ... The Commando Supremo's supply organisation in Rome reacted to the severe losses to the heavily escorted convoy on 19 October by switching the main supply route to the short run from Palermo round Cape St Vito then direct to Cani Rocks some twelve miles from Bizerta. From Cani Rocks their supply ships could go either to the port of Tunis or Bizerta as required.
>
> Air reconnaissance soon made this clear to us and intelligence told us that new minefields had just been laid on either side of this route from close west of Marittimo almost to Cani Rocks. This meant that to attack the main flow of supplies, submarines had to enter a narrow strip of sea 100 miles long and 20 miles wide with minefields preventing retirement north-west or south-east, and

---

[1] David Wanklyn had been lost on 14 April when on his twenty-first patrol, which was to have been his final one before taking the *Upholder* back to the UK.

operate against a fast shuttle service of fleet destroyers now carrying personnel, and heavily escorted supply ships. This was a natural development but a highly dangerous one for the attacking submarines.[1]

Four days after sailing from Gibraltar I received from Shrimp a signal ordering me to 'proceed on the surface at discretion' towards a position on the line Cape Bon – Marittimo which we reached forty eight hours later. I can distinctly recall going into the asdic office shortly after we had dived to listen to a certain unusual hydrophone effect emanating from a north-westerly direction. After a bit I realised that the sound was being caused by the motion of the current striking the shallows of the Skerki Bank. This confirmed our position and, sure enough, after twenty-four hours in the billet, a float plane appeared, weaving about in the direction from which our target was expected. About twenty minutes later I sighted what I took to be two supply ships escorted by two destroyers as well as another aircraft. Being almost right ahead of the convoy I was able to select my mode of approach, and decided to steer straight towards a position between the two columns of the convoy, then turn so as to be able to fire a bow salvo at one ship and my stern torpedo at the other.

The surface of the sea was darkened here and there by a light breeze but there was strong sunlight and I decided to go deep between periscope observations so as to minimise the chance of being seen from the air. We could hear the nearest escort's asdic transmission and when I next came to periscope depth I saw that I was 1,500 yards on her starboard bow. In the control room everyone held their breath. Would we be detected? Just then we heard an explosion, followed by five more; I thought that the submarine must have been sighted from the air so I went deep again. As there were no more explosions I came back to periscope depth and was thankful to see that the approaching escort had altered course away. This allowed me to complete my turn to the firing course just in time. I had told Robert to set 12 knots on the fruit machine, but as I began to fire a three torpedo salvo, aiming the first one a quarter of a length ahead of the target – a large, grey-painted freighter with a deck cargo of motor transport – I began to wonder whether I had got his speed right; so I turned the P228 to starboard, firing the next two torpedoes individually; then, because I had a feeling that all the torpedoes were missing ahead, I fired a fourth.

[1] Simpson, op. cit. p. 268.

Swinging the periscope right round I was just in time to put in a shot with the stern torpedo at the ship in the port column.

My patrol report reads:

> Fifty seconds after the fourth torpedo was fired there was an explosion, giving a running range of 1,300 yards ... Approximately ten minutes after the attack a very powerful explosion was heard which shook the submarine, followed by a report from the asdic operator of 'a series of small explosions'. There was no counter-attack.

Having seen only two supply ships in the convoy before I attacked it I was surprised and disappointed when, some time later, I came back to periscope depth and saw, in the distance, still two supply ships. I had to assume that, after all, I must have failed to hit my target. Within the next couple of hours John Stevens in the P46 and John Bromage in the P212 each torpedoed and sank one of the two ships. However, post-war analysis showed that the convoy had in fact consisted of three supply ships escorted by four torpedo boats when it left Sicily and that P228 had indeed sunk the ss *Sant' Antioca* (5,048 tons). Being loaded with ammunition, she had blown up, as I had originally believed.

That night the P228 was ordered to take up a new patrol position and warned to expect a convoy. Our navigation must have been accurate (and the intelligence also) for on 17 December a merchant ship was sighted coming from the direction of Naples towards Bizerta. She was escorted by four aircraft and two destroyers. I ran in at full speed for ten minutes, had another look, then pressed on in for another seven minutes, trying to get as near to the target as possible before firing. There was enough breeze to disturb the sea so that I was not too worried about my periscope being sighted. The trouble was that the destroyer nearest me was zig-zagging: instead of my being nicely between her and the target when I fired, she had come between me and my quarry which I could now see was camouflaged black and buff with a raked stem. When I began firing the salvo of six torpedoes the destroyer formed a continuous target line with the supply ship and I therefore spread the torpedoes to cover both ships. Two explosions a few seconds apart were heard at the torpedo running time for a range of 2,500 yards and then two more. HE from both the destroyer and the merchant ship ceased. The counter-attack from the other destroyer was slight. I was quite certain that I had hit the destroyer twice and the merchant ship twice.

HM Submarine *Splendid*'s officers, Algiers, February 1943.
Left to right: Harold McMillan, Robert Balkwill, the author, Gordon Hardy, Kenelm Burridge.

Alas, it was later revealed that although I had indeed hit the destroyer, which was the *Aviere*, twice and sunk her, I had missed the supply ship. I believe that when the *Aviere* was hit the supply ship was able to put her wheel hard over in time to avoid the rest of my torpedoes. Although I did not know it at the time, the supply ship was the German ship *Ankara*, the only vessel able to embark and discharge Tiger tanks for the Panzer divisions. She had been ferrying them to Tunisia with clockwork regularity. After several escapes from torpedoing she had become known to the Axis as the 'ghost ship'.[1] Having dodged my torpedoes the *Ankara* also managed to avoid those of Mike Lumby, whose P212 had been positioned by Shrimp to back me up. That night a note of exasperation was discernible in Shrimp's signal to me ordering the P228 to move to a new patrol position off Cagliari, the main port in the south of Sardinia. 'Aim at the destroyer next time,' Shrimp's message said. Perhaps he thought that I had aimed at the supply ship, missed it and hit the destroyer by a fluke.[2]

---

[1] Simpson, op. cit. p. 272.
[2] Edward Young in *One of our Submarines* (London, 1952) recorded this incident incorrectly. The destroyer was sunk by, and Shrimp's signal addressed to, the P228, not the P212.

I know now that Shrimp was included in the select band of operational commanders who were privy to intercepted and deciphered enemy signal traffic. But of course the last thing he could do was indicate in any of his own signals that his dispositions were based upon such up-to-date and reliable intelligence. No doubt he was acting on this when he ordered P228 to patrol off Cavioli Island, Sardinia, where I lurked about all day near the entrance to the known swept channel into Cagliari Bay, keeping clear of a minesweeper which was stationed there. Then, at last, almost half an hour after sunset, we heard the unmistakable sound of a submarine blowing its main ballast tanks. Diving stations! Nearly thirty tense minutes passed before HE was reported and a moment later I sighted a U-boat proceeding seaward silhouetted against the after-glow. I had only one torpedo left, having already fired four at one target, six at another (the double target) and one from the stern tube. The U-boat was zig-zagging, but I managed to get a shot at him which must have passed fairly close. I saw him alter course 90 degrees at the time my torpedo would have reached him, and he was heard to report on his radio that he had been attacked by a submarine. I was deeply despondent at missing yet another U-boat – even an Italian one.

On 21 December we left patrol and three days later arrived in Algiers, where the 8th Submarine Flotilla, with Barney Fawkes in the *Maidstone*, was now based. I do not think that Captain (s) 10, in ordering the P228 to leave patrol in time to reach harbour on Christmas Eve, was prompted by any consideration other than his knowledge that I had expended all my torpedoes. There was no reason why he should have known that 24 December was my wedding anniversary – the fifth. But it was a great day on which to arrive, both for my crew and myself. After reporting briefly to Barney Fawkes and having a word or two with Bertie Pizey and Joe Cowell, I was free to relax. It is impossible to recapture the ineffable bliss of being back in harbour after two or three weeks of physical discomfort, imminent danger and continuous concentration. The pleasures of a hot bath, clean clothes, a few drinks and an edible lunch, followed by several hours of uninterrupted slumber, could not have been surpassed. Mail from home with good news of Somers and the boys completed my contentment.

If any of the P228's people had felt sufficiently restored by the evening to want to sample the delights of Algiers they were out of luck. Rumour had it that someone had assassinated Admiral Darlan and it was feared that there might be trouble between various factions of the French citizenry so all leave was cancelled. It transpired that the admiral had been appointed by the Americans, representing the Allies, to be the High Commissioner in Algeria and Commander-in-Chief of the French forces, following the 'Torch' landings. As a 'collaborationist' with the German-dominated Vichy government Darlan was a traitor in the eyes of all Frenchmen who believed that only an Allied victory could restore France's independence. Darlan was shot by a young French patriot, René Bonnier de la Chapelle. Such was the political confusion and so uncertain were loyalties, that the French and American security police, still under Darlanist influence, arrested Bonnier and had him immediately court-martialled. Despite an initial pardon from General Giraud, he was executed next morning.

Shore leave was restored before New Year's Day and it was possible to take a look at Algiers. Amongst the ships in harbour was the cruiser *Argonaut*, which had been hit by two torpedoes from the Italian submarine *Mocenigo*. Her bow and stern had been severely damaged and it was a wonder that she had been got back to port. Her second-in-command at that time happened to be Commander Peter Pelly and I was delighted to receive an invitation from him to dine on board. Peter had been my term lieutenant in the cadet training ship *Erebus* ten years previously. He was a short, slim, good-looking man with fair, wavy hair, always impeccably turned out, many of whose caustic comments on the shortcomings of us cadets remained fixed in the memory. One Sunday when we were lined up in our best uniforms for inspection Peter studied my feet and remarked, 'You had better do something about those rustic boots, McGeoch.' However, he was good enough to recommend me in due course for transfer from the engineering to the executive branch of the navy so that my ambition to command one of HM ships might one day be fulfilled; and he must also have had a say in my being awarded the King's Dirk for the best all-round cadet of the year. It was typical of Peter that when I arrived alongside the battered *Argonaut* in the *Maidstone*'s motorboat he was standing at the head of the gangway ready to receive me, perfectly turned out in mess undress – 'bum-freezer', waistcoat, starched white shirt and butterfly collar, black bow tie and patent leather half-Wellington boots. We had much to talk about. It was largely thanks to his damage control organisation that the *Argonaut* had been saved, as I later found out.

On another day about this time the naval Commander-in-Chief, Admiral Sir Andrew Cunningham, sent for the submarine COs who were in harbour. We put on our best uniforms and drove up in service

85

transport to his fine villa in the best part of Algiers. During the previous week action had been started, perhaps reluctantly, by the First Sea Lord, Admiral Sir Dudley Pound, in response to Winston Churchill's minute of 19 December 1942:

> I am still grieved to see our submarines described as 'P212', etc., in the daily returns. I thought you told me that you would give them names. It is in accordance with the tradition of the Service and with the feelings of the officers and men who risk their lives in these vessels. Not even to give them a name is derogatory to their devotion and sacrifice.[1]

The submarine cos had had a certain amount of fun proposing names for their boats. Ours had to begin with 'S' but otherwise we had a free hand – or so I thought. The name which immediately suggested itself was *Scorpion*, for two reasons. Our initial war patrol had been based on Gibraltar and it was well-known that the slang term for inhabitants of the Rock is 'scorpion' or 'scorp'; and secondly, it had so happened that the P228's first torpedo to achieve a hit on the enemy was fired from her stern tube – a real sting in the tail. Unfortunately, when submitting the proposal that my submarine should be named the *Scorpion* I was unaware that a certain Lieutenant Andrew Cunningham had assumed command of a destroyer called the *Scorpion* on 11 January 1911 and remained in command of her for the next seven years.

The four or five of us, having been met by the flag lieutenant, were ushered into the presence of our renowned C-in-C wondering what was in store. The not very tall, red-faced, grey crew-cut admiral stood up and welcomed us warmly enough. Emerging from behind his desk he began to pace up and down the room as if it were the quarterdeck, paused, looked at us fiercely and said, 'One of you wishes to call his submarine *Scorpion*.' I instinctively tried to shrink from view and heard the great man go on, 'I have telegraphed [that was the archaism he used] to the controller that on no account should any submarine be named *Scorpion*. That is a destroyer name.' He then turned to some other matter. I have no recollection of anything else which 'ABC' said on that occasion, the only one on which I met – if that is the word – our most famous naval leader of the war. When we got back to the *Maidstone* and I went to ask Joe Cowell what the hell was going on he

[1] Winston S Churchill, *The Second World War* (London, 1951) Vol. IV p. 815.

The ship's company of the *Splendid* in Algiers, February 1943.

said, 'Oh, you've got the message, have you? No submarine is ever to be called *Scorpion*.' 'Yes,' I said, 'I'm just going to talk to my chaps about it and come up with another name.' 'No good,' responded Joe. 'Barney's already made a signal to the Admiralty proposing that you be called the *Splendid*.' So that was that. We all thought that it was a ghastly name, and decided to hang a large sign over the side of the conning tower when in habour reading 'Hotel Splendid'.

Shortly before we were due to go on patrol again I was sent for by Barney and introduced to a tall, fair major, named Dodds-Parker, who was master-minding a secret operation which required the use of a submarine. The P228 had been selected for this and we were to sail on 5 January. The orders for the operation, which was called 'Converse', were marked MOST SECRET. I was to embark four unnamed individuals together with an inflatable dinghy which I was to use, manned by two of them, to land the other two on the east coast of

87

Sardinia. I was then to withdraw to seaward, report and await further orders.

The night before we sailed Douglas Dodds-Parker, a Wykehamist, ex-Sudan political service and wartime Grenadier, called for me in a car and we drove for miles into the dark hinterland of Algiers, finally arriving at a large farm house. Here I met two swarthy individuals who were busy preparing a meal of roast chicken and *tagliatelli* with a rich tomato sauce, while an attractive young woman in uniform – one of Dodds-Parker's famous FANYS[1] – looked after the drinks. The chicken was superb. No one mentioned the forthcoming operation, but I gathered from Dodds-Parker on the way back to the *Maidstone* that the two men who had produced the meal were the ones whom I was to put ashore in Sardinia.

Operation 'Converse'[2] went at first according to plan, but as dawn approached the dinghy had not returned. I could not risk being seen from the shore as that would inevitably have compromised the operation. So I moved silently offshore for a couple of miles and dived the P228. I had arranged with Leading Seaman Taylor – he and his mate Able Seaman Webb were naval commandos – that if they missed the submarine they were to pull seaward on a certain line so that I could find them. Just after noon, as we were proceeding very slowly towards the shore along the agreed line, Robert said incredulously, eyes glued to the search periscope, 'There they are, sir!' It was a sunny day with a calm sea. We were four miles from the land. I came to the conclusion that, quite apart from humane considerations, it would be better to surface and risk being seen rather than let the dinghy be found drifting about with two Cornishmen in it, who would have difficulty in providing a convincing explanation for their presence. As my report said:

> 1223 Surfaced. Embarked boat and its occupants who were
> understandably relieved that we were not a U-boat, the
> periscope having looked at them, they said, in a hostile way.

We were quickly dived again. Robert had leapt over the side to rescue the dinghy paddles which were floating away and could have aroused

---

[1] FANY stood for First Aid Nursing Yeomanry, the first of the women's services, which was re-formed to support SOE in the Second World War. Many of its members took part in dangerous missions in enemy-occupied territory.

[2] According to SOE records at the Foreign Office: 'About the time of Scamaroni's arrival in Corsica, Operation "Avocat" was mounted by SOE's Italian section at Massingham to infiltrate two agents into Sardinia.'

suspicion if found, and the dinghy had been slashed with a knife so that it would deflate quickly. A tot of rum soon restored the morale of the brave Cornishmen, who thereafter seemed to be entirely unmoved by their adventure. No enemy activity followed our brief stay on the surface and a couple of nights later, when well away from the scene of the crime, I was able to signal to Captain (s) 8 the completion of Operation 'Converse'.

Within a few hours I received a signal from Captain (s) 10 ordering me to patrol off Naples. Four days later, having so far found no targets, another signal came from Shrimp ordering the P228 to be four miles south-west of the focal point near Ischia by sunset. Being mid-winter it was dark by 6pm and although the moon had risen and was in its second quarter it was almost continually obscured by cloud, so there could be no question of achieving a dived attack. I stayed on the surface and was rewarded an hour or so later by sighting a convoy of two supply ships escorted by destroyers. This was for me the moment of truth. Years before, in peacetime, I had become convinced of the capacity of a submarine to exploit, by attacking at night on the surface, the smallness of her silhouette in comparison with that of surface warships. But, whereas the German U-boats had been designed with this mode of operation in view, our boats were relatively bulky and carried periscope standards which projected several feet above the bridge structure. As the nearest escorting destroyer approached I kept the P228 pointing towards her. It was hard to sustain the belief that we would not be seen, dark as the night was. According to an account written not long after the event by Ken Burridge, our newly joined sub-lieutenant, who was officer of the watch:

The Captain crouched by the voice-pipe and held the submarine close on her course as the destroyer came ahead, and then, sickeningly near, crossed the bow of the submarine, rolling gently on the waves. The Officer of the Watch breathed in sudden gasps: he could see the escort's gun crew hunched round the platform on the foredeck; the streamline of the bridge and the steamy wisps of smoke around the funnel top. A soft blue light shone dimly on the end of her main yardarm, and a figure walked clumsily along the weather deck towards the stern.

'Stone the crows!' gasped the starboard lookout, 'we'll be inboard soon!'

Hypnotised by the nearness of it, the sub-lieutenant gazed fixedly at the escort's swaying funnel. His stomach was numbed. Gripped around his gut was an iron band which seemed to squeeze and then relax its hold in union with the engines' beating rhythm. The submarine was surely seen . . . but the sea was heaving up in silver-crested waves . . . the night was dark, and the boat was ballasted low. Destroyer's wash and chopping seas met in a high curved concealing wall which hid the submarine from view . . .[1]

The narrative in my patrol report was somewhat drier:

P228 altered course to starboard on to a 90 degree track after keeping end on to the starboard wing destroyer as it passed, distant 1,000 yards. P228 then increased speed to close the range, and at 1927 fired five torpedoes spread over two ships lengths, being at that time about 1,500 yards right ahead of the starboard beam destroyer. The mean firing range was estimated at 2,000 yards. P228 dived immediately after firing and one explosion was heard, at the running time of 1,500 to 2,500 yards, depending on which torpedo hit. The pattern 12040 night sight was used for the first time in action and was entirely satisfactory.[2]

As we withdrew slowly upwind in order to minimise the risk of detection by the destroyers' asdic, we heard a few depth-charges, dropped apparently at random. Half an hour later I surfaced. The starboard diesel engine was out of action, having lost lubricating oil pressure just before we had started the attack on the convoy. The main battery, also, was unduly low after a day patrolling in rather a rough sea and some swell, followed by the attack and withdrawal. But I could dimly see the torpedoed ship lying stopped with a destroyer circling round her and was able to keep the target in sight while charging the battery with the port engine. She was a large important vessel laden with tanks and other war material. Naples was less than thirty miles away – we were using the red glow above the crater of Vesuvius as an aid to navigation – so the damaged ship might well be towed into harbour. It was imperative to administer the *coup de grâce*. The trouble was that in the strong breeze prevailing the ship, lying broadside on, was drifting away from me at two knots or more, while periodically

---

[1] James Casing, *Submariners* (London, 1951) pp. 21–22.
[2] I could not resist this comment, having submitted a year before the war came that our submarines should have a proper night sight, designed one and had its prototype made in the depot ship's workshop.

the moon would be obscured so that maintaining contact was difficult.

In the event, I took advantage of a period of moonlight to attempt a dived attack but before I could close to decisive range it became dark again and I had to surface so as not to lose sight of the target. After a somewhat tense wait the moon appeared once more and I dived for another attack, hoping at last to approach near enough to make sure of a second hit. Owing to the motion of the surfaced submarine it had not been practicable to reload the torpedo tubes and only one 'fish' remained ready to fire. While the range looked to be still well over 2,000 yards I saw the destroyers (there were now two in sight) exchanging signals by flash lamp, whereupon one of them came towards us pinging on his asdic. It seemed that he had gained contact as he suddenly increased speed but this, luckily, caused him to lose it. However, things were getting rather unhealthy so I fired the single torpedo and hoped for the best. We were out of luck. We heard it explode at the end of its run several minutes later.

When I brought the *Splendid* to the surface again after a while I could still see the target, now about four miles away, with one destroyer standing by her and two more sweeping towards Ischia. During the rest of the night I was able to keep the damaged ship in sight while charging the battery with the one good engine by proceeding slowly towards her on one motor. At 6.00am I dived the submarine and went deep so that the torpedo tubes could be reloaded without the motion caused at periscope depth by the swell. At 7.15, having at last been able to get downwind of the target so that she was drifting towards and not away from me, I came to periscope depth. There she was, lying beam on to the wind and sea. To quote my patrol report once again:

> As the target was approached a tug was seen going alongside her and soon afterwards the tow was begun. Fortunately, in pointing her towards Naples, the target was pulled through nearly 180 degrees towards P228, which at 0835 was able to fire a torpedo at short range. At the running time for 750 yards a very heavy explosion occurred, followed by unmistakable breaking up noises. Ten minutes later the destroyer, the tug which had been towing the target, and another tug were all in sight, but the merchant ship had gone.[1]

---

[1] It turned out to have been the *Emma* (7,931 tons).

We retired to the north-west, following the sage advice of Chiefy McMillan. Owing to momentary inattention to the depth-keeping and the fact that even at 70 feet the swell affected the boat's behaviour, she suddenly began to lose depth. Before the officer of the watch, who had not previously experienced such conditions, could regain control, the P228 momentarily broke surface. A minute or two later, one depth-charge (or it could have been a bomb) exploded fairly near and HE and asdic transmissions sweeping were heard. I immediately ordered diving stations and altered course to disengage if possible. But the enemy gained contact and came in to attack. A pattern of eight depth-charges landed fairly close astern. The submarine was soon down at 350 feet and the hostile destroyer lost contact with us. When I came to periscope depth that afternoon there was no ship or aircraft in sight, but it had been our closest shave so far.

An hour later we received a signal from Captain (s) 10 ordering P228 to proceed to the east coast of Sardinia to intercept coastal traffic. That night the starboard engine was repaired – an airlock in the system caused by the heavy rolling of the submarine in the bad weather was thought to have been the trouble.

On 18 January, having made a landfall on Cape Comino, the light-house on which was showing with normal characteristics, we began to cruise southward looking for targets. I had noticed that the best anchorage on the east coast of Sardinia and the only port served by a railway was Arbatax, which could accommodate a 4,000 ton ship. I planned to approach it, dived, during the following night, surface close in and bombard the port installations plus any ship that happened to be there. The nearly full moon would enable us to see the targets, but moonset would be shortly after the action and this would help us to evade any retribution.

At 5.25 am we surfaced and I told Robert to engage a small vessel which was lying at anchor off the harbour. Infuriatingly, it was found impossible to load the 3-inch gun. Three separate rounds were tried but none would enter the chamber fully. I thought the target too small to justify the expenditure of a torpedo and decided forthwith to abandon the operation, which depended upon the achievement of surprise. This was lost now that we were on the surface in bright moonlight.

That afternoon, while we were coast-crawling southwards, smoke was sighted on the horizon ahead. Then the masts of a schooner appeared a little to seaward. I described the ensuing action in my patrol report as follows:

1415 Surfaced and attacked 200 ton auxiliary A/S schooner with gunfire. The 3″ gun came into action at once and did not fail throughout the engagement.

1422 Schooner stopped and burning. Altered course to close a trawler, three miles to the southward, which was firing wildly in the direction of P228. Speed was now 14 knots.

1427 Opened fire on trawler which, after being hit several times, made smoke and headed for the beach, still firing.

1432 Trawler ceased fire.

1432 P228 ceased fire and, a minute later, dived to avoid casualties from the fire of rifles and some kind of pop-gun at a beach defence post 1,000 yards away. Proceeded to attack a 2,000 ton laden merchant ship[1] which had taken refuge in a bight, and lay stopped over a $4\frac{1}{2}$ fathom patch.

1440 An aircraft arrived on the scene.

1505 Smoke was sighted to the North and South near the coast: the wreck of the schooner was still burning.

1518 Fired one torpedo at the merchant ship: it was seen to hit her amidships after running 2,000 yards. The vessel broke in two and sank, leaving bridge, funnel and poop visible above water. P228 altered course to seaward.

1523 Two aircraft bombs landed some distance away.

1605 Periscope depth. There were several aircraft in sight and the masts of a vessel to the Northward, near the coast. The wreck of the schooner was no longer visible, and she may have sunk. Went to 70 feet and withdrew on course 110 degrees.

1858 Surfaced and continued to withdraw.

1923 Altered course to 180 degrees and proceeded to leave patrol as ordered by Captain (s) 10. This day, 19 January, was the first anniversary of the launch of P228, and her ship's company were glad to have had the opportunity to mark the occasion with a firework display.

At 10.20 am on Friday 22 January 1943 the P228 secured to the *Maidstone* in Algiers.

A couple of days after our return Douglas Dodds-Parker, now promoted to lieutenant-colonel, came aboard the *Maidstone* to receive my report on Operation 'Converse'. He seemed to be satisfied and was kind enough to invite me to dine with him at the Club des Pins the following

[1] Later found to have been the *Commercio* (765 tons).

week. This was a well-appointed group of buildings set back in the sand dunes at Guyotville, a few miles west of Algiers on the shores of the Mediterranean. It was to be the training and mounting base for the Special Operations Executive (SOE) in the Mediterranean theatre with Douglas Dodds-Parker in charge. The dinner was excellent, reflecting Douglas's declared war aims: *'Chasser l'ennemi et chercher la cuisine francaise'*. The charming presence of a number of FANYs helped to create a certain impression of exclusivity – a combination of White's with the *Tour d'Argent* – redolent of cigars, champagne and Chanel No.5. Before dinner I met a couple of most congenial merchant bankers – David Keswick, a taipan if ever there was one, and 'Mouse' Glyn, both in army uniform. At that time I knew very little about the organisation by which I was being entertained. Much later I came to realise that, in response to Winston Churchill's 1940 directive to 'set Europe ablaze', men of high international standing were acting as the link between the clandestine activities of SOE and people of political importance in occupied territories. In the place of honour at the dinner table was Major-General Colin Gubbins, the head of SOE, who was on a brief visit from London. I was placed on his right. The talk was free-ranging within the bounds of security, but what I remember most clearly is the after-dinner entertainment. This consisted of going out in the moonlight to an open space amidst the sand dunes, with our drinks in our hands, and witnessing a parachute jump by a score or more individuals from three or four Dakotas, which flew overhead at extremely low altitude. I felt exhilarated to be helping SOE and it was pleasing to read Douglas Dodds-Parker's reference, written many years later, to the practice of:

> ... landing agents from submarines and picking them up. HMS *Maidstone*, under Capt. 'Barney' Fawkes, provided additional transport unsurpassed in verve. Our debt to them running so many risks for us outside the normal line of danger and duty, was immense. Our only loss was one FANY, married to a submariner.[1]

A spell of nearly three weeks in harbour followed our third war patrol. It was during this period that Rawdon Bannar-Martin, my most efficient, loyal and cheerful first lieutenant, who had been running the boat for me since we had commissioned, was selected to do his perisher. I am happy to record that he qualified and on 14 October 1944, when

[1] Douglas Dodds-Parker, *Setting Europe Ablaze* (Windlesham, Surrey, 1983) p. 119.

in command of the submarine *Viking*, sank a German supply ship of 1,286 tons in a convoy which he attacked off the coast of Norway. Robert Balkwill, who had been understudying Banger, relieved him as first lieutenant, while Gordon Hardy continued as navigator (he had had a good deal of experience by now). Sub-lieutenant Ken ('Buster') Burridge, who had joined us for the previous patrol as a 'makee-learn', now relieved Robert as armaments officer.

By this time a rest camp had been organised for the submarine crews when in harbour. Although not quite so palatial as SOE's Club des Pins, it was a great boon for the ship's company. From the point of view of the wardroom, Robert, Gordon and I felt that we ought to have a flat ashore. We had a strong desire to get right away from the service atmosphere of the depot ship – the constant and inescapable clatter of clumping naval feet, the frequent and inevitably strident broadcasts on the ship's Tannoy system, the bantering small talk in the mess and, above all, the need to be in uniform. It was the practice in Malta for the officers and ratings of the 10th Flotilla boats to have flats for use when in harbour; but, as far as I know, we were the first boat to have one in Algiers. To make sure of Barney's compliance with our formal request to 'sleep ashore' we invited him to a house-warming party, which he seemed to enjoy – he was a great party man.

The owner of our flat, which was quite reasonably furnished, was a French dentist. He was kind enough to make available to us to help keep the flat clean and do some laundry a nice young woman called Angèle, who became a sort of mascot. I cannot remember doing any cooking, but I do recall eating pleasurably at a modest but clean little restaurant across the road, called *l'Alsacienne*, where the tablecloths were of red and white check gingham. We certainly steered clear of the bar at the Arletti Hotel, having found it crammed with American, French and British officers, all in army uniform. The grosser delights of the Casbah held little attraction for us either, smug though that sounds. All in all I think we regarded our time in harbour between patrols rather as going into retreat, in order to unwind from tensions built up during a period in which we had faced 'the perils of the sea and the violence of the enemy'. We felt the need to recreate around us, however vicariously, an oasis of civilised life.

We sailed from Algiers again on 13 February, having become on 31 January HM Submarine *Splendid*. Early on 17 February we were in our patrol billet off Cape St Vito at the north-west corner of Sicily. That evening, while we were still dived, we sighted a convoy of two supply ships with an escort of two destroyers and a sloop heading for Tunisia.

I decided to attack from the landward side, with the larger of the ships as target, while the stronger escort was on the far side of the convoy. By good fortune I was able to slip between the nearer escort and the supply ships. Just before firing I found that the two supply ships were lined up so as to form a continuous target. I fired a salvo of six torpedoes, each one individually aimed, and was rewarded by seeing the second and third hit the nearer of the two ships. After the correct running time, we heard the first torpedo hitting the further ship. I did not wait to see what happened but headed for the open spaces of the Tyrrhenian Sea. Seven minutes after my attack the counter-attack began, during which three patterns of six and one of twelve depth-charges were dropped not all that far away from us. No damage resulted, probably because I had taken the *Splendid* down to 330 feet and the enemy's depth-charges were not set deep enough. According to the post-war records, only one of the supply ships was sunk.[1]

The next five days were frustrating as I maintained patrol in the area ordered, which encompassed the focal point off the north-west corner of Sicily. There were aircraft in sight most of the time, anti-submarine vessels carrying out sweeps and potential targets appearing, but always out of reach. It was on the sixth day, 24 February, that our luck turned. Early in the morning a couple of small tankers with a destroyer escort came our way. There was barely enough light to see them. One, which was a vessel of about 2,000 tons, was a long way astern of the escort and I was able to move in close enough for an attack, which was unsuccessful. Twenty-five minutes later, having returned to periscope depth, I sighted what at first looked like another tanker but which turned out to be a water carrier of the *Dalmazia* class.[2] As she was passing astern of me I hopefully fired the stern torpedo at her. But the range was over a mile and with a single torpedo an error of as little as 2 knots in the estimation of the target's speed would have been enough to make it miss, which it did.

One of the remaining torpedoes was found to have a defect, later attributed to faulty preparation by the torpedo maintenance party in the *Maidstone*. Now I had only one torpedo left. Early next morning I reported this situation to Captain (S) 8 and received his order to return to Algiers, where we arrived on 27 February without further incident.

The period in harbour following the *Splendid*'s fourth war patrol was unremarkable. Algiers was calm – at any rate outwardly. There was

---

[1] *XXI Aprile* (4,787 tons). The other ship was the *Siena* (4,000 tons).
[2] Owing to the shipping shortage these water carriers were being used as fuel carriers.

some social life, however. One of the people whom it was a surprise and pleasure to meet was Michael Mason, wearing the uniform of the RNVR. In the mid-thirties, when I was a sub-lieutenant doing courses, I had navigated his superb 50-ton yawl, *Latifa*, which had been designed and built by the celebrated William Fife of Fairlie. I do not think we won many races because the handicapping rules of the Royal Ocean Racing Club at that time did not favour so large and robust a vessel. But I have never before or since experienced the thrill of being at the wheel of so powerful a sailing yacht in a fresh breeze. Michael was most tolerant of my sometimes elementary mistakes in navigation, when I knew more about the theory than the practice. In harbour, by the light of the paraffin lamps which he favoured in the *Latifa*'s finely panelled but austere saloon, Michael would spin roguish yarns of tough times in the Klondike and other adventures. He was one of a small group of young Britons of independent means – Augustine Courtauld, Gino Watkins and Peter Fleming were others – who in the 1930s ventured here and there around the world – wintering in the Arctic, sailing the oceans, crossing deserts, climbing mountains, penetrating the jungle – in protest, perhaps, against the encroachment of suburban values and the erosion of individualism. These men were the stuff of which SOE was made, and Michael Mason had been recruited into that organisation by Douglas Dodds-Parker, who had found him at Djidjelli on the coast to the east of Algiers, training on landing craft. I have since learned from Dodds-Parker's book *Setting Europe Ablaze* that Michael, while working for the British Secret Intelligence Service (SIS), had 'eluded capture' in the Balkans. But that story may never be told.

During this period in Algiers we said farewell to our much-loved, vastly experienced and highly competent Chief, Mr McMillan. He had stood by the P228 when she was building and had shared with us the hard work and excitements of her career to date. But he was suffering from phlebitis and had to go to hospital. Our new Chief was Lieutenant (E) D E Laidlaw, who quickly fitted in to our team.

On 11 March the *Splendid* sailed from Algiers for her fifth war patrol. Our billet was to be off the north-west corner of Sicily; once again I felt conscious of taking an active part in the 'intrinsic sea and air offensive ... to sink Rommel's supplies' for which I had called in a letter published in *The Times* of 14 July 1942. This had elicited from Admiral Sir Herbert Richmond, Master of Downing College, a magisterial counterblast about the nature of sea power. My determination to succeed was therefore reinforced by the compulsion to give effect to my words. I had long since been convinced that sound military strategy demanded the organised mutual support of all arms, land, sea and air. It was exciting to be in the thick of a three-service campaign such as the eviction of the Axis forces from North Africa.

Barney Fawkes, in explaining the strategic background of the patrol, had indicated that a British offensive in Tunisia was imminent and stressed the urgency of the Axis need for petrol and their lack of tanker tonnage; he had also said that a large tanker would probably try to slip through within the next few days. It was at this time that (as our C-in-C knew from Ultra[1]) the sinking of three supply ships:

> caused Kesselring to ask Goering to improve convoy escort and to order special protection for a convoy due to reach Tunisia on the 12th (March). Three of the ships were sunk nevertheless. Hitler accepted Kesselring's advice on the 14th, when he told Doenitz that the Sicilian narrows 'must teem with ships to protect the convoys'.[2]

My observations during our previous patrol, plus intelligence gleaned from the reports of other submarines, had provided accurate knowledge of the inshore route being used by the Axis traffic in the vicinity of Cape St Vito. It ran within a mile or two of the shore, and I positioned the *Splendid* 3,000 yards or so from it. That afternoon, 16 March, we received from Captain (s) 8 what purported to be an air-reconnaissance report, but may well have been an Enigma decipherment of Axis operational radio traffic, alerting me to the presence off Palermo of a large west-bound tanker. In case this vital target should try to get by during darkness I did not withdraw to seaward that night to charge the main battery but remained close inshore while doing so. Just after midnight we sighted a couple of vessels rounding Cape St Vito. I proceeded at full speed to intercept them, but when they came in front of the land we lost sight of them. I pressed on towards the coastal route. To my dismay there were no ships in sight. As it was moonlight I dived the submarine and waited. An hour or so later, assisted by hydrophone effect, I made out four shapes heading our way. In case one or more of them should be a worthwhile target I surfaced, keeping end on, which was just as well as they turned out to be motor anti-submarine boats. It was not until a couple of hours before noon next day that persistence was rewarded. Round Cape St Vito came the convoy for which I was waiting. It consisted of one large

---

[1] Ultra was intelligence gained from breaking high-grade cyphers.
[2] Ralph Bennett, *Ultra and Mediterranean Strategy 1941–45* (London, 1989) p. 212.

and one medium tanker and an ocean-going tug, escorted by two aircraft and four destroyers. The larger tanker, with three destroyers, was about a mile ahead of the other. It was one of those blue Mediterranean days, with bright sunlight and catspaws rippling here and there the limpid calm of the sea. I was conscious that my periscope might very well be spotted if I was not more than usually cautious in using it; and I knew, also, that unless I could move in to very close range an aircraft would see the torpedo tracks and alert the target in time for it to put its wheel over and avoid being hit. As an added consideration I knew that tankers are hard to sink, being designed to carry a liquid cargo, and that I must therefore be certain of at least two hits if I was to make sure that this one was not merely damaged, to be towed into harbour and soon repaired.

For these reasons I manoeuvred the *Splendid* directly towards the inshore track which I felt sure the convoy would follow. Sure enough, half an hour or so after first sighting it, I was able to fire a salvo of four torpedoes from a range of 600 yards. This gave the target no time to avoid the 'fish', and enabled me to see the first one hit it right forward, sending up a plume of spray. I told the first lieutenant to take the boat down while we altered course so as to get away to open water as quickly as we could. Two more torpedo hits were heard closely following the first and it seemed reasonable to assume that the tanker had been sunk.[1] The counter-attack was fairly heavy, but once again, thank goodness, it was inaccurate. The enemy destroyers did not easily give up and when I came circumspectly to periscope depth above five hours later I could see a couple of them not far away, 'systematically searching an area which did not happen to enclose *Splendid*', as I put it in my patrol report.

I had the recollection from my spell in the spare crew at Malta in 1941 that boats sometimes had blank patrols – that is to say, found no targets, or missed any they had attacked. One of the forces driving me was the determination to achieve at least one success in each patrol. There were perhaps more opportunities in 1943, when the traffic was being funnelled directly across the short passage from Sicily to Tunisia, than there had been in 1941. Having sunk the tanker, I felt somewhat relaxed and set course for a quieter area, near the island of Ustica, so that next day the torpedo petty officer and his men could haul back and test the reload torpedoes. On 19 March at around noon the officer of the watch sighted smoke to the westward; an hour later

---

[1] Later confirmed as the tanker *Devoli* (3,006 tons).

masts and funnels appeared, with two aircraft patrolling around. The mirage was most pronounced and it was not until the convoy was within two miles that I could make out what it consisted of. Suddenly I realised that it was a tanker, in tow, escorted by an auxiliary anti-submarine vessel and a couple of motor torpedo boats. The tanker was down by the bow and appeared to have been hit forward by a bomb or torpedo; it was yawing widely to and fro so that it was a bit of a problem to know what director angle to use to ensure a hit. It was disconcerting also that when the moment came to bring the torpedo tubes to the 'stand-by' condition, for some unexplained reason the bowcaps could not be opened. We had to take some water in, speed up in order to retain control over the boat and then use the pump, the noise of which inevitably risked detection. I was not surprised when eventually we managed to open the bowcaps to find a motor anti-submarine boat a few hundred yards on each side of me obviously investigating a contact. The target was by now past the originally determined bearing for me to fire on, so that I had to twist the boat round violently through thirty degrees to get on to a firing course again. The sea, as for the previous attack, was like glass, but this time the target, being under tow, could not alter course to avoid the torpedoes. Although the range was 2,300 yards, one of the three torpedoes which I fired was a hit. I had by now identified the target as the Italian naval auxiliary *Cerere* of 2,730 tons.[1]

I did not hang around waiting to observe the result of the attack but told Robert to take the boat swiftly down to 300 feet. This was just as well. About forty depth-charges were dropped in quick succession, probably because the point at which the torpedo tracks originated could easily be seen on the flat calm sea. At any rate we all felt pretty sure that if we had not gone to our maximum operating depth at once we should have been damaged.

It seemed to me, after we had spent a peaceful day well away from the coastal route, that I might try a different part of it: from the signals I had received it appeared that we did not have a submarine on patrol anywhere on the north coast of Sicily at that time. I moved further east and spent 23 March unproductively off the northern entrance to the Straits of Messina. That night I received Captain (s) 8's signal ordering me into that part of the coastal zone which included Palermo. This suited me. I still had five torpedoes left in the bow tubes and the stern torpedo also. Next afternoon, as we were moving slowly along

[1] It was in fact the Italian tanker *Giorgio* (4,887 tons).

the coast, we came upon a schooner. Believing it to be another anti-submarine auxiliary, I ordered gun action stations and we surfaced in the usual way with a rush and at very short range. As I studied the target I realised that it was very small and almost certainly a genuine fishing vessel so I broke off the action. By then, sadly, the schooner's dinghy had been smashed and some of the crew wounded, but I could not jeopardise the safety of my submarine and her crew by remaining on the surface for a moment longer – there were far too many aircraft about in that locality, one of which might come at us out of the sun at any minute. We later saw that the sailing vessel was proceeding inshore, well under control. I hope all her crew survived.

For the first time in five patrols I was conscious of being over-tired. I believe that my officers noticed it, although I do not recall any of them making a comment to that effect. No doubt all of us had had enough of being keyed up to concert pitch. Thinking about this later, I felt that my total capacity to master events was a finite quantity; and although some of it was restored during each spell in harbour between patrols there was an overall and cumulative loss – like a steel spring that when fully compressed and released fails, by an increasing amount over time, to return to its original shape. I was quite glad to receive a signal from Barney telling me to leave patrol and proceed on the surface to Malta, following a carefully prescribed route in order to keep clear of the latest known enemy mine fields.

Our luck held and on 28 March we secured alongside the Malta submarine base, now HMS *Talbot*. In the Great War Commander Talbot had been a distinguished submarine captain. It was tragic that in this war his sons Frank and Bartle had already both been lost in submarines. Their father, for his part, was serving in the rank of vice-admiral, as Director of Dockyards, a post which he filled with outstanding ability. Frank had served with me for a couple of patrols in the *Clyde*. We had laughed a lot and listened many times with much joy (not shared, I fear, by the rest of the wardroom) to his record of the Boswell Sisters singing 'How high the moon'.

The purpose of the *Splendid*'s visit to Malta was to go into dry dock for the six-monthly examination of her hull and fittings, maintenance of her engines and auxiliary machinery and various repairs. The base engineer officer was no longer the whimsical and ingenious 'Sam' McGregor. He had been relieved by Commander Tom Sanders, another of the exceptionally able engineers we were lucky enough to have in the submarine service. But Tom lacked Sam's imagination as well as his highly developed sense of humour. When Denis Saunders, my

Somers and Angus McGeoch with the author in 1940, a picture used by the *Glasgow Herald* on 7 April 1943.

LIEUT. M'GEOCH with his wife
and one of his two sons.

D.S.O. for Scots Sub. Commanders

NAMED by the First Lord of the Admiralty last month as one of the Navy's ten outstanding submarine commanders, Lieutenant Ian Lauchlan Mackay M'Geoch has been awarded the D.S.O.

Bracketed with him in last night's " London Gazette " is Lieut. John Henry Bromage, D.S.C., another submarine commander, who also wins the D.S.O.

They have been waging an unremitting and successful offensive against ships trying to run supplies to Rommel.

Lieutenant M'Geoch is a son of Mr and Mrs L. A. M'Geoch, Glasgow. Mr M'Geoch is chairman and managing director of William M'Geoch and Co., Ltd., ironmongers and electrical engineers, Glasgow.

Married in Malta

Lieutenant M'Geoch, who is 29, attended Larchfield School, Helensburgh, before going to Pangbourne College when 13. He entered the Navy four years later.

His wife is a daughter of Canon Hugh Farrie, of Sliema, Malta, who has been on the George Cross island since the beginning of the war. His marriage took place at Malta, and he has two sons. Lieutenant M'Geoch's home is at Danbury, Essex.

Lieutenant Bromage is 27, and his home is at Kirn. Like Lieut. M'Geoch, he has played an invaluable part attacking Axis shipping in the Mediterranean.

During recent patrols the submarine under the command of Lieutenant Bromage sank three supply ships and a number of smaller vessels. She also bombarded and damaged a seaplane hangar.

superb chief ERA, reported to him that *Splendid*'s main engine cylinder liners were very deeply corroded owing to galvanic action and should be replaced, Tom replied, 'Don't worry, Chief, they'll last as long as you'll need them.'

It was good to find Lieutenant Commander Hubert Marsham still running the Lazaretto base, with Lieutenant Commander C ('Pop') Giddings providing the victuals; between them they had kept the much-battered place in being throughout the worst days of Malta's siege. As soon as I had reported to Captain Phillips (who had taken over from Shrimp Simpson) and made my number on Philip Francis, who had relieved Bob Tanner as Staff Officer (Operations), I set off up the hill in Sliema to find out how my in-laws had fared. Poor Hugh and Gladys Farrie, and Mary Ward their housekeeper, had obviously had a terrible time. They had all lost several stones in weight. But their morale was high. We compared notes as to which of us had had the most recent letter from Somers. It was me, I think, as our mail had been diverted to Malta and given priority. I heard, too, about the recent visit of the much-loved Bishop of Gibraltar, Harold Buxton, who had contrived to get himself around his vast diocese in the war zone by accepting transport in RAF bombers.

26 March had been my birthday and it was decided that a party could be managed for my ship's company – as long as I provided the beer and any food that seemed to be appropriate. The party was held in the garden of Bishop's House and was good fun. I did not stay with the Farries as the civilian population was still severely rationed. However, being able to relax in Bishop's House and attend Holy Communion and other sevices in the church in which I had been married made my time in Malta truly restoring. I called in to see the Tenches and was stimulated by their company, as ever. Wingrave Tench had done a superb job in organising the feeding of the besieged and starving populace.

Quite suddenly it was 18 April and the day to say farewells. That evening the *Splendid* sailed from Malta, followed the searched channel round the south and west of the island and set course for Naples. Having been in dock, it was necessary to carry out a deep dive in slow time to make sure that everything had been put back correctly. The news had come through while we were in Malta of various decorations which had been awarded to us, probably as a result of recommendations made by Barney Fawkes to Sir Andrew Cunningham after our third war patrol.[1] We had certainly clocked up a substantial

[1] See Appendix B.

score. In fact, now that all the records have been sifted and cross-checked,[1] we know precisely what we achieved between the 'Torch' landings on 8 November 1942 and the end of organised German and Italian resistance in North Africa on 9 May 1943. The *Splendid* (P228) sank by torpedo six escorted supply ships (including two tankers), totalling 26,424 tons; in addition, she sank by gunfire one supply ship of 3,576 tons, which had been damaged by the RAF; she torpedoed and sank the destroyer *Aviere* and damaged the destroyer *Velite*, as well as sinking by gunfire the anti-aircraft patrol schooner *Sao Paolo* and a trading schooner and damaging an armed trawler. In addition, like many other submarines during the period, she carried out a special operation, in our case Operation 'Converse'.

Between twenty-five and thirty British and Allied submarines were operating in the Central Mediterranean during the final phase of the war in North Africa. Although the *Splendid* failed to sink either a U-boat or a large surface warship during her five patrols, she did account for more tanker and supply ship tonnage than any other boat in the period November 1942 to April 1943. This was probably the most intensive period of British submarine operations during the Second World War, having taken place in narrow waters where there were numerous targets.

Of the forty boats we lost in the Mediterranean other than in harbour throughout the four years from mid-1940 to mid-1944, ten including the *Splendid* were sunk between November 1942 and May 1943. Of the total of forty, nineteen were sunk by depth-charge, fourteen struck mines and the remainder were 'cause unknown'. As the official naval historian wrote:

> The great contribution of the submarines to cutting the Axis supply lines to Africa has been emphasised earlier in our story. It was continued unremittingly throughout the present phase, but in these shallow waters it was inevitable that a heavy price would be paid by the submarine service.[2]

The *Splendid* was about to pay her share of that price.

---

[1] *Submarine Operations*, HMSO. J Rohwer and G Hummelchen, *Chronology of the War at Sea, 1939–1945*, translated from the German by Derek Masters (London, 1972).
[2] S W Roskill *The War at Sea* (London, 1956) Vol. II p.431.

5 · A leap in the moonlight

I do not remember seeing the *Splendid* sink. Later I learned that, a few minutes after Robert and I had abandoned her, the bow of our submarine had risen vertically into the air before she slid down stern first and disappeared. Not long after that the German destroyer's motorboat came and picked us up. Two other survivors – I cannot remember who – were already in the boat and we were soon on board the German ship.

'For you ze vor iss ofer.'

No it bloody well isn't, I thought. Vague notions of an early break for freedom were already in my mind. So I made no reply. Instead, seeing that the young blond *Oberleutnant zur See* who had been put in charge of me was wearing an Iron Cross, I asked him what it was for.

'I sank your destroyer *Vortigern*,' he said with justifiable professional pride. 'I commanded a *Schnellboot* – you call them E-boats.' I happened to know that the *Vortigern* had indeed been torpedoed and sunk the previous year. It seemed a good idea to keep the conversation going. I soon learned that the young officer's parental home was Cologne and that the city was suffering terribly from British bombing. 'Ve should agree now to stop ze vor,' he said.

'You started it,' I said, 'and if you have had enough you can stop it.'

Silence.

Looking around the upper deck of the destroyer I could see, down aft, several members of my crew swathed like myself in blankets. They were evidently being looked after properly. I asked the *Oberleutnant* how many men had been picked up. He did not know, but said that several were wounded and being given medical care. As we proceeded at high speed across Naples Bay, leaving a long, ruler-straight, dazzling white wake upon the blue expanse, the *Oberleutnant* was informative – surprisingly so, considering our situation. The destroyer was indeed

British-built. But I had been wrong in identifying her as probably the Italian ex-Yugoslavian *Dubrovnik*. She had been built just before the war for the Greek navy.[1] When the Germans invaded Greece they had sunk her by air attack. Later they had salved her, refitted her and renamed her *Hermes*.[2] In command now was *Fregattenkapitän* Rechel, who in 1940 had been captain of one of the big German destroyers sunk by us near Narvik and later of the new destroyer z29. According to the *oberleutnant*, Commander Rechel, after the *Hermes* sailed from Salerno earlier that day, had refused his first lieutenant's request to send the crew to cruising watches and ordered him to keep them at action stations. Hence the five or more lookouts on each side of the ship, all equipped with powerful Zeiss binoculars. I had come up against the German first eleven.

This was confirmed half an hour or so later when the *Hermes* was brought smartly and with no fuss to a berth stern to the quay in the small harbour of Pozzuoli near Naples. Within a few minutes the ship was secured in position and a gangway was in place, with Commander Rechel and his officers manning it. Then came the shrill note of the bo'sun's call as a smiling *Kapitän zur See* was piped aboard. It was the familiar naval custom. We stood to attention. The officers saluted as we would have done; the senior officer, pausing for a moment as he stepped on to the destroyer's steel deck, returned the salute. Only one of the ship's officers, I noticed, gave the Nazi salutation.

Quickly our wounded shipmates were landed, to be taken away in waiting ambulances. The rest of us were somewhat brusquely bundled into an open three-ton truck and driven off. We had not gone far before the truck stopped and the driver got out. The single guard jumped down and they conferred. I looked round. Nearby there were trees, and many Italian citizens going about their business. No one seemed to be taking the slightest notice. Could this be the moment to make a dash for it? With the truck between me and the guard and driver I might make it to the nearest corner, then mingle with the crowd. But what then? I stayed put. In a minute or two the driver climbed back into his seat and the guard into the back, and we were off again. Eventually the truck arrived at the gateway of a large compound containing several huts. Robert and I were ordered into one of these. We had been able on the journey to get some notion from the survivors about who else might have been saved, besides the

---

[1] The *Vasilev Gorgios I*, built by Yarrow at Scotstoun in 1938.
[2] The *Hermes* was immobilised by Allied air attack off Cape Bon on 9 May 1943 and sunk shortly afterwards in a Tunisian harbour by further bombing.

The *Splendid* engaged by gunfire after being depth-charged, 21 April 1943.

wounded who had been with us on board the *Hermes*. An Italian patrol craft had appeared on the scene in time to pick some people up. We had also reminded ourselves and our shipmates, from whom we were now separated, that in accordance with the Geneva Convention we could not be required to tell the enemy anything other than name and rank or official number.

By far the worst aspect of life in the transit camp was having to use field latrines of truly nauseating filthiness; and a single cold water tap had to serve for our ablutions. The food, consisting mainly of slimy pasta provided in what seemed to be old kerosene tins, was edible only as the alternative to starvation. Yet the relief at being alive, after being so near to death, made hardship of little account. Nor was the process of interrogation, which we had awaited with some apprehension, at all daunting. A mild-looking middle-aged German, or rather Austrian, officer opened the batting by remarking, after I had given my name and rank, that he presumed that I came from Scotland. This did not seem to call for a reply. He went on to ask how well I knew London. For his part, he said ingratiatingly, having worked in London for several years he had come to be very fond of it – especially South Kensington. This, from his almost too perfect English accent and

Survivors of the *Splendid* on board the German destroyer *Hermes*, 21 April 1943.

speech, I could believe. Tempted though I was to make some rather abrasive remark, I kept quiet and after a few more conversational gambits my interrogator gave up and I was ushered from his presence. According to Robert Balkwill, whose turn was next, the interrogating officer opened with, 'Is your captain always rude?' 'Fortunately,' said Robert when telling me this, 'I did not have to answer the question.'

We had learned by now that we were in Capua, some 25 miles to the north of Naples, and in ancient times a city second only to Rome in renown. Far more important to us all was the visit of a tall bearded Roman Catholic priest, bent upon putting us in touch with our next of kin. Thanks to him I was able to get a letter off to Somers, naming those whom I knew to have survived. It reached her in due course, through the Red Cross.

Within a day or two of our arrival I received a visit from a smartly-dressed RSM of the Buffs, the senior NCO in the other ranks part of the camp. He informed me of various important matters, in particular that, as POWs taken by the Germans, we must expect to be shipped off to Germany as soon as the transport could be made available. Meanwhile, I had become aware that all was not well with my right eye. Severe irritation, inflammation and loss of sight in it boded ill, and I asked for medical attention. Next day or the day after, I found myself sitting beside the stolid-looking German driver of an otherwise empty three-ton truck heading, as I understood it, for a hospital. As we bumped and rattled through the winding cobbled streets of Capua, every now and then stopping and starting again as the traffic dictated, I thought how easy it would be to jump out of the truck. Surely I could disappear into the crowd and somehow lie up until dark. Thereafter I would try to take a train going north and get to Rome with the prospect of gaining the sanctuary of the Vatican City. Even as I looked at the door handle – and as it was to my right I had to turn my head in order to do so – I began to have second thoughts. To start with, I was afraid that my bad eye might become septic and infect my good eye; secondly, I was clad in a nondescript battledress and British army boots; and thirdly, Italy was still at war with us, so that a POW on the run in broad daylight could not expect to be harboured by the local populace even in order to frustrate the German forces.

I stayed put.

Very shortly the truck joined a main road heading south-east and speeded up. We soon turned left off the main thoroughfare just short of a vast eighteenth-century building.[1] A moment or two later we turned left again and stopped at a guarded gateway. A carabiniere sentry sauntered up and my driver, leaning out of his cab, handed him a bit of paper. I was invited to step down. I had arrived at the hospital. The three-tonner backed away, and that was the last I saw of the Germans until four months later.[2]

A second carabiniere now emerged from the primitive guardhouse adjusting his uniform and beckoned.

'*Andiamo*,' he said, and I learned my first word of Italian.

As we walked the few yards to the nearest building I observed that running from the gateway in either direction was a barbed-wire barricade, which had been erected a couple of yards inside the perimeter wall of the hospital grounds as a temporary measure. The building in which I found myself was one of a cluster which had evidently been put up to meet the wartime emergency. They were made of wooden frames, clad in asbestos or some such material, and stood clear of the ground on piles. I was taken up to the first floor and into a ward containing four beds, a small table and four chairs. It was early afternoon and only one of the beds was occupied. Two more

[1] The palace of Caserta, built in 1752 by Charles III. Later in 1943 it was chosen by General Eisenhower as Allied headquarters for the campaign in Italy.

[2] I learned in due course that, shortly after I had been removed from the transit camp to hospital, the Italian authorities had sent a large armed guard with orders to take the *Splendid*'s survivors away from the Germans and into Italian custody, on the grounds, apparently, that the *Hermes* was under Italian operational control when she sank the submarine.

KM *Hermes*.

inmates were dressed and sitting at the table. One of them rose and held out his hand. 'I'm Bill Griffiths,' he said, 'SBO[1] and padre, and this is Colonel Henri of the French Foreign Legion.' We nodded towards each other and smiled. 'In bed and not feeling too good – he's got bad dysentery – is Tom Roworth. He's a Sapper major,' went on the padre. I looked over to where a very pale roundish face, beneath close-cropped hair, was visible above the sheet. Roworth managed a smile.

'Now tell us about you,' said the padre, sitting down and indicating a chair at the table.

I said who I was and briefly how I had become a POW. As to why I had been brought into the hospital, I asked the padre to take a look at my right eye since it continued to irritate. 'It's certainly inflamed,' he said, 'and it's turned brown but I can't see anything in it. I hope they'll look after it properly here. They're not bad.'

I never did find out what the padre's ailment was nor that of the Foreign Legion colonel. That evening a *tenente* of the carabinieri appeared and asked in a reasonably friendly way in tolerable English how I was getting on. The *dottore* would see me in the morning.

It was now the first week in May 1943. The sunshine seemed to be perpetual and not too hot. My inflamed eye responded to treatment

[1] Senior British Officer.

and gradually became less bothersome, while I was becoming fully accustomed to being deprived of its sight. One day a consignment of Red Cross parcels arrived. A chain of the more mobile other ranks, including men of several nationalities, was formed to pass the handy-sized Red Cross boxes from the truck to a store on the ground floor of our building. Observing from our window the activity down below, I was diverted to see that about every tenth box was being swiftly passed, as if it were a rugby football going out to the blind side, to a pair of hands strategically located at a ground-floor window. It was the belief in our ward when I mentioned the matter that the guileful group engaged in securing more than their fair share of the Red Cross parcels were Poles. But as we each got our parcels we saw no reason to complain.

About ten days after my arrival Tom Roworth took a considerable turn for the better – although he saw no reason to let the medical staff know of his returning strength. Sitting round the table in the evenings the four of us talked about the war, mulling over how it had gone so far, speculating upon its outcome and exchanging snippets of life history. Bill Griffiths came from East Anglia, had become a chaplain to the forces, served with the Eighth Army and had the misfortune to

Korvettenkapitän Curt Rechel.

be rounded up with his battalion during one of the sudden reversals of fortune which marked the desert war. Henri, the Foreign Legion colonel, was extremely reserved, no doubt in the tradition of the Legion, both as to his background and the manner in which he had fallen into enemy hands. We got the impression, however, that he had been with General Koenig's 1st Free French Brigade at Bir Hacheim (famous, when its history came to be written, for giving rise to Rommel's comment, 'Nowhere in Africa was I given a stiffer fight.')

Major Tom Roworth was more forthcoming. A Yorkshireman, he had read English at Cambridge and been recruited by Tom Harrison to help the innovative research into human behaviour which became known as Mass Observation. He had joined the Royal Engineers at the outbreak of war and by 1942 was serving in North Africa. Early in 1943, as the stubborn Germans with their much less enthusiastic Italian allies were clinging grimly on to Tunisia, Tom was detailed to blow up a bridge in order to pin them down. But his luck deserted him and he was, as he put it, 'hoist with my own petard'. What precisely went wrong with the operation I never found out. The result of it must have been satisfactory to the Allied command, however, if not to Tom personally, as he was in due course awarded the DSO.

It was Tom who steered our evening talk towards literature. I think that Cambridge had imbued him with a love of Chaucer. Certainly, he could declaim a good deal of the prologue to the *Canterbury Tales* and much else. I had not realised Chaucer's debt to the Italians – to Dante especially and to Boccaccio, whom he probably met during a visit to Italy. It was not just the earthiness, the uninhibited expression, or the superb style which Tom loved, but the observation of human nature and the humour.

Colonel Henri also came out of his shell. His forte was the modern novel, Proust for example, of whom the rest of us knew little. George Eliot was one of Henri's favourite English writers and much admired, apparently, by Proust. When the talk turned again to poetry we were urged to read Paul Valéry, *La Jeune Parque* especially. For my part, having read little in comparison with the others, I enthused about the Russians. I recalled taking from a bookshelf at home when aged ten or so a largish volume, upon the sunlight-faded pink spine of which *The Brothers Karamazov: Dostoievsky* was printed in gold. I was at the stage of reading everything and anything that I could lay my hands on for the simple purpose of finding out about life and how people lived it. I remembered being totally absorbed in Dostoievsky's bizarre story of murder, mystery, epilepsy, innocence and guilt without, however, being rewarded by any convincing insight into provincial life in the west of Scotland. By the time I came to read Tolstoy, I had experienced enough of life, not excluding love, to respond without reservation to his genius. And I could recall with exactness the blue Mediterranean afternoon in the spring of 1934 when, taking a sailing skiff from the destroyer *Boadicea*, anchored then off St Maxime, I had sailed over to the little fishing harbour of St Tropez. Having found a quiet sunlit corner out of the wind I had stowed the sails and settled down to read the book which I had brought with me – *Anna Karenina*. I recalled the impact of those celebrated opening sentences of Tolstoy's: 'All happy families resemble one another; every unhappy family is unhappy in its own way. Everything had gone wrong in the house of the Oblonskys.'

One day we were visited by a fine upstanding Yorkshireman, Sergeant Peacock of the Green Howards, a coal-miner in civilian life who had had the bad luck to be wounded in North Africa and taken prisoner. Having established his credentials with us and been satisfied with our reception of him, Sergeant Peacock had produced from under his shirt a French automatic pistol and a clip of ammunition. A day or two before, finding that he could not persuade the lavatory to flush properly, he had lifted the lid of the cistern and on plunging his hand in to investigate had been rewarded by finding the pistol. Would we like to have it? The answer from me was 'Yes, thank you', although at that moment I had no idea of using it to shoot my way to freedom – just a feeling that the weapon might come in handy. Our acquaintance with Sergeant Peacock had the effect upon Tom Roworth and me of concentrating our minds upon the question of escape. Why not tunnel our way out? It was, I believe, the fact that the sergeant was a miner that clinched the matter, especially as he was ready to recruit Private Keir, also of the Green Howards, and Lance Corporal Marsden of an anti-aircraft unit. It was far from an original idea but potentially feasible owing to the temporary nature of the construction in which we were housed. The usual problem with tunnelling as a means of escape is how to dispose of the earth when it is dug out. In our case all we should have to do was to spread it around in the space between the ground and the floor of the hospital. From our window we could see that it was only about ten yards to the barbed wire fence. A yard or so beyond that and we could emerge on a pathway, with only an ordinary stone wall to climb over, then vanish into the darkened streets of Caserta.

It so happened that I had to visit the surgery on the ground floor of the hospital daily but not at any particular time. I soon found that, as a matter of routine, the surgery was unoccupied during the lunch hour and early afternoon. Furthermore, I located a trapdoor through which one could descend to the space below the building. In a very short time our tunnel had been started, the team consisting of Sergeant Peacock, Private Keir, Tom Roworth and myself. I was the only amateur. Using improvised implements of various kinds and working in pairs, mainly during the prolonged lunch-cum-siesta hour of the Italian hospital staff, progress was at first quite rapid. In a week or so we had sunk the entry shaft to a depth of about six feet and begun the horizontal stretch. Then, alas, and not surprisingly in view of their manifest recovery from wounds which could not have been very serious in the first place, our two soldier accomplices were discharged from the hospital. Tom and I were on our own. That is to say as far as the actual digging was concerned, but the padre and Colonel Henri (until he also was discharged) provided moral support and, even more important, acted as our intelligence arm. The padre, given his non-combatant status, was precluded from attempting to escape; but this enabled him to move freely and unremarked around the hospital and, better still, to foster a special relationship with the security officer.

Towards the end of June, Tom estimated that we had tunnelled far enough to emerge beyond the barbed wire. Bill Griffiths was to help us establish beyond doubt where we had got to. It was the time of full moonlight, occurring, what is more, in the early part of the night. Bill had acquired a gramophone and some records which he was in the habit of playing for our benefit. We found that on a still evening the strains of 'Che gelida manina' or 'Una voce poco fa' (Italian opera predominated) floating out of the open window of our ward could be heard by the above-ground member of the tunnelling team as he crouched or lay at the top of the mine-shaft.

On the night in question I had crawled along the tunnel as far as I could, becoming more and more apprehensive lest the whole thing suddenly fall in upon me. For we had taken the risk of doing without the customary pit props and roofing; the distance had seemed short enough and the soil, as we filled old Red Cross boxes with it for our mate to haul away and empty, felt firm and damp. I had with me a wand about five feet long, flexible, but sufficiently tough, we hoped, to be pushed up through the earth to appear close to the barbed wire fence.

I was lying on my side, trying to keep bits of falling tunnel out of my mouth and about to drive the wand upwards, when the line on the Red Cross box was given a succession of sharp tugs – the signal for me to get back to base. It is hard enough to crawl forward inside a narrow tunnel; it is even more difficult to retreat along it. When I had extricated myself I heard Tom's urgent whisper, 'The music stopped in the middle of an aria ...' This was the danger signal to be given by the padre if discovery seemed to be imminent. 'Listen!' hissed Tom. Silence. No sound of shoes shuffling on the surgery floor above us. No shouts. No alarm bells. Nothing. In a few moments our hearts were once again beating normally. But it seemed prudent to return to our ward and turn in, pausing only for a quick shower and clean-up on the way.

Back in the ward the padre put on another record. Then he told us what had happened, trying to keep his tone as conversational as possible despite ill-suppressed convulsions of laughter. It appeared that just about the time when he had judged I would be pushing the wand up through the earth, one of the sentries had wandered along the path outside the barbed wire, paused, looked around and then lain down with his ear to the ground. Bill had forthwith lifted the needle off the gramophone record, as agreed. As he continued to watch from the window, the sentry seemed to be settling himself more comfortably to listen. Having given the warning signal there was nothing more the padre could do. Five or so minutes later Nemesis descended – but not upon us tunnellers. It was the sentry, by now sound asleep, upon whom retribution fell, as an officer accompanied by an NCO with a torch appeared on his rounds and all but tripped over the prostrate form. The wretched man, hauled to his feet and illuminated by the NCO's torch, was quickly on his way to the guardroom.

Thanks this time to the padre having his ear to the ground as it were, we heard a day or two later that the POW inmates of the hospital were shortly to be moved elsewhere. Soon we were informed officially that we would be leaving the hospital the following evening. This gave Tom and me time to make careful preparations. In readiness for getting out through our tunnel we had collected a small hoard of Red Cross chocolate and certain sundries. I had obtained an army compass in return for my cigarette ration, and the padre had secured for me a large piece of surgical rubber out of which I had made a shoulder holster for the French automatic pistol. Tom had a small store of medicaments.

Overleaf:
Letter from the author to his wife written in a prisoner of war camp at Capua, 30 April 1943.

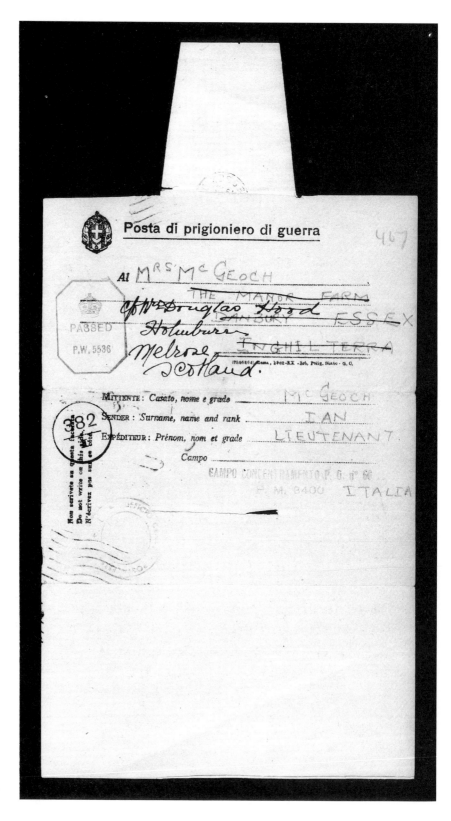

Posta di prigioniero di guerra

467

Al MRS MᶜGEOCH
~~THE MANOR FARM~~
~~C/o Mr Douglas Hood~~ ~~BANBURY~~ ~~ESSEX~~
~~Holmburn~~ ~~ENGHILTERRA~~
Melrose
Scotland.

MITTENTE: *Casato, nome e grade* — MᶜGEOCH
SENDER: *Surname, name and rank* — IAN
EXPÉDITEUR: *Prénom, nom et grade* — LIEUTENANT

Campo

CAMPO CONCENTRAMENTO P. G. n° 66
P. M. 3400 ITALIA

PASSED
P.W. 5536

382

Non scrivete su questa facciata
Do not write on this side
N'écrivez pas sur ce côté

30/4/43 Dearest Muffs, it's not too bad here and I think I shall be able to stick it quite well. I have seen, and spoken to Balkwill Burridge and Laidlaw but not Hardy yet; the behaviour of the sailors was first class, a fine crew to the last. You may have had a cable saying I am going to a German camp; but until you hear more please write to me here and pass this on to the family when you've finished with reading it. I do hope you and Angus and Alec are very well and that you will enjoy staying in Scotland. I know the following are safe. DIXON WORTHINGTON FROST WARREN SOUTH HARRISON COLLINSON DIMSDALE WILLIAMS AINSLIE STRUDWICK RAMSDEN GOODALL FOULKES KING PAINE Eleven others were saved but I don't know who they were Heaps and heaps of love from your stupid Ian

Realising that in all probability we would be searched as we left the hospital, we took pains to conceal these important effects about our persons. At least Tom did. I decided to use a suitably reconstructed Red Cross box which provided a sort of tray upon which I laid out my toilet gear, chocolate, butter tin and so on, hiding with care only the automatic pistol, snug under my arm. We were in khaki battledress and had army water-bottles, which we filled before exchanging good wishes with the padre and mustering at the main gate. The search by a bored sentry was cursory. Then we were on our way. Ambulances took the badly-wounded men, but Tom and I, being well able to walk, joined a file which led past the great Palace of Caserta, across the Via Appia and down to the railway station, where a hospital train was drawn up in a siding.

Tom and I had agreed to keep together and at a suitable moment during the night jump off the train and make our way across country to the Adriatic, moving during darkness and lying up by day. Our cover story, if engaged in conversation by the locals, would be told in broken Italian with a German accent by Tom. We were to be German soldiers enjoying a few days' leave in the Italian countryside, earned by our exertions and terrible privations in North Africa – and as proof we would be wearing Afrika Korps peaked caps, which we had fashioned in the hospital and brought with us. It is true that our footwear did not support this: Tom had on his ultra-British officers' desert boots of brown reversed calf and I was wearing black army boots which had obviously been broken in on a barrack square in Aldershot. But then you couldn't, we philosophised, have everything.

The train consisted of a large number of coaches, at least eight. We were urged up the steps and into one of them, near the rear. The interior was gloomy but blessedly cool. Along each side were tiers of bunks and there, in almost the first one I came to, was the familiar cheerful face of Ken Burridge, my sub-lieutenant in the *Splendid*. He had been fairly severely wounded by shell-fire in the action with the *Hermes* – I heard much later that, despite his wounds, he had kept one of his shipmates afloat until they were both picked up. He said that he had been well looked after by the Italians and was making a good recovery; he gave me news, also, of one or two other members of my crew who, like him, had been wounded. In the next or next but one coach we found two vacant bunks, one above the other. Tom took the upper one and we lay down, having removed our footwear. This did not please the orderly who now appeared. He was rather officious and indicated strongly that we should take off our clothes, put on the pyjamas which he held out and turn in. It would not have suited our book to comply. So Tom staged a fine act (which he had no need to rehearse) of the consequences of severe dysentery, while I feigned total exhaustion as I lay stretched out on the bunk, muttering '*Aqua freddo, per favore*' and '*Quando parte il treno – dove andare?*' The orderly had better things to do than try to persuade a couple of stubborn, not to say stupid, POWs to do what they were told and we were left in peace.

It was almost dark by the time the hospital train pulled out of the station. We were straining every nerve to ascertain where we were going. Out of the window by my bunk I could just, by craning my neck, see some sky and stars, while it seemed after a few minutes of rattling and sinuating over many sets of points that the train was indeed heading north-west because the last flush of summer sunset was on the left. I dozed. Despite being rather hot in my battledress I was comfortable enough. My injured eye had long since responded to medical treatment and gave me no trouble. What I must not do, I kept telling myself, was fall asleep and miss the moment for preparing to jump and run for it. It was dark inside the coach as well as outside. The orderly did not reappear. The train seemed to be making good progress. The question was – what was its destination? Suppose it were to haul into a siding and stop before we had leapt from it. What then? Such a good chance to escape might not recur. However, on went the train non-stop through the night – 'clickety-click, clickety-click, clickety-click, clickety-click'. It was hard to tell its speed. But we knew that from Caserta to Rome, to which all rail as well as ordinary roads were said to lead, was not much more than a hundred miles. If we were not careful we would be there before we had jumped.

After what seemed like another hour, Tom leaned over and said, 'We'd better go soon.' I put on my boots and stood on the carriage floor. My head was just above the level of Tom's bunk. As I watched, he opened the window, which ran the length of his bunk, and began to squeeze out through the narrow space. It did not look easy and the train seemed to have speeded up. Suddenly the whole enterprise began to appear rather dangerous. Then Tom disappeared out of the window altogether. I climbed on to his bunk and prepared to follow him. The night air was cool as it rushed by. Looking down I could sense rather than actually see the ground going past. When I was fully outside, clinging on to the window ledge and feeling around with my feet for something to stand on, I could see Tom to my right, edging his way towards the rear of the coach. He was standing on a running board, holding on, as I now was, to a narrow gutter above the windows. In a minute or two we were both hanging on to the corridor connection between the coaches, with our feet on the steps over the buffers.

Through a small window in the coach which we had just vacated, I could discern the shape of the orderly slumped on a seat. Many years later Ken Burridge, who was there to witness the discomfiture of the orderly told me that when the train arrived in Rome and the unfortunate man had to explain why he was two 'patients' short all hell was let loose.

The trouble about jumping off a train in hostile territory is that one wishes to do so when in open country rather than in a built-up area. But in open country, as a rule, the train is going fast – much too fast it appeared to us that night – and the trick therefore is to wait until it begins to slow down and then grit one's teeth and leap clear. It seemed to be ages before our particular train began noticeably to lose speed. The brakes were quite certainly being applied. The ground which, as the moon was now up we could see clearly, was going by at a less daunting pace. We lowered ourselves down and round the corner of the coach, so as to get on to the running board abreast the door. As the train came out of a long righthand curve into a straight stretch of line we passed buildings of some kind by the track. It was now or never. 'Come on!' said Tom and jumped. I followed a split second later. The ground was hard, but we managed to keep relaxed and roll over as we hit it. The impact would probably have been much the same had we been landing by parachute in a strong wind.

'Are you OK?' said Tom. I had landed a few feet beyond him and was picking myself up. 'I think so. No bones broken, at any rate. You OK?' I replied. 'Yep. I'd rather have a parachute though.' 'Next time ... damn! My water-bottle's bust. I must have fallen on it.'

We crouched for a minute or two watching with incredulity mixed with glee the disappearance into the distance of the red light at the end of the train, which was very soon all that we could see of it. The noise died away. We looked around, conscious of the silence, trying to orientate ourselves. The night was still, the moon full and the sky cloudless. With the help of my compass we saw that we should have to cross the railway before pressing on north-eastwards towards the Adriatic coast. We set off over the tracks, and were somewhat dismayed to find before us a row of cottages. To outflank them we turned right, in the direction from which our train had come. We had not gone far when we came to a patch of long grass. It was tinder-dry and as we trod upon it the crackling noise shattered the stillness of the night. In a moment all the dogs in Creation seemed to be barking and barking and barking.

Suddenly we felt extremely exposed standing there in the moonlight, the answer to a watchdog's prayer. To have started running would have compounded our intrusiveness and confirmed the dogs' worst suspicions, bringing into their routine barking that note of genuine anxiety combined with hostility which would alert the householders. We kept off the grass, walking in Indian file until we could leave the railway and take a line left-handed, well clear of the dogs and the habitations, across open scrub-land. Gradually the canine clamour died away as we trudged on in a north-easterly direction, aiming to put as much distance as possible between us and the railway before daylight.

By dawn we had reached a high embankment, near the bottom of which was a clump of bushes – a thicket almost. It seemed as good a place as any to lie up; besides it was too late to look for anywhere else. We lay down, ate a piece of our Red Cross chocolate, took a swig from Tom's water-bottle and reviewed the situation. We had covered about three miles since leaving the railway but had no idea where we were, apart from the conviction that we were some distance south-east of Rome. 'Might be worse,' was Tom's verdict.

He had spoken too soon. All of a sudden there was an ear-splitting roar as a fighter biplane swept over the embankment just above our heads, so that we could see the wheels of the undercarriage still turning. We had chosen the edge of an airfield! A few seconds later came another fighter, then another – it was evidently the dawn patrol. We could do nothing. Despite the appalling noise every so often of the air-cooled Fiat engines at full revs we were reasonably safe; the chances of our being spotted from the aircraft taking off just over us were nil.

But there were other hazards. Attracted possibly by the chocolate, a fair-sized snake came slithering through the grass towards my face as I rested on an elbow with my head in my hand. I jumped up and back, treading on Tom and crying, 'Snake, look out!'

Tom was both displeased at being stood upon and scornful. 'Grass snake', he said, '*absolutely* harmless.' I relaxed. The snake had meanwhile vanished, apparently even more frightened than I had been.

As the sun rose higher the heat began to be oppressive. The shrubs behind which we were concealed could not give us shade. The nearest trees were hundreds of yards away. We simply had to stay where we were. But was it all up anyway? For what now assailed our ears, there being a lull in flying operations, was the baying of hounds. This was bad. The baying got louder and louder. Tom peered cautiously through the shrubs. 'Three couple of – of – well, I don't know quite what. Bloodhounds, I suppose. Three carabinieri. They're being dragged along by the hounds. Damn. I think they're on our trail.' Tom crouched as low as he could. I did the same. The baying grew to a crescendo. At any moment we should know what it was like to be at the receiving end of half a dozen slavering jaws. By a miracle some other scent took the hounds' fancy and the hunt swept by. Gradually the baying became fainter, then died away, drowned out in any case by the shattering roar of yet another fighter getting airborne.

After that narrow escape surely, we thought, it must be our lucky day. We might well remain undiscovered and be able to make more ground away from the railway that night. Incredibly, within about half an hour of the hounds going by, there came the brazen notes of a badly-played bugle. This time I was the one who peered cautiously through the shrubs. A file of a dozen or so men, in uniform of sorts, accompanied by an NCO, was marching in our direction, bugled on by one of their number who was in the lead. The others, I could see as they came nearer, each had a bugle slung round his neck. Not fifty yards away from our hiding place the squad was halted, turned right into line and fallen out. Then the bugling began in earnest. For a couple of hours, with amazingly little respite, those wretched recruits practised bugle calls. The din was truly dreadful.

Shortly before noon, with a final frenzy of breathy fanfare, the bugle squad was marched away. The sun was now extremely hot and there was no wind, not even the slightest zephyr. It was sweltering. The aircraft had to use maximum take-off to get into the still air. They kept coming over the very end of the runway at the top of the embankment, so low that we felt that by standing we could have reached up and given their wheels another spin. The long afternoon passed somehow, dusk came and with it cool air and quietness. It was time to be on our way.

The sky was cloudless, so that the stars gave us our direction. But to begin with it was so dark that finding a line to follow was not easy. We had to skirt the perimeter of the airfield, crossing a road in the process, before we could stick to our north-easterly course with the aid of my compass. The country was now undulating and we came upon a pasture where there were many fig trees. Never was the ripe green fruit more welcome. We ate a good many of those figs before pressing on. Once the moon had risen progress was a good deal more rapid, and I suppose that we had covered about ten miles in the course of the night before a faint sign of the approach of dawn caused us to look urgently for another hiding place. We had been climbing gradually since leaving the fig orchard and found that we had come to the brink of what seemed to be a huge crater. There was no cover anywhere nearby, but Tom discovered a narrow path leading over the edge of the crater and down to a rocky but quite wide ledge. It would have been ideal had there been a cave to give both concealment and shade but we had to make do with a small declivity, which at least kept us below the skyline. Here we lay down. We were fairly tired but reasonably cheerful. The only immediate trouble was lack of water. The loss of my water-bottle was more than tiresome. In Italy, in mid-summer, there isn't much drinkable water about. Even the small amount of chocolate which we now ate added to our thirst. A couple of swigs each from Tom's water-bottle had to suffice. It was not enough.

By the end of the second whole day in the broiling sun we were thirstier than ever, as well as being extremely sore and stiff from unaccustomed walking and from lying for hours on end on the unyielding ground. However, not a soul had come into view all day nor any beast either. We had at least got clear, we now had reason to believe, of the initial search for us. The thing to do was to press on throughout another night, hoping against hope that we would find potable water as we went. The sun had set but twilight remained when we scrambled to our feet and set off up the path towards the top of the crater, which seemed a good deal smaller by daylight than when we had come upon it in the dark. Having skirted the edge and orientated ourselves towards the north-east once again, we had not gone far when the ground fell away. Before us lay a large town. Despite the blackout, lights were visible here and there, and before it had become pitch dark we could see that the town was clustered at each end of a bridge, which seemed to span a gorge.

So far Tom and I had been making our decisions without delay and with little discussion, let alone argument. We had agreed upon our intention: to walk by day and lie up by night until we reached the shore of the Adriatic, there to steal a boat and sail across to Yugoslavia, where we expected to find friendly forces. Now a council of war had become essential. The question was, what to do about the town that lay across our line of march. If we attempted to skirt the place, either to the north-west or to the south-east, we should in all probability be faced with a large river but no bridge. To go through the town, even in the blackout, would certainly be risky but would enable us to use the bridge. Provided that there wasn't a curfew, Tom said, we ought to be able to pass through the town unnoticed. I agreed.

It seemed a long wait until the moon came up and lighted us on our way. The going was rough for a bit and then we came upon a track, which in turn brought us to a roadway leading to the town. We put on our Afrika Korps caps and strode out purposefully, keeping step as military people do. Soon we were in what seemed to be the main thoroughfare. There were plenty of people about – no curfew, evidently. It was strange to be walking along, mingling with people, hearing them talk, seeing their faces clearly as they stepped out of the shadows into the moonlight. It was quite a long way into the centre of the town, but when we reached it the approach to the bridge showed up. Praying that it was not guarded we went towards it. There was no sign of a barrier. We did not pause to admire the view from the bridge, tempting though it was to look down at the river below.

Once across, the choice of roads to follow became somewhat embarrassing. None seemed to be heading in the desired direction. Taking the one which looked most promising, we followed it for a short distance and came upon a railway station. This we entered with caution. TIVOLI. So that was where we were. The name rang a bell, though quite what bell neither of us was sure. 'Why don't we bum a ride on one of these trains?' said Tom. We had found the 'Signori', splashed some water from a tap over our faces, had a most welcome drink and refilled Tom's water-bottle. 'No,' I said, 'the railways don't run to and fro across Italy – they run north-west to south-east. We would find ourselves either in Rome or back at Caserta.' Tom saw the force of this, so we slipped out of the station and took to the road again, leaving behind us the clank of wagon couplings and the puffs of a shunting engine as a freight train was made up.

Fairly soon we had reached the eastern outskirts of Tivoli and were following a road which seemed to be bearing gradually left and hence towards the north-easterly sector. On one side the ground sloped steeply upwards; on the other it appeared to fall away equally steeply although it was not easy to tell in the semi-darkness. So far there had been no traffic. But as we walked we became aware that the road ahead was completely occupied by a large flock of sheep. Some of them had bells which tinkled agreeably. A shepherd was dimly visible. We were balked. We did not wish to be engaged in conversation by the shepherd. Our Afrika Korps story would sound a bit thin. Nor was it feasible, given the lie of the land, to circle round the flock. Besides, there must be at least one sheep dog and they would not take kindly to strangers. There was nothing for it but to slow right down to the gentle pace of the unhurried sheep and hope that they would soon reach their pasture and leave the road to us.

I doubt if we had got much more than five miles beyond Tivoli when at last the shepherd and a lad he had with him turned the flock off the road on to some level ground. By then we were in trouble. Dawn was already breaking. There was no sign of any cover. We walked on, becoming more and more anxious. It was getting lighter every minute. We were just about to leave the road and take to the fields on our left when we realised that we had come to the outskirts of a village. Not far ahead was a small barn. It looked dilapidated, unused and – what seemed particularly attractive – it had a flat roof. I don't think there was a door and certainly nothing much inside. But there was a ladder to give access to the roof. Up we went. There was a parapet about two feet high – enough to screen us from the road if we kept down. Lying about on the roof were large seeds of some description, evidently left there to dry. We relaxed, ate some more chocolate – almost the last of it – and drank a little water from Tom's bottle. The sun was now well up and warming us. We dozed off.

Abruptly we sat up, alerted by the same sound. Someone was coming up the ladder. A moment later a head appeared with an ancient felt hat on it, followed by the large body of a man, whom we took to be the proprietor of the barn. He looked at us, seemingly without any emotion, but enquiringly, as well he might.

'Soldaten ... Tedeschi,' began Tom hopefully, pointing to his Afrika Korps cap and adding a few more fictions in fractured Italian. The farmer looked contemptuous but said nothing. He turned the seeds over, picked up a few and examined them, gazed very hard at us once again and disappeared.

This was bad. At the very least the chap was bound to tell his wife and probably the neighbours that he had found a couple of doubtful-looking characters hiding on the roof of his barn. The sooner we got clear the better. So down the ladder we went, across the road and away towards the hills to the north. We were now in a fully cultivated area. We were toiling round the side of a field of lucerne when we heard a shout. In the middle of the field was a ragged old man. As we looked he shouted again – something incomprehensible. Tethered nearby was a donkey. The fellow was a vagabond if ever there was one. Tom shouted, 'Abitare qui?' at him, followed by 'Abbiamo vacanze ... Andiamo a passeggio.' (Do you live here? We are on holiday ... We are going for a walk.) We waited for a moment, not so much with any hope of understanding what the old man was shouting as to appear nonchalant. Then with a '*Buon giorno*' we pressed on up the hill beyond the field. It was fairly easy going and we thought that we were doing rather well. It was even slightly cooler than hitherto. The sky was clouded over. All of a sudden it grew rather dark and rain began to fall. Next came the rumble of thunder. We walked on. Then the storm broke – lighting, torrential rain, more thunder-claps, the lot. We were soon soaked to the skin. But, like the storm passage in Beethoven's 'Pastoral' symphony, the thunder quickly died away, the rain ceased and the sun blazed again. We decided to take our clothes off and spread them on the ground to dry. The spot which we selected was no more than a dip in the gentle slope up which we had been walking. There was little cover, just a few shrubs here and there. But it seemed remote enough, and we had already forgotten about the old man in the field with his donkey. Not surprisingly, we both fell asleep in the sun.

*   *   *

The carabinieri were grinning, even as they pointed their carbines at us. To come across your quarry in a manhunt, after a hot toiling search over the hillside, not only asleep but stark naked was most satisfactory – and what a story to tell over the vino! '*Soldaten . . . Tedeschi . . . Afrika Korps . . . vacanze*,' said Tom with, in the circumstances, commendable dignity as he sat up, putting one hand over his private parts and reaching with the other for his Afrika Korps cap. The carabinieri were unimpressed. They continued to smile. Their scepticism was unconcealed. '*Inglese*,' said the NCO with assurance. '*Prigionieri di guerra*.' By this time Tom and I were on our feet and starting to get dressed. There really was no option. It was a fair cop. The feeling of utter powerlessness of a totally unarmed person surrounded by armed captors has to be experienced to be understood. Tom and I were lucky. We were not political prisoners. We were not even spies. And we were the beneficiaries of that continuity of civilising impulse which, in Europe, had given rise to laws of war including, above all, the Geneva Convention. We were chagrined, but not frightened.

Admittedly there was a moment, as the NCO's eye lit upon my automatic pistol lying on the ground, when I felt somewhat apprehensive. But he picked it up, inspected it and put it his pocket without comment. His chief concern, clearly, was to hand Tom and me over to the proper authority as quickly as possible. Quite soon we found ourselves standing to attention, like a couple of schoolboys who had run away and been caught, in front of a large desk in the sparsely furnished office of the local carabinieri. Behind the desk sat the capitano. On the wall behind him was a large poster to the effect that information leading to the apprehension of escaped prisoners of war would be rewarded with a very large sum. Standing beside the capitano, looking extremely pleased with himself, was the old villain with whom we had exchanged greetings earlier that day.

As there really was nothing to be said at this stage of the proceedings Tom and I said nothing. But the NCO, in reporting to his superior, must have passed on as being whimsical if nothing else our story about being German soldiers on a walking tour. Because the capitano, having failed to get anything out of us in reply to his questions, suddenly stood up, came round the side of his desk, reached down and grabbed my right ankle, then lifted my foot as if he were a blacksmith about to shoe a horse. The broad arrow on the sole left no doubt.

'British army boots,' he said in English.

There was a small group of mildly excited villagers waiting outside the police station when, after a couple of hours in a cell, we were led out and hustled into the back of a black car. It was already evening and by the time we reached Tivoli it was dark. We did not stop there, but went on through the town and were soon in the open again. In half an hour or so we were in the outskirts of a city. '*Roma?*' enquired Tom. '*Si, Roma.*'

Neither Tom nor I was well acquainted with the Eternal City. Nor, did it appear, were the country-bred carabinieri who were in charge of us. For, after many twists and turns, accompanied by much animated conversation, our car was driven off the road, under an archway and into a small courtyard. Here the NCO alighted and disappeared. Left on their own the two junior carabinieri got out also, lit cigarettes and began to argue about something. Then one of them lifted up the bonnet of the car. Both peered in, although what they could possibly see in the dark was hard to say. After a moment or two they seemed to have forgotten about us. The door on my side of the car was invitingly open, although I should have to negotiate it before heading for the exit from the courtyard. Tom had evidently had the same idea. I felt rather than saw him cautiously trying the door handle on his side. He looked round and nodded.

'See you in the Vatican,' he whispered.

'OK – now!' Simultaneously we leapt out of the car and started to run like riggers. Whether to blame my British army boots or not I do not know. At any rate I had not gone ten paces when I slipped on the cobbled yard and came a purler. Before I could get off my knees an outraged carabiniere had jumped on top of me, trying to hold me with one hand while with the other he was striving to draw his revolver from its holster, which had slipped round and seemed to be difficult to reach. A shout of 'Bastard!' from Tom indicated that he, too, had been unable to make his getaway.

All four of us were now somewhat out of breath, and the carabinieri were behaving with that mixture of anger and relief evinced by nannies when their little charges disobey the injunction not to run into the road. By this time, however, our 'nannies' were pointing their revolvers at us and thoughts of 'shot while attempting to escape' flashed through my mind. The worst that happened was that my infuriated and shaken guard so far forgot himself as to put a fist into my face rather hard, but not hard enough to break any teeth. Tom had already had a bit of a dust-up with his man, but was no more damaged than I was. We were bundled back into the car, while the carabinieri marched up and down with revolvers at the ready, awaiting the return of the NCO.

Ten minutes or so later back came the NCO, to be assailed with almost hysterical accounts from our guards of the episode in which they had triumphed over us two desperadoes. The words *prigionieri molti pericolosi* featured once or twice, I noticed. Thus briefed, the NCO, as if to reassert his authority, leant into the back of the car and gave me a sharp slap on the face, accompanied by some words which sounded distinctly ungracious. He climbed into the driving seat and started the car. Emerging from the archway into the street we turned right. Our destination was entered through an archway, like the courtyard which we had just left. But this time there were gates which shut behind us. Once out of the car Tom and I were separated, and I did not see him again until well after the war. I was prodded a bit and found myself at the top of a curving staircase, on a first floor landing. It was dimly lit. As I waited there while a carabiniere unlocked the door of a room on the left I heard an English voice, saying 'Watch out for . . .' but I could not quite catch the name. Then I was pushed into the room, the door was locked and I was left to myself.

6 · Stone walls

The guard had been decent enough to switch on the light. It was a single bulb in an opaque glass bell-shaped shade, hanging by its flex from the middle of the ceiling. By its dim glow I could see that I was in a single bedroom of modest size, furnished with an iron bedstead positioned lengthways along the opposite wall beneath a makeshift blackout curtain behind which, presumably, there was a window. The rest of the furnishings were equally institutional. On the wall to my left was a small chest of drawers; on the wall to my right an antediluvian but comforting commode and a small bookcase; and in the centre a table with – surprisingly – two chairs. Having every expectation of doing thirty days solitary confinement (Tom Roworth had told me this was the accepted consequence of an abortive attempt to escape) I wondered vaguely who the second chair was for. But I was too tired to concentrate. It had been quite a day. I took my boots off – the boots which had betrayed me – and lay on the bed. The light was still on, but I went to sleep almost at once.

What awoke me was the sound of a stentorian voice floating up, or erupting rather, from somewhere outside my window. An NCO's commands – combining as they do the notes of authority, encouragement and scorn – are both characteristic and barely comprehensible in any language. Not until I had stood on my bed, pulled back the blackout curtain and peered out between the bars did I discover what was going on. The NCO, dressed as a cavalryman and from time to time adding emphasis to his words by slapping his riding boot with a swagger cane, was standing in the middle of a *manège*, around which were trotting a dozen or so horses, on each of which was mounted, bareback, a young man. After a moment or two studying the form, I could see that the riders were recruits. They were undergoing precisely what I had experienced about ten years previously when, as an acting sub-lieutenant on 'courses' at the Royal Naval College, Greenwich, I had volunteered for riding instruction at the 'Shop' – the headquarters of the Royal Artillery at Woolwich. A proper seat on a horse, we were firmly told, could not be acquired without seemingly endless 'circuits and bumps' – riding bareback round and round at the trot to loud cries of 'Grip with your knees! ... Sit right down! ... Keep your heels down!' As I found out some forty years later when I revisited Rome I was not incarcerated in a cavalry barracks as I had supposed but in the Rome headquarters of the carabinieri, which then maintained, as it does to this day, a mounted contingent.

I was lying on my bed again, contemplating the dusty, fly-blown ceiling and cream and green décor of the room, when the door opened and in came a man in British battledress.

'Good mornin'. You must be Lieutenant Mac-something.'

'McGeoch – OhSeeAitch, och as in loch, McGeoch,' I said, accustomed as I had become to elucidating my surname for the benefit of almost everyone whom I met. 'But call me Mac, it's much easier.'

'Right, Mac,' said the individual. Something ingratiating – an air of *faux bonhomie* – in his manner rang a warning bell in my mind. He continued, 'I'm George Richards, captain.' Here he indicated with a gesture the three pips on his shoulder-tab. 'I'm the Senior British Officer in this place. Anythin' you want, within reason of course, just let me know and I'll see what I can do with the Eyeties.'

'Thank you,' I said. 'I suppose I'll be here for thirty days, so there's bound to be something. In fact, right now I could do with a pee and a wash.' 'Of course,' he said, and went to leave, adding, 'you are entitled as an officer to proper treatment. You'll have to bang on the door to get the guard when you need something.'

In the corridor outside he spoke in what seemed to be fluent Italian, in which the word *gabinetto* featured strongly, whereupon the guard came in and conducted me a short way to a water closet in a very small space. It had a ventilator but no window, I noted, automatically on the lookout for any possible means of escape.

Back in my room I found that a jug of hot water, soap, towel, a Gillette razor and some blades, shaving soap, toothbrush and a tin of tooth-powder had appeared on the commode. I began to be reconciled to my recapture. I wondered what had happened to Tom and made a mental note to ask Richards when he next appeared. I now connected him in my mind with the disembodied English voice warning me to 'watch out' for someone. That 'someone' was, I felt certain, this 'Captain' Richards RASC – if indeed his name, as well as his rank, was not phoney. In short, he must be a stooge. His traitorous task would no doubt be to extract from me, in the course of uninhibited conversation between comrades-in-arms, as much information as he could about British submarines, their latest equipment and mode of operation. I had better be careful what I said to him.

As it happened, the captain did not turn up for a couple of days. No doubt the idea was to let me settle in and start to feel bored with my solitary state, so that I would welcome his company. But I was not bored by solitude: the reverse if anything. Both by temperament and by upbringing I had always, for as long as I could remember, found my own company quite congenial and on the whole sufficient.

'Mornin', Mac. Everythin' OK?' It was Captain Richards again. 'Good morning,' I replied, a little stiffly. 'Thanks – might be worse.' Richards sat down at the table. 'Good,' he said, 'but don't forget – if there's anythin' at all, just say so.' He leaned over the table and added in a lowered voice, 'We can talk safely enough. Tell me, they picked you up with that other chap in the country somewhere, didn't they, after you'd jumped off a train?'

'Yes,' I replied, 'do you know what's happened to Roworth, my chum?'

'Same as you – thirty days in the cooler.'

I asked the captain to give Roworth a message from me to the effect that it was fun while it lasted and wish him luck. Then, no doubt in order to put conversation on the right track, Richards said, 'You were skipper of a submarine, weren't you?' This set the warning lights flashing in my mind.

'As a matter of interest, how much do they tell you about the POWs who come in here?'

'Officially, name and rank or number only,' he replied. 'That's all they're entitled to know. But I can usually squeeze more out of the capitano, Belli – he's not a bad chap. He knows you're a submarine officer.'

'What about you?' I asked.

'I was in Tobruk,' he said, and seemed reluctant to say more. I wanted to ask him how he had found himself here as Senior British Officer, but refrained. Instead, I enquired where he came from. It seemed that he was from Reading, and I was led to understand that in peacetime he had been a wages clerk in a large factory where a lot of women and girls were employed. He went on to tell me, in lubricious detail, of the amorous advances to which he had frequently been subjected – indeed in some cases 'exposed' would be a better word – by females trying to seduce him into giving them an extra-large pay packet. I could hardly have helped showing some interest in these revelations and the captain turned to the matter of Italian women. It was clear that he regarded women as a commodity, to be deprived of which was by far the worst aspect of being a POW. And there was a suggestion that if you played your cards right even a POW – and one in solitary confinement at that – might be permitted some feminine company.

Having dropped this hint, Richards got up to go.

'Must be gettin' along,' he said, 'or it won't look too good. But I'll be back. I've never met a submarine skipper before. I'd be shit-scared, cooped up like that below the water. Sure there's nothin' you want? Food OK?' I went to the door with him, opened it quickly and found the carabiniere guard lurking outside. It was just as well that I hadn't knocked the captain out, put on his battledress and cap, and walked out. The idea had occurred to me. '*Arrivederci*,' said Richards. 'By the way, why don't you learn a bit of Italian?' Before I could think of a suitable reply the door was shut and locked.

With another twenty-seven days to go, it really was necessary, I felt, to make some effort to use the time systematically. I had abandoned any serious intent to try to escape while in my present situation. The only window in my cell was barred and in any case faced inward over the riding school. If I was lucky enough to nip through the door when the guard was looking the other way I would have no idea how to get out of the building; and supposing I were somehow to achieve an exit, where then? Could I really find my way unnoticed to the Vatican, in broad daylight? No. It was not on. The alternative was to adopt some mental discipline. To start learning Italian might not be such a bad idea. I had no notion what would happen to me after my thirty days 'solitary' was completed. No doubt I would be transferred to some POW camp. Another opportunity to escape might then present itself. But I would be on my own. Not to be able to understand basic Italian could be my undoing.

I went over to have another look at the little row of books lying, some upright and others on their sides, in the bookcase. Unfortunately for my good intentions I now saw that the title of one of the books, which being upright I had not noticed before, was in English: *An Introduction to Modern Architecture*. I pulled it out. It was a Penguin edition, published in 1940. The author was J M Richards. Without putting it back on the shelf I examined the other titles, hoping to find one which looked as if it might be a useful primer in Italian. The only one I can recall was *I Promessi Sposi*.

Having leafed through *An Introduction to Modern Architecture* and noticed among its illustrations the photograph of a building which I had so often passed without, to my shame, even being aware of it, I began to read. It was the Glasgow School of Art, the architect being Charles Rennie Macintosh. I discovered that Macintosh had designed the furniture for a private house also, built to his plans not far from where I was born and had lived for many childhood years. This was in Helensburgh, the town created by a far-sighted Colquhoun of Luss, overlooking the Firth of Clyde within rail-commuting distance of Glasgow. I took the book over to the table and sat down to read it from the beginning.

'Mornin', Mac, how's everythin'? What's that you're readin'?'

'A book on architecture – it's the only one in English,' I said, waving towards the bookcase.

'What about learnin' Italian?' said the captain. 'I thought you were going to.'

'That'll have to wait.'

But Richards was not to be put off. 'I could help you learn some Eyetie,' he said. I felt inclined to ask him how he himself had learned to speak it so well, but decided against it. I wanted to keep him at a distance without giving him an excuse to turn nasty. Suddenly I had a brainwave. 'George,' I said, permitting myself to use his first name in order to retain his confidence, 'you know that you said you could probably get me anything I wanted, within reason?' The captain, who had seated himself at the table, leaned across. 'Sure,' he said, hopefully, '*che cosa?* – sorry, I mean, what is it?'

'Well,' I continued, 'you may think it ridiculous, but I have a terrific yen to learn to play the piano-accordion. Do you think that you could borrow one for me from someone?'

'A piano-accordion? What the hell!' He was silent for a moment or two. 'I'll see what I can do. Don't go away – oh, sorry, Mac, I shouldn't have said that.'

'Don't worry, I don't suppose you can get away any more than I can.' The captain, departing quickly, avoided answering the loaded if rhetorical remark. I was by now quite sure that he was a stooge, through whom the Italians and possibly the Germans hoped to acquire intelligence derived from my careless talk.

Looking back, I did take myself rather too seriously in those days. Quite apart from the very strong urge to return as quickly as possible to my wife and family, which was normal, I did feel at times that my own actions could actually have an effect upon the outcome of the war. Tolstoy's description of how the Irish mercenary soldier at Borodino, fired by fighting spirit, had single-handed held a bridge till reinforcements came, so that it was at least as much he as the dispositions of Napoleon or Kutuzov who had determined the outcome of the battle, had seized my mind. Mortified as I was at having lost my submarine together with many of her crew, I rejoiced at having sent to the bottom many cargoes of armaments and fuel desperately needed by the Axis forces in North Africa. But the war was still raging. It was not only a sense of duty which, coupled with uxoriousness, kept prompting me to escape; nor was it entirely my detestation of the Hitler gang for daring to seek conquest everywhere. It was to a considerable extent the desire to rehabilitate myself professionally.

Having decided against trying to escape from the solitary confinement in which I now languished, the regime which I proposed for myself was beginning to take shape. If Captain Richards did indeed manage to get me a piano-accordion, that would provide both a pastime and a means of countering his efforts to persuade me to talk freely about submarines and other naval matters. But I should still have time to pick up some Italian and, in my spare time as it were, to improve my knowledge of architecture. This had been founded happily, if somewhat insecurely, on Osbert Lancaster's brilliantly written and deftly illustrated pre-war skit on architecture in Britain entitled *From Pillar to Post*. Somers and I in our courting days in London had rocked with laughter at Osbert's perceptive and witty evocation of styles such as 'By-pass Variegated', 'Wimbledon Transitional', 'Bankers' Georgian', 'Pont Street Dutch', 'Stockbrokers' Tudor' and, most sublime, 'Pseudish'. The very fact that a POW, and moreover one who had misbehaved by trying to escape, should find in his cell any books at all, let alone a Penguin about modern architecture, reflected the paradox of civilised European countries fighting each other in a war to determine which of the two barbaric regimes, the Nazis or the Communists, would prevail. How lucky I was to be in Italy, I thought, and not in Germany.

I ought to have rationed my reading to one chapter a day. But my self-discipline was not good enough. I read the book on architecture at a sitting and was reduced to reclining on my bed and just thinking. Two or three days passed. Then the door of my room was thrust open and in came Richards, lugging a box-like object.

'Hello there, Mac,' he breezed, plonking the thing on the table. 'Look what I've brought you! How's that?'

'Bloody good effort,' I said. 'How on earth did you do it?'

'Oh,' he replied, 'I told Belli that you'd be less likely to try to escape if you got stuck into learnin' the squeeze-box.'

I got off my bed, went over to the table and picked up the accordion. It looked quite new and had a broad strap which I slung over one shoulder. Having more or less adjusted the instrument so that I could finger the keys with my right hand, I inserted my left under another strap so as to cover the array of chord buttons. I released a catch and let the bellows fall open. I then began to squeeze them closed. The result was a loud, sad, prolonged, confused noise. I tried again, this time attempting to pick out with one finger of my right hand the notes of 'Stardust', that almost indestructible and conveniently slow melody. The result was very far from being even tolerable. I looked enquiringly at the captain.

'At least it works all right,' he said. 'I'll leave you to it. The best of luck.' And he was gone.

It did not take me long to realise that I was not going to master the wretched squeeze-box quickly, if at all. Not only was it extremely hard to control the bellows, but the rows of buttons, each of which, when pressed, contributed a chord to harmonise (or not, as the case may have been) with the air being played on the keyboard, called for special expertise. Give me a clarinet or a saxophone and I can (or could in those days) produce a tolerable tune; but without guidance I was not, it was obvious, going to make much progress with the piano-accordion.

Next day the captain came to find out how I was getting on. I think that he must have heard from afar the dismal groans and squeaks. Maybe there had been complaints from the guards or their officers, other POWs even, perhaps quoting the Geneva Convention's rule against torture. At any rate he was somewhat subdued. I began again to try to play the instrument. 'You see how it is, George,' I explained, 'I can't seem to get the hang of these buttons that make the chords. What I really need is one of those instruction books – *Teach Yourself the Piano-Accordion* – that sort of thing. It won't matter if it's in Italian. It will probably have a diagram of the beastly thing, some simple exercises like scales and a few simple tunes – "Way Down Upon the Swanee River", or "Singin' in the Rain".'

As I was talking Richards had sat himself down. 'OK,' he said, 'mebbe I can get that too. But,' he went on, 'I still haven't heard what happened to your submarine. Is it true you were clobbered by a Hun destroyer? That's what Belli says.' It looked as if Captain George Richards was being pressed by his masters for results. I was almost sorry for him. 'The fact is,' I told him, careful not to give anything away, 'it was a grim business. I lost, near as I can make out, eighteen of my people. I know that everyone had left the boat before I did, except for one poor chap who was killed just as he was getting out of the conning tower hatch. The Germans – and I can't blame them, really – were shooting at us from short range with everything they could bring to bear. One or two direct hits with the main armament caused most of the casualties; and not everyone, I'm afraid, could swim. I don't really want to talk about it. War is war. Them or us.' But the captain persisted. 'Yes, OK, but I just want to know what it's like to be in a submarine. How deep can it go? How long did you have to spend at sea? That sort of thing. What's the food like? I'm just a bloody "brown job", I don't know anything about the navy, let alone submarines.'

'Well,' I said, 'that's fair enough. Some day maybe I'll feel like spinning you a yarn, as we say. But you'll have to tell me what things were like in Tobruk. Can't have been much of a picnic. Right now, George, I'm determined to get the better of this bloody squeeze-box. Can you bring me that instruction book?' I started practising again. It was not difficult to make an excruciating noise. The captain departed.

This time he was back the same afternoon and he had with him a glossy publication which certainly contained, as a quick flip of the pages revealed, just what I needed to know. 'Many thanks, George,' I said, 'now I can begin to make some progress. Just give me two or three days and I'll be able to play you a scale or two. No good trying to run before you can walk.' Richards still hoped, perhaps, that my enthusiasm for the squeeze-box would flag and that rather than remain solitary I would be glad of his company and be willing to talk about submarine warfare. 'What about this learnin' Eyetie?' he asked. 'Have you given up that idea?'

'Not really,' I said, 'but how much longer can Italy stay in the war?' The date was 10 July. Although I did not know it, the Allies had landed in Sicily that morning. The captain must have begun to wonder what the future held for him. 'I've no idea,' he replied after a pause, 'ma – as they say here – *speriamo la guerra finira subito. Buon giorno.*' Then he left.

I didn't, in the end, get around to learning Italian.

*   *   *

It is part of the technique of prison security, I imagine, or if not it certainly should be, to deny prisoners any advance knowledge of the intention to move them. This prevents them from planning how best to make a bid for freedom during the transit, when a lapse in security is most likely to occur. I had not been told officially how long my sentence would last. Thirty days, as I have mentioned, was the norm. I was not prepared in any way, therefore, when after only ten days, that is to say on 11 July, an officer came in and said in quite good English, 'Lieutenant, I have come to escort you to a different place. Make ready at once, if you please. I shall be back in ten minutes.' I thought that the chap was a cavalryman. Certainly his riding boots were well-polished; he wore a sort of sash and carried both a pistol at his belt and a sword. He was in fact a carabiniere officer.

'Making ready' didn't take long. I had no luggage as such. I piled my toilet gear and the few garments which I had acquired on the table and waited. When the officer returned, he brought with him an other rank who had with him a small cheap suitcase into which he swept my things, shut it and, I was glad to note, held on to it. In Italy at that time officer POWs were still officers and they were not expected to carry their belongings. The journey itself was uneventful although, as it was now mid-July, the heat was thoroughly disagreeable. After being driven by car to the main railway station in Rome, we boarded an important looking train at the platform signposted 'Genova'. It is not far short of 300 miles from Rome to Genoa. It seemed a very long day before we arrived there. I was watched like a hawk, even when I went to the lavatory. At Genoa we changed trains and in half an hour or so got out at a place called Arquata. Here a car was waiting, and we set off into the hills. It must have been about six in the evening when we drew up at the entrance to an extremely imposing castle, built on a hill outside a village. I had not tried to talk to my guards, preferring to keep my mouth shut and my eyes open. So far the names of various railway stations *en route* had helped me to keep track of where we were going. But what was this village called, I wondered.

'*Dove?*' I asked the officer. '*E Gavi, Gavi, questa villagio,*' he replied, adding, '*Campo cinque,*' then, slowly and with emphasis, '*Campo Concentramento Numero Cinque – e per li prigionieri di guerra molti pericolosi.*'

Without delay I was taken in charge by the Campo Cinque guards and found myself in the welcome shade of the castle guardhouse. There was another POW there who must have arrived shortly before me. He was a tall dark officer, whose face was vaguely familiar. I stood in the guardroom waiting my turn to be searched. 'OK – *ecco fatto,*' said the guard, motioning the other towards the door. 'We've met before,' I remarked as he passed me. 'Bellamy,' he said, smiling. 'DCLI. Weren't we racing together in the *Diadem* with Ralph Hawkes? You're Ian Mac-something, aren't you?' 'You've got it,' I said. 'See you later no doubt.' By this time my guard was getting grumpy. '*Subito!*' he exclaimed, taking hold of my arm and propelling me towards the middle of the guardroom. I had nothing to hide this time, which was just as well because this guard was not at all friendly.

Various forms having been filled in, we set off up a winding track towards the great castle – fortress almost – on the hill. We entered through a formidable gateway, watched by more guards, and found ourselves in a spacious courtyard surrounded by buildings; here there were scores of POWs strolling about in the evening sun. We followed a paved ramp circling round and up to a higher level, where there was another extensive courtyard. The scene before us here was both heartening and amusing. A cricket match was in progress. Facing me, clad in near-white flannels and cricket cap and wielding an oddly-shaped bat, was no less a figure than W G Grace himself – or so, for a moment, it appeared. But behind the flowing beard was the person, well-known to me, of Lieutenant-Commander David Fraser. He had had the misfortune to have his submarine, the *Oswald*, sunk in August 1940; I was very glad to see him alive and obviously well. The redeployment to the Mediterranean from the China Station of our large, slow-diving submarines of the 'O', 'P' and 'R' classes had brought to light the dire consequences of ignoring, both in design policy and in training, the potential of the submarine for surface night attack. In consequence several of our large submarines, including the *Oswald*, had been caught on the surface at night and destroyed.

During the next few days I became acclimatised to 'Campo Five'. It was rather like joining a new school. First of all I was shown where I could stow my belongings, Red Cross parcel and so on; then where I would sleep and eat; then I had to meet the 'Headmaster', in this case the Senior British Officer, who was in fact a New Zealand brigadier. He was a most helpful man and undertook to complain at once to the Italian commandant on my behalf regarding the neglect of proper medical attention to my damaged right eye. I soon became aware that Campo Five was rather more like a club than a school in that its inmates were all POWs who had escaped and been recaptured at least once and thus merited the esteemed category of '*prigioniero di guerra molto pericoloso*'. I was not surprised to be invited quite soon to appear before the Escape Committee. Its chairman was, I believe, a group captain. The proceedings were serious and businesslike.

'Everyone in this POW camp wants to escape,' I was told. 'Our job is to appraise plans, decide priorities, coordinate support, prevent mutual interference and, above all, to ensure the strictest security.' The brigadier had evidently informed the Escape Committee of his intention to raise the matter of my injured eye. It was assumed – and I did not demur – that until some action had been taken by the Italians to provide proper treatment I would not wish to become involved in any escaping plans.

Within a fortnight I was sent for by the brigadier to be told that an appointment had been arranged for me next day with an eye specialist in Alessandria, about 25 miles away. The guard kept me under very close supervision. We travelled by bus to Novi and then on by train. Our fellow passengers, either from courtesy or preoccupation with their own affairs, took no notice of the carabiniere and his prisoner. The specialist looked carefully into my damaged eye and shook his head. 'It's bad. I cannot do anything.' He went to his desk and scribbled a note, which he put in an envelope, addressed and handed to my guard. We left the *ospedale* and took the next train back to Novi, returning to the camp by bus.

During the next few days I heard from some of the old hands in Campo Five stories of various attempted escapes. Two, in particular, remained in my mind. The most ambitious, by far, had taken place the previous winter, after many months of fearfully hard work by dedicated teams, directed by a South African mining engineer. The stone-flagged floor of the dining hall in the lower part of the castle had given forth a hollow sound when tested by the expert. In due course, using crowbars made out of parts of iron bedsteads, one of the flag-stones had been levered up, to reveal a rock-bound water storage area. Professional surveys by sappers, carried out over several weeks, had established the mode of construction of the castle and the thickness of various parts of its walls. It was thought feasible to make a hole at the outward side of the water tank, through which escape could be effected. But in order to make the hole it was necessary for a pair of particularly hardy POWs to go down into the tank, swim across it and light a fire so as to heat up the rock wall. When an area was judged to be as hot as it could be made, cold water was thrown over it, which caused a crack to appear into which a crowbar was thrust. Using the leverage thus obtained it was possible, from time to time, to dislodge a small piece of rock or stone. Hectic games of volley-ball, accompanied by frenzied shouting, were laid on to distract the attention of the guards and drown out the noise of rock-chipping.

Eventually, by which time it was mid-winter, a hole had been made, large enough for men to get through; the trouble was that they would emerge on a cliff face with a drop of thirty feet or so to more or less level ground; and the landing area would be near the guards' living quarters. As usual, in order to give the escapers as many hours' start as possible before their absence was discovered, an elaborate scheme of deception was worked out by which virtually the entire POW population cooperated in a system of standing (or rather lying) in at the evening count by the duty officer of the carabinieri.

Infuriatingly, snow began to fall shortly after the operation had been set in motion. The agonising decision had then to be taken to call it off, since the escapers' tracks in the snow would inevitably give them away. It said a great deal for the morale and security-mindedness of the Campo Five POWs that no hint that a mass escape was imminent reached the camp commandant. Three weeks later a second attempt was made to exploit the hole in the rock face. This was partly successful. A number of POWs emerged but one of them fell from a considerable height and broke his leg. By sheer misfortune the carabinieri were out and about in the vicinity of their quarters near the 'dropping zone'. None of the escapers had enough start to enable him to get clean away and all were recaptured. The main instigator and leader of this spirited and determined effort was, I believe, Lieutenant-Colonel David Stirling of Long Range Desert Group fame.

The other escape attempt of which I heard was, by contrast, strictly a one-man effort. An officer who had been in the Indian Army and in consequence was deeply sun-tanned on top of a naturally somewhat swarthy complexion, conceived the idea of impersonating a similarly-complexioned priest who came to the castle on Sundays to celebrate Mass for POWs of the Roman Catholic persuasion. To this end, the officer in question made himself a soutane and a hat to match (a biretta, fortunately, was not required); he then shaved off his moustache and had his hair shorn at the last moment of the first Sunday morning after he had made ready and received the blessing of the Escape Committee. By some strange mischance the real priest failed to turn up that particular Sunday. As the guards had not checked a priest coming in, they could not be expected to check one going out. That evening, at roll-call parade, the duty officer exploded with laughter when he saw the moustacheless officer with the semi-tonsured head and made some wry comment on the lines of '*molto simpatico – avere troppo caldo?*' There was not much prospect of having a second bite at that particular cherry.

Although very strictly controlled, special broadcasts from England could be received in Campo Five. Towards the end of July, it had become known that the Allied landings in Sicily had led to the downfall of Mussolini. Despite the continuing bombastic tone of the Italian news bulletins, which were relayed to us on a primitive but loud public address system, we felt that the Italians might soon be out of the war. Allied forces might land any day on the mainland of Italy. Well aware of the situation the German High Command – spurred on by Hitler himself – had already begun to prepare for this contingency. Thus it was that late one sunny afternoon in mid-August, as I was having a cup of ingeniously brewed tea with Lieutenant Desmond Callaghan, I saw from his window a most sinister sight. Over to the westward, winding down the narrow road leading from the direction of Turin, there had appeared a long column of troops, with artillery, in the dreaded field-grey uniforms of the German army. True, the guns were horse-drawn, but the implications were not good. Others had also seen the unwelcome spectacle. It looked as if the Germans were getting ready to react vigorously if and when Italy should cease to fight. As we watched, the German field guns were drawn up in a neat row in the village square of Gavi just below us. 'Italy will become another German-occupied country,' said Desmond, 'and we'll be taken over – sent to Poland, probably.'

Although I knew that the brigadier had represented most strongly the need for proper and immediate attention to my injured eye, I could hardly believe it when he sent for me and said, 'I think that you may be in luck, Ian. It seems that there is about to be an exchange of wounded between us and the Italians. If it comes off there is a sporting chance that you will be on a train before long, heading for Lisbon or wherever it is that the exchange is to take place.' I thanked the brigadier most warmly for his efforts. 'That's OK,' he said, 'but if I were you I wouldn't count on it coming off. I only hope it does.'

Two days later I began to wonder if my luck would hold. We were all seated at the tables in the large mess-hall when in came a group of German officers. The buzz of conversation died away. We eyed them and they eyed us. The atmosphere as the German officers, erect and unsmiling in their long greatcoats, walked past us was chilling.

On 3 September 1943 I was told that I would be going to join a Red Cross train somewhere in the north of Italy, for onward transport to a neutral country and from there back to Britain. The place turned out to be Piacenza, about 50 miles east of Gavi and on the main railway line from Bologna to Milan. There, in a hospital, I joined a number of other wounded POWs who had been gathered in from various quarters to await the Red Cross train. By this time speculation was rife. If the Italians threw in the sponge, as seemed likely, would the Red Cross arrangement hold? Was it true that the Allies had tried to land and been driven into the sea? Seldom has the medical profession been seen in a better light. Many of our party were grievously wounded and unable to fend for themselves. Somehow, despite the uncertainties, the hospital staff coped – wounds were attended to, meals were produced, order prevailed. One of the soldiers, a 'Desert Rat' who one night had been unlucky enough to find himself, with his tank squadron, forming part of a column of the Afrika Korps after losing touch with his own formation, had been in a POW camp – Sulmona, I think – with some naval officers, of whom I was glad to have news.

On the morning of 7 September word at last came that the Red Cross train had arrived in Piacenza. By mid-afternoon we were entrained. But the train remained in the station for what seemed an eternity. It was dark by the time we reached Milan, to be shunted about for most of the night. From Milan to Bergamo is only about 20 miles, but we did not arrive there until late afternoon on 8 September, having spent most of the day in a siding on the outskirts of Milan.

As we drew in to Bergamo we could see on the platform upturned smiling faces and flags being waved – Italian flags. Moments after the train stopped a man appeared in the long, bunk-lined coach shouting, 'E finito la guerra! E finito la guerra! E finito la guerra!' as he rushed by. I ran along to where the representative of the Red Cross, a Swiss, was standing, calm enough and smiling but obviously taken as much by surprise as ourselves, despite the fact that we had all been expecting Italy to lay down her arms. One would have thought from the general air of celebration that the Italians had just won the war instead of having discovered, rather late in the day, that they had backed the wrong horse. I asked the Swiss whether, if I should manage to find my way into Switzerland, I would be permitted to move on from there at an appropriate moment in order to get back to Britain. He said that if I reached Switzerland I could stay there just as long as I liked. That was good enough for me. The Swiss official also showed me a map, from which I was able to make a rough tracing of the area of immediate interest, between Bergamo and the Swiss frontier.

I assume the Germans must have boarded the train fairly soon and told Mr Piu the Red Cross representative that the exchange of prisoners was cancelled. Next day we were all taken off the train and put into a hospital on the outskirts of Bergamo. The Italian hospital staff rallied round nobly. In the morning I sought out the Senior British Officer – there was some doubt about who this was, given our situation – and asked permission to leave the hospital and take a chance on crossing into Switzerland. No objection being raised, I made what preparations I could. The main thing was to get rid of my British army boots. I was obsessed by the fact that they were a dead give-away. After wandering round the wards for a bit I found a chap in bed with a pair of desert boots beside him. It appeared that the poor fellow couldn't walk, so he agreed to swop his boots for my army ones. When I tried them on they seemed to be comfortable enough, if just a shade on the small side. We had been provided with lightweight chocolate-coloured trousers and white shirts to wear in the hospital. About mid-afternoon, thus clad and wearing my new boots, I went to the door of the hospital. Only a few yards away was the main gateway, which led to a busy road. There appeared to be no one guarding it, or for that matter the front door. As I watched the road, some German mechanised personnel carriers went quickly past, full of steel-helmeted soldiers. I waited a bit longer and then, praying that there would be a lull in the military traffic, I walked smartly out of the hospital. I did not have far to go before I found a path leading towards an open hillside. I believed that I had got clear away, and felt lighthearted as I climbed up the steepening pathway. But I kept on going at a good pace.

It was a hot day in the late summer and I was not feeling cold in my very lightweight clothing, especially as walking fast was warm work. But it occurred to me that if I should have to spend the night in the open air, as seemed quite probable, I could expect to feel rather chilly. Coming across a scarecrow in a field, I removed what seemed to be quite a respectable black linen jacket. It was too small for me and I felt rather like Charlie Chaplin without his walking stick. I must have been a quaint sight and I can only marvel when I recollect the unblinking courtesy with which I was bidden to enter a farmhouse that I came upon shortly afterwards. Quite possibly the scarecrow's jacket had belonged to one of the household.

Having failed to learn more than a few words and phrases of Italian I was not immediately able to explain myself. But in a minute or two there appeared a young Italian army officer in uniform. His arm was in a sling. Speaking a certain amount of English, and aiding my vestigial knowledge of Italian by gestures, he apprised me that his name was Roberto, and that he was on leave pending recovery from a wound – he indicated the sling. I was able to establish that I was a *tenente degli Marina Britannica* called Mac who had been a *prigioniero di guerra* in Gavi and was hell-bent on escaping to Switzerland before the Germans caught me. I was soon installed in a comfortable chair in the living room, listening in due course to the BBC. It seemed that the Allied landing in Salerno had come up against very stiff opposition. There was no news of a landing further north. My options were either to set off southwards, with over 400 miles of German-occupied Italy to cover before reaching the Allied lines, or alternatively to make at once for the Swiss frontier, about 40 miles away. There was the added consideration that Swiss eye specialists were known to be excellent.

Roberto, whose surname I did not find out, was clearly a son-in-law. It became evident that he was putting my case favourably, first to his young wife Marisa and then to her parents. The atmosphere was friendly. The young couple took me in a car a few miles to a little railway station called Sedrina. I had no money at all. Roberto, having bought me a ticket to the end of the line, insisted that I also take a fistful of banknotes. There were not many people on the station, which was just as well because, when a train puffed and clanked into view round a bend in the single track, we could see that it was already so crowded that passengers were clinging to the outside of the coaches, and three or four were even perched on the front of the small tank-engine. I managed to find a toe and handhold on one of the coaches. Turning round to where Roberto and Marisa were standing, I called out '*Molte grazie, molte grazie, buona sera, arrivederci*', or words to that effect, to which they replied '*Buona sera, buon' viaggio, arrivederci. Viva Inghilterra!*' As I was returning the compliment with a heartfelt '*Viva Italia!*' the train began to pull out. It was rather an emotional moment. Despite our very short acquaintance, devoted entirely to the practical problem of setting me safely on my way out of Italy, I had found Roberto and Marisa *molte simpatico*. At the risk of falling off the train I took one hand off the window ledge and waved. They waved back, and then the curving track left them out of sight.

One of my fellow passengers, sensing that the overcrowding of the train demanded some explanation, kept saying to me '*molti Tedeschi, molti Tedeschi a Bergamo – molti canone*' and so on. It was evident that the Italians feared, not without reason, that the Germans were in a vengeful mood, not taking at all kindly to being deserted by their allies. After stopping at San Pellegrino, where a good many people left it, the little train chuffed on up the valley to its terminus at San Martino di Calvi. It was now almost dark. I was pondering what to do next when

I spotted a group of a dozen or so men striding off along the road towards the head of the valley, in the general direction of the Alps and hence the Swiss frontier. I followed them, and could see that they were wearing those dashing conical hats with feathers in them and breeches of a special cut, which identified them as Bersaglieri, or more probably Alpini. Pretty obviously this was a bunch of Italian soldiers who had been demobilised – or, more likely, had demobilised themselves – and were on their way home. After a while they began to sing one of their marching songs. They were in the highest of spirits. '*E finito la guerra!*' was the keynote. In the darkness I attached myself to the tail of the group.

In about half an hour, during which my recently acquired desert boots not only began to pinch but were clearly unsuited to the hard surface of the mountain road, we came to an *albergo*. In we all went, and very soon the wine was flowing. I have only the dimmest recollection of that remarkable evening, spent in the company of the Alpini. But it was certainly a joyful occasion, with many a *Viva Inghilterra!* and *Viva Italia!* and absolutely no sign that Italy had been on the losing side, let alone that the war was by no means over, despite the euphoria.

When I came to early in the morning there was no one about. I slipped out of the inn and followed the road northwards, out of the tiny village, which turned out to have been Piazza Brembana. I had something of a hangover from the previous night's carousing and my desert boots were starting to hurt again, but as the sun came up and began to warm me I felt that all was going reasonably well. The rough sketch map that I had originally had was of no further use, being too small a scale. But I could see the road winding on, up the hill towards the Alps. Surely it must lead to a pass into Switzerland. After an hour or so I sat down by the side of what by now was not much more than a track, to rest my feet. I was really worried now. The worst of the climb was still ahead of me, and another twenty miles in those wretched boots would reduce my feet to pulp for sure. As I was casting around for something sharp with which to remodel my boots, a man came walking up the track, leading a mule. '*Buon giorno,*' I said, standing up. The man, who was tall, dark, rugged-featured and dressed in practical-looking civilian clothes, replied, somewhat to my surprise, 'Good-a-morning,' adding, 'I am a guide-a, for the mountain. I take-a English people sometimes-a.' '*Io sono,*' I began, having been preparing to try out my Italian, and went on, 'I am a British officer – was a *prigioniero di guerra*. I am going to Switzerland.' 'OK,' said the guide, 'I will show

145

you.' '*Mille grazie,*' I replied, and extended my hand, which he took, saying that his name was Paolo. I then indicated my desert boots and said, 'No good, too small – *piccolo,*' accompanied by a spirited pantomime to indicate that surgery was needed. This message got home and my new-found friend produced a penknife with which he cut the front of the uppers off. Putting the boots on again, I found that I could wiggle my toes freely. '*Molti grazie,*' I said, '*sta bene,* OK, *andiamo.*' I was now keen to press on. Paolo had a much better idea and pointed to the mule, which had been trying to find some vegetation on which to graze, without much success. 'OK,' I said, 'thank you.'

I was soon mounted on the mule, which was docile enough, and we set off up the track. Around noon I began to feel the pangs of hunger, not having eaten a meal since the far from substantial breakfast provided by the hospital in Bergamo about thirty hours previously. Not long afterwards we came upon a hut. '*Ecco,*' said Paolo. 'My mamma will give us some pasta.' I dismounted from the mule, which Paolo tethered before leading me towards the door. Entering from the brilliant sunlight it was impossible to see anything at first but in a little while I could make out an old woman in dark clothes standing by a cooking stove. Paolo greeted her and explained my presence. I could catch odd snatches: '*prigioniero di guerra ... tenente nel Marina Britannico ... Svizzera ...*' We sat down at a small wooden table and in a remarkably short time a heaped dish of steaming pasta was before us. '*Poliatelli,*' said Paolo. '*Molti grazie, signora,*' I said to his mother with real feeling as I tucked in. Silence reigned as we ate, but it was a companionable silence. We drank water with our pasta and were soon on our way again up the steepening track. I had tried, without much conviction, to tell Paolo, that extremely grateful as I was for his help so far, I was sure that I could now get along all right on my own. Paolo merely smiled, and motioned me to climb aboard the mule. I had debated in my mind whether or not to offer money in return for my pasta, but decided against it. These kind people might well have been offended. We were on the same side now in the fight against Fascism.

It must have been about six in the evening when we reached the summit of the pass and saw, on the more or less level ground before us, a long low stone building. '*Cantino di San Marco,*' said Paulo, pointing. 'This is the *Passo di San Marco,*' he went on. 'You go down the other side-a and it is *Svizzera.*' For a little while we stood silent taking in what to me was the most stunning view I had ever seen. This was Paolo's country, and no doubt the beauty of it was part of his everyday existence. We shook hands again and wished each other *'buona sera'*. I thanked him as much as I could, patted his mule – an exemplary member of his sometimes maligned species – and with *'Arrividerci, Paolo'* and *'Arrividerci, tenente'* we parted. I watched Paolo stride off down the track, leading his mule. He turned and gave me a wave. I waved back. Then I walked over to the cantino.

The place seemed at first to be deserted. When my eyes had adjusted to the gloom, I could see a long room with a fire burning at the far end. At the sides were bunks and in the middle a couple of long tables. The air smelled of wood smoke. I sat down at one of the tables. After a while an old woman appeared from somewhere, greeted me and, so far as I could gather, asked me where I had come from and where I was going. I had by this time mastered a few phrases in Italian, which enabled me to satisfy, to some extent anyway, her curiosity. Despite having ridden on a mule most of the way up to the pass, I felt somewhat tired and certainly sleepy. So I indicated one of the bunks and the old woman nodded her head. I climbed in and fairly soon went to sleep.

It was dark, with just the light from an oil lamp on one of the tables, when I woke up. A group of men had arrived. Although I could not recognise any of them in the gloom, their breeches and assorted shirts and jackets seemed to be familiar. If not the same bunch as I had been drinking with the previous night, in the *albergo*, they were certainly troops on their way home from the war. I went to sleep again. The bunk was hard, with only a straw palliasse to lie on, but there was a blanket of sorts.

Daylight was showing when I awoke. Peering from my bunk I saw that one or two of the soldiers were already up and about. I turned out and went to the door to see what sort of day it was. If the view the previous evening had been stunning, this, with the sun not yet risen but the sky suffused with pink and gold and the mountainsides still in deep violet shadow, was stupendous. But it was chilly. It took some plucking up of courage to go over and await one's turn at the water-tap beside the doorway, under which the soldiers were sluicing their heads. Ooooh!! How cold that water was! I was beginning to feel somewhat frayed at the ends. Even in Campo Five it had been possible to have hot water for shaving, a shower now and then and to clean one's teeth. A change of clothing at reasonable intervals had also been taken for granted. None of these amenities were now available and I had little idea when they would be. The momentary magic of the scenery had quickly worn off. Back inside the cantino the soldiers were sitting around drinking red wine and eating brown bread. I joined

147

them, and was handed some wine and a chunk of the bread. There was not even the smell of coffee; no butter; no marmalade; no honey . . .

I was not able to brood for long over the inadequacies of the Cantino di San Marco as a hostelry, however welcome it might be as a refuge for the benighted traveller overtaken by bad weather. For even as a shaft of sunlight in the doorway heralded sunrise, there were murmers of '*Allora, andiamo,*' and a pushing back of benches as the soldiers prepared to depart. I pressed into the old woman's not unwilling hand a couple of the notes which Roberto had given me. Then I set off down the mountain track towards the north-west, in the wake of the by now quite carefree soldiers. I was happy to be going in what seemed to be the right direction but my wretched desert boots were beginning to give me acute discomfort. This was because the track was mainly downhill and in places quite steep. My feet were constantly being forced into the boots, accentuating the constriction, even though the toes had been cut out. However, I felt that I must at all costs keep up with the Alpini as I was sure that they would be heading for their home villages; and that would mean the possibility of finding a bus in which to reach the frontier.

After stumbling down the rough track for a couple of hours we came upon a roadway – a proper metalled road – running more towards the north. We rested at the roadside. Presently a discussion arose. Some of the soldiers were for continuing along the road on foot; others, more sanguine, seemed to take the view that a vehicle was bound to come along sooner or later, so why exert oneself. On account of my desert boots I belonged unequivocally to the latter group. We had not been hanging about for more than a quarter of an hour when we heard a motor vehicle approaching from the desired direction. Round the corner rattled an ancient three-ton truck. It was empty. The driver, an elderly farmer by the look of him, drew into the side of the road and stopped, exchanging as he did so animated greetings with one of the soldiers who had run up to the driving cab. In a moment or two we were all aboard. My presence seemed to excite no interest at all at this stage. As we bounced and swayed along the soldiers began to shout and sing. It looked as if they were nearly home and, sure enough, we had only been going for twenty minutes or so when we came to a village and stopped. Immediately the entire community surrounded the truck. Down went the tailboard and out jumped a couple of the soldiers, to loud cries of 'Pietro!' 'Guiseppe!' as they met and embraced men and boys, women and girls alike. Quickly wine was brought and passed around so that those still in the truck could join in the libations.

After half-an-hour or so of this jollity the truck moved on, amidst cries of farewell and goodwill, to arrive within a quarter of an hour at another village, where much the same scene was re-enacted. I believe that we stopped to discharge passengers in two more villages, in each of which a celebratory cup was provided for us all. The final stage of our riotous progress was to the town of Morbegno. Or so I discovered when I awoke from wine-induced slumber to find myself sitting in the truck, which had been abandoned in the centre of the town. I climbed out, feeling far from my best, and began to wander about, trying to get my bearings. Approaching a passer-by I asked, '*Dove la ferrovia, per favore?*' and was rewarded with, '*La Stazione? . . . prenda la terza strada a sinistra.*' I walked out of the square with that feeling of one's feet not quite touching the ground which is attendant upon an advanced hangover. I took the third turning on the left as instructed. There, facing me, was Morbegno railway station. I was standing near the ticket office wondering where to go next and whether I would have enough money to buy the ticket, when a middle-aged man approached. I wondered if I ought to make a run for it. I need not have worried. '*Buon giorno,*' said the man, smiling. Putting a hand to the collar of his jacket he turned it back and revealed a small oval badge with an enamelled union jack on it and an inscription which I could not read. 'British-a Legion,' he said. 'Allies.' It seemed that he was referring to the Great War, when the Italians were certainly our allies. He spoke a little English, from which I gathered that he had spotted me entering the station and guessed that I was British and making for the frontier. '*Andiamo,*' he said, 'I have a *ristorante,*' and he piloted me there in a few minutes. The Almighty was undoubtedly on my side.

My latest friend soon had his wife and helpers scurrying round on my behalf. I felt I did not deserve any more such luck. The lunchtime service was evidently over, as the tablecloths had been removed and the chairs placed upon the tables. A carafe of white wine appeared and two glasses. For once I felt that I could manage to have a meal without wine and be none the worse; but Pietro would not have understood. So I allowed my glass to be filled and we drank various toasts. A cheese omelette was put before me, with delicious fresh bread, butter and a green salad, well-dressed.

Back at the railway station Pietro bought me a ticket to Tirano, accepting the money I offered, which may or may not have covered the cost. Fairly soon after that a train arrived, going in the direction of Tirano, that is to say eastwards along the valley of the Adda. It must have been very crowded because I had to stand in a baggage compartment. There were many people milling about on the platform and I lost sight of Pietro so that I was not even able to shout goodbye to him or wave. The train started and soon worked up speed. The doors of the baggage compartment, which I was sharing with many assorted articles including bicycles and a poor little calf in a sack, were open. The sun-bathed countryside flashed past. We stopped at Sondrio, where the calf and some of the bicycles were removed.

There was one more stop before the train reached its terminus at Tirano. I joined the queue of alighted passengers making for the station exit, holding my ticket ready – almost smugly. By now I was completely unaware of my bizarre appearance, dressed literally like a scarecrow, and was entirely confident of passing through the ticket collector's gateway. As I handed over my ticket, however, the dreaded figure of a carbiniere loomed out of the shadow of the station building, stood in front of me and said firmly but politely, '*Documenti?*' One's instinct on such occasions is to flee. But that being physically impossible I stood my ground, as indeed the carbiniere desired that I should, held my hands open, shrugged my shoulders, turned down the corners of my mouth and replied '*Niente*'. I thought it wiser not to reveal further my lack of Italian, although the fact that I was a POW on the run was no doubt obvious to the carbiniere. The next move quite patently being his, I was glad when he beckoned, and with the inevitable '*Andiamo*' took me off to see the capitano.

This official greeted me civilly enough in his office, white-walled, sunlit and provided with a portrait of Mussolini in glorious technicolour which I was surprised to see still in place. The capitano soon sized up the situation and, Mussolini notwithstanding, proceeded to give me precise instructions as to how I should get myself safely into Switzerland. He began by making it clear that a direct approach to the frontier post would be fatal. Without papers of any kind I would not stand a chance of being admitted by the Swiss. That being so, I would have to cross the frontier well clear of the guardpost. Furthermore, he explained, it would be no use crossing the frontier and giving myself up anywhere within a kilometre or two of it; I would be hustled back into Italy. What I must do, he said with emphasis, was to follow the route the smugglers used. This would mean a stiff climb up the mountain – he took me to the window to point out the direction – until I reached a track which followed the contour round to the north-west slope. By proceeding far enough along this track before beginning the descent to main road level I should find myself at least seven kilometres inside Switzerland, with a much better chance of being allowed to remain in that country.

It was about five o'clock in the afternoon when I went on my way with the capitano's blessing. I soon found the track up the mountainside which he had indicated. I felt no need to hurry, as I intended to cross the frontier during darkness. There were grapes everywhere – luscious ripe grapes, almost ready to be harvested and transformed, in due course, into the renowned red wines of the Valtellina, the Sassella, Grigioni, Inferno, and Grumello. Once I was well above the vine-line, and having eaten my fill of the grapes, I found a shady spot and sat down. The panoramic view, though lacking the awesome extent of that from the Passo di San Marco, which was about 8,000 feet high, was certainly most beautiful. The town of Tirano lay tidily arranged and delicately coloured in the immediate foreground. To the right and left ran the verdant valley of the Adda, with glimpses of the silvery river here and there, enfolded on my left by the Alpine foothills leading up to the Stelvio pass. To my front lay the northern slopes of the Italian Alps, which I had just crossed.

I must have gone to sleep at this stage. I awoke feeling distinctly chilly and found that the sun was going rapidly down. I had not yet located the smugglers' way, which I knew to be very high up on the mountainside. I pulled myself together and set off up the track again. Before long the going got rougher and steeper. My desert boots were once again beginning to hurt my feet. Quite suddenly, the state of euphoria in which I had imagined myself to be virtually home and dry evaporated. I was worried. Darkness was closing in rapidly, so that it was becoming more and more difficult to discern the track, and I was beginning to stumble painfully from time to time. I found myself wondering if I should ever find the transverse pathway that I was looking for. I was in among trees now – conifers. The going underfoot was better, but it was too dark to see the way ahead. I stopped to take my bearings. It was windless and quiet. The sound of church bells, which before sunset had floated up from Tirano, had ceased. I felt rather lonely. I had no torch and no matches. I would have been drummed out of any self-respecting Boy Scout troop. All that I could do was try to find a way through the trees, going always upwards. It was toilsome and very slow.

I had just decided that I must look for a place to lie down and await the dawn, when, as quickly as the sun had set, the moon rose. I could see my way now quite well. In the event, I did not find a transverse track as such but became aware that I was gradually going round the mountain. The moon was full and, when I emerged into a clearing, away below me and towards the south-west was a guardhouse, glistening white in the moonlight. I could even make out the Swiss flag above it. I took this to mark the frontier, so that I had another seven kilometres before I dared descend to the roadway, the line of which I could now discern.

From now on, the light being so remarkably good, it was just a matter of keeping going. I judged that I was covering about a couple of kilometres an hour. I had no watch, but the transit of the moon across the sky gave me some idea of the passage of time. Every now and then I found a comfortable place to sit down and rest for a while. I did not want to go to sleep again. Not only might I be found by some person or persons less favourably disposed towards me than the Italians whom I had had dealings with recently, but I was anxious to reach a Swiss authority without further delay. I was cold and hungry, and my feet were killing me. Eventually dawn came. I took a very long hard look at the country spread out before me. There was the road winding away northwards up the Alpine valley. I set off down the mountainside towards it. The going was rough as there was no track. Nor was the visibility very good. The sky had clouded over and light rain had begun to fall. At last I reached the road and began to walk along it, limping a good deal. It curved between steep hillsides so that I could not see far ahead.

I rounded a bend and came upon a road-block. There were two or three soldiers manning it. I walked on towards them. One of them – a young-looking man with red or sandy hair visible below his cap – stepped up and said in English, 'Good morning.' I replied, 'Good morning. I am a British naval officer and would like to report my arrival to the British military attaché.' 'Have you any papers – identity card, passport?' the soldier, who appeared to be a lance-corporal, now asked. 'No,' I replied, 'nothing at all.' 'We had better go and see my officer,' he said, indicating where I could pass the road-block. As we walked to a house a hundred yards or so along the road I complimented the young lance-corporal on his excellent English. 'Well, sir,' he said pleasantly, 'I was a waiter at the Ritz before the war.' Not having been an habitué of the Ritz I was unable to establish my bona fides by dropping a famous name or two, such as that of the maitre d'hotel, or the chef; nor, for that matter, could I test the lance-corporal's. So I fell back on, 'Where is this place?' 'It's Poschiavo . . . we're in the Bernina, not far from St Moritz. I expect you've skied there.' Fortunately I was spared further revelation of my social shortcomings by our arrival at the house. I could see that it was a private dwelling which had been commandeered. A large Swiss flag on a pole drooped in the drizzly still air.

The author on Pont Rousseau, Geneva, September 1943.

7 · Silken dalliance

The reputation of the Swiss as superb hoteliers was in no way diminished by my experience that day. Scruffy and as yet unidentified, I was nevertheless provided with an excellent breakfast of coffee, fresh bread, butter and honey. After that I was brought before a young officer – a lieutenant in the Swiss army. I told him who I was and where I had come from. He seemed to be in some doubt as to what to do. A neutral country has its obligations under international law; it must also be careful not to provide an excuse for a belligerent to invade it. The lieutenant was clearly seeking some evidence to support my story and, the rain having stopped, he decided that to stroll with me on the well-trimmed lawn beside the guardhouse might provide the relaxed atmosphere in which I could unwind. In a few minutes we had discovered mutual acquaintances. A family whom I knew and whose name I fortunately remembered, used to go to Lausanne from time to time to play tennis and the lieutenant had met them there. This seemed to be all that was needed to validate my story, and I had of course stressed my desire to be attended to by one of the Swiss eye specialists whose international reputation was so high. A minute or two later he was on the telephone back in his office, while I was invited, politely enough, to wait in one of the other rooms.

It was not long before the lieutenant put his head round the door and explained the arrangements he had made. Next day, after being given a good breakfast, I entrained with a Swiss as a 'minder' and had a comfortable journey to Bern. Here I was deposited at the British Legation.

It is a commonplace that life, especially for a man, is one continual repetition of going to a new school. One reaches at dame school the privileged status of afternoon lessons and then one is propelled into prep school, there to be made to feel a new boy and the lowest of the low. Five or six years later, having somehow graduated into the top form at prep school and passed one's Common Entrance, one arrives at public school to be made immediately aware that one is once again at the bottom of the pile. Entry into the Royal Navy via a cadet training ship at the age of nearly eighteen, was a comparatively easy transition; the real relegation, yet again, to rock-bottom status, came with one's appointment as a midshipman to the gunroom of a battleship. But, having since then reached and held for some years the rank of lieutenant in the Royal Navy, and in addition commanded one of His Majesty's submarines, I was not mentally, let alone psychologically, prepared for the reception accorded me by the British military attaché in Bern, in whose forbidding presence I now found myself.

Colonel Harry Cartwright, I later found out (I do not think that I could reasonably have been expected to know at the time) had greatly distinguished himself as an escaper from Germany during the Great War, and with a fellow-escaper, MCC Harrison, had written a book called *Within Four Walls*. To him an individual such as myself – always supposing that my story was true – having merely walked across the frontier from Italy and being the equivalent of a junior subaltern in rank, rated very low indeed. Whether consciously or not, Cartwright heightened the impression he gave of dismissive authority by sitting in an almost dark office behind a huge desk piled with papers, wearing a green eyeshade and with the sleeves of his white shirt rolled up, just out of the pool of light cast on his blotter by a powerful desk lamp. He looked like a tough newspaper editor in an American movie.

'Well – how do you pronounce your name, MacGoff is it?' I corrected him. 'We've got hundreds of people coming over now. The Swiss are setting up a camp.'

'I need some attention for my eye, sir,' I said. 'What's the matter with it?' he asked brusquely. I told him. 'Oh, well, I'll see what can be done. Now go and have a wash and brush-up. The Minister and Mrs Norton have invited you to dinner in the legation and they'll put you up for the night.'

It was many months since I had dined at a polished table and enjoyed coffee and liqueurs. There were just the three of us – Clifford Norton, HM plenipotentiary, diplomatically refraining from expressing a firm opinion on any of the topics, mostly war-related, which cropped up; his wife, whose name was Peter, and me. When I explained that one of the reasons why I had come to Switzerland was to have my injured eye attended to, Peter said that she would arrange for me to go to Geneva to see Professor Franceschetti.

Captain Reed, the military attaché's assistant, had provided me with

Meg Todd-Naylor.

some civilian clothes. I journeyed by train to Geneva, where I was met by a female member of the British Consulate General. She seemed to have no difficulty in picking me out from the crowd of travellers with whom I had alighted. There was no mistaking the Englishness of the young middle-aged woman of medium height, with perfectly regular features, fresh complexion owing nothing to artifice, beautiful grey, almost white hair, navy-blue coat and skirt, sensible shoes and no hat. She was smiling.

'I'm Meg Todd-Naylor,' she said, coming towards me and extending a hand. 'You look as if you might be Lieutenant McGeoch, if that is how you pronounce it.' It was.

'Hello,' I said, 'yes, I'm Ian McGeoch. How very kind of you to come and meet me.'

'I understand that you will be seeing Professor Franceschetti about your eye. I do hope that he will be able to do something for you. He has a great reputation and is very pro-us. But he can't take you into his clinic until Friday, so I've arranged some digs for you. We might as well go straight there. We'll take a taxi.'

As we went along Meg said, 'I hope that you'll be all right *chez*

Pénard. They're rather a quaint old couple. She is large and rather bossy – and extremely strait-laced. He is small and does what he is told. I've been there for a couple of years. They don't overcharge. Have you got any money, by the way? If not, I can let you have some.'

'Thank you, but they let me have an advance of pay at the legation.'

'Here we are – 14 rue de Candolle. Quite central, even if not fashionable.'

Meg refused to let me pay for the taxi. 'The Consulate can stand it,' she said, entering the building. The Pénards lived on the first floor. They were most welcoming. '*Soyez le bienvenu*,' said Mme Pénard and chattered on, explaining the amenities of her establishment and what she would require of her latest lodger in return for his use of them. I quickly found that my French could not cope. Meg, realising this but not wishing to show me up, interposed laughingly in her fluent and perfect French, with an occasional comment to me in English to keep me in the picture. We trooped upstairs to the second floor, where I was shown a comfortable, if small, bedroom, an equally small sitting room and a bathroom. Meg, it appeared, lived above, on the third floor.

The following day I sallied out to explore Geneva. My first impression, which has remained, was of a beautiful city, especially favoured by its location at the edge of the lake, so that one may gaze across at the always snow-covered Alpine peaks of Les Dents du Midi. To my right a fine bridge spanned the river Rhône as it debouched from the lake, to be divided by the Ile Rousseau, the trees on which, this mid-September day, had begun to assume their autumn tints. It was fortunate that the shoes provided by Captain Reed fitted better than my desert boots had done, because I walked for miles revelling in the freedom to do so. I began to formulate my plans for the continuation of my journey back to England. First of all I had to have my eye seen to. Next I ought to brush up my French. The Germans had extended their occupation to the whole of France shortly after the Allied landings in North Africa in November 1942. Switzerland was completely isolated. Colonel Cartwright had not given me any hope of an early transfer back to Britain. If I was going to get home I should have to cross occupied France, either under my own steam or with help of some kind. Either way, not to be able to understand and speak French reasonably well might let me down badly in an emergency. Then I would have to have some identity papers to enable me to circulate freely in German-controlled France. Geneva would be the ideal jumping off point for the venture.

That evening I wrote to Somers, giving no hint of my intentions.

Meg had said that all mail leaving Switzerland was liable to be censored by the Germans. Many weeks later, it transpired, Somers received the letter but, despite my care, several pieces had been snipped out.

Professor Franceschetti inspired confidence in me from the start. He was so businesslike and friendly that I did not have any qualms when, having kept me under observation for a couple of days, during which he examined my eyes minutely and at length, he caused me after due preparation to be firmly secured to an operating table. But I was not prepared for the next step. This consisted in bringing closer and closer to my eye a large electro-magnet on a trolley, so mounted that its angle of presentation to the eye could be varied precisely. As I had not been given a general anaesthetic I was able to watch, out of the corner of my good eye, the process whereby a jagged sliver of rusty steel, about half a centimetre in length, was extracted by the magnet from the back of my eye along the path by which it had entered through the lower eyelid. It was, I think, a bit of the periscope standard of the poor old *Splendid*. At any rate the professor's precautions against infection were successful. These had included, I believe, injection with boiled milk! His main concern, he had told me, was to make sure that my good eye remained quite unaffected by the damage to the other. But he did not hold out any hope of sight being restored to the injured eye. The splinter had damaged the retina beyond the possibility of repair. I had not really expected to get the sight back and was by now fully accustomed to coping without it.

I was positively enjoying my stay in the well-run Clinique Opthalmologique in the rue Alcide Jentzer and did not demur when told that the professor would like me to remain for a few more days. I think that I slept a good deal. Meg Todd-Naylor had evidently been keeping in touch, for as soon as I had begun to perk up she arrived to see me, bringing chocolates and grapes. Meg let it be known that I could receive visitors and a day or two later the delightful Princess Schwarzenberg, a friend of Peter Norton, came. Prince Schwarzenberg was head of the Red Cross and I was able to ask his wife to pass on from a grateful recipient my heartfelt thanks for the benison of the Red Cross parcels which, through such brilliant organisation and devoted work, reached so many POWs.

By 18 October I was able to write to Colonel Cartwright to say that I was to be released from the clinic in a few days and requested his permission to remain in Geneva in order to study French at the university. The military attaché consented to my plan and on 25 October I was back at Mme Pénard's rooms. At the consulate the next day I met a young man called Eddie Luff, whose father was British and mother Belgian. In 1940, when the Germans arrived, the family had remained in Brussels where Eddie was at university. He had been taking part in the production of an underground newspaper when he was warned that he might shortly be pulled in by the Gestapo. He had found his way into Switzerland some months before the Germans occupied the whole of France. Eddie was very keen to get back to the United Kingdom and offer himself for military service, and in the meantime had enrolled in l'Ecole des Hautes Etudes Internationales to complete his study of modern history. He had been trying to obtain from the British Consulate some papers which would enable him to pass as a Frenchman in order to cross occupied France, but these had not been forthcoming.

Over lunch in a modest restaurant Eddie and I decided to team up. I had written again to Colonel Cartwright, this time to say that I was fit to travel whenever his organisation could take me. In his reply the colonel had stated that I must not expect to go soon as there was a priority list and some people had already been waiting for over a year. One of these, I later discovered, had been F W E Hammond, a submarine engine room artificer who had managed to escape from Germany; he had been living in the Hotel Wilhelm in Montreux and I had not been able to see him. If only we could acquire some false passports Eddie and I could, we felt, make the transit of France to the Pyrenees on our own. For the time being, we agreed, Eddie would continue his studies at L'Haute Ecole and I would brush up my French at the university. Eddie seemed to have enough money to keep him going, and had rented a one-room flat not far from the Cornavin – Geneva's railway station. He told me that he had found a way of making himself useful in the consulate, which was to help to process 'navicerts'. These were documents which formed part of the measures which the British government had introduced in both world wars as an instrument of the economic blockade against Germany and her allies. Any vessel on her way to or from a port through which goods might reach, or come from, enemy territory or enemy armed forces must be provided with a navicert valid for that voyage. Otherwise the ship would be liable to seizure. I decided to volunteer my services to help with the navicert work, which entailed checking long lists of Swiss exports for nature, origin and destination, as this would provide me with a reason for being frequently in the consulate.

When I asked Meg to arrange for me to do the navicert work she thought it a good idea and the following week I began working with

Left, Eddie Luff in Geneva *c.* 1943; right, Yolanda *c.* 1943.

Mr Bloor, one of the proconsuls. I also met Victor Farrell, the passport control officer, who was a vice-consul. He was friendly, and introduced me to a delightful New Zealand brigadier called Hargest, whose countryman in Campo Five, Brigadier Clayton, had managed to get me on to the Red Cross train. I had absolutely no idea that James Hargest, who had escaped from Italy six months before, was just about to set off across occupied France under Farrell's auspices; still less that Farrell was in reality the leading member in Geneva of MI9. This was a branch of military intelligence set up in August 1939 as MI1a for the purpose of facilitating the escape of British POWs and the return to the UK of those who succeeded in evading capture in enemy occupied territory. When I asked Meg that evening if she thought Farrell might help me to leave Switzerland by providing me with false papers, she smiled enigmatically and said, '*Ça se peut.*' I felt that it would be unfair as well as fruitless to press Meg for information about clandestine activities in which our consular officials might be engaged. Later, when I became associated with the French Resistance, I was thankful that I knew so little, lest I should fall into Gestapo hands and be subjected to torture to extort information.

It was Victor Farrell who told me, when I was in the consulate a day or two later, that two of my officers from the *Splendid*, neither of whom I had seen since I went to the hospital in Caserta, had made their way into Switzerland. Denis Laidlaw, our recently-joined engineer officer, and Gordon Hardy, the navigator, had both jumped successfully from trains when being transferred to Germany from POW camps in Italy. I was able to make contact with both of them later. My work in the consulate also brought me into touch with a Mr Van den Heuvel, who ranked as a consul with the overt task of press attaché at the British Legation in Bern and was, I now know, the head of MI6 in Switzerland. I was delighted when he asked me to help him with the debriefing of a brave French naval officer who had managed to photograph a German U-boat in Toulon dockyard. As the Frenchman was a naval aviator I, as a submariner, was able to help a little in describing several of the devices with which the U-boat was equipped; one of these, it turned out, was the search receiver, which enabled the U-boat when on the surface to intercept the radar of our anti-submarine aircraft and dive in good time to avoid destruction. The French officer told me of the care with which the contents of wastepaper baskets at German military headquarters were examined; and of a skilfully organised fracas in a crowded street in the course of which a German officer, about to step into his staff car, was relieved of his briefcase.

I had begun on 1 November to take a course in idiomatic French which was on offer at Geneva University. I sat at the back of the class, which consisted of earnest young Genevois and Genevoises. I took notes but I don't remember being able to bring any of the idioms into my conversation. I was hoping to pass for a French-speaking Swiss. It was not at all easy to exercise colloquial French although Meg was helpful not only in making me talk French but in correcting my accent, grammar and vocabulary in the nicest possible way, so that I did not feel too much of an oaf. It was at this time, also, that I began helping Eddie Luff by typing drafts of the thesis he was working on at the School of Higher International Studies – a history of the Little Entente.

Invitations to cocktail parties and dinners had begun to arrive. The very first of these was the one which counted most, by providing an entrée to the most pro-British as well as patrician element in Geneva society. I received a note from Kathleen Schwarzenberg asking me to supper. It was a memorable evening. A few days later I received an invitation from a Madame Maurice Bourquin. Happily I was able to accept and thus got to know another couple to whom, for their

Lieutenant (E) Denis Laidlaw.

hospitality and stimulating company, I remain eternally grateful. Maurice Bourquin was Belgian, an international lawyer whose work for the League of Nations had earned him widespread respect around the world; he was a professor at the School of Higher International Studies. At his invitation I attended his lectures on 'The Congress of Vienna'. They were brilliant.

I was now beginning to find myself speaking French in company where English was not the first though a frequently-used language, as for example at dinner with Princess Kourakine, the beautiful Genevoise wife of the immensely tall and good-humoured Prince Kourakine. Until the fall of France he had been serving with the French cavalry and would have dearly liked to join his fellow Russians, or rather Ukrainians, in the battles to drive the Germans out of his still-beloved even if 'Red' country. Indeed, when the war news broadcast by the BBC confirmed beyond a shadow of doubt that Kiev was once again in Russian hands, Sergei Kourakine threw a party in his small flat in Geneva (the Kourakines lived in a rather grand villa at Gex, on the outskirts of the city) to celebrate the great event. Every Russian exile in Geneva must have been invited, and I was lucky to be there. A vast panoramic photograph of Kiev was mounted across the entire width of one wall of the living room. Vodka and blinis were in ample supply, and a good deal had been drunk before the moment came for the prince to call the party to order, face the picture of Kiev and propose a toast. I did not get to bed until very late that night. The gallant prince had recovered sufficiently a day or two later to suggest a game of golf. It was a dreary day towards the end of November and our golf was dreadful – in fact we had time for only nine holes before bad light stopped play. But it helped me to see how the frontier ran.

The highlight of my social season was undoubtedly a party in an extremely smooth night club given by one of the Schwarzenberg's friends, Charles Im Obersteg. I have never forgotten the *Rognons de boeuf à la Charentaise*, the fine wine which accompanied it or the impact made upon my susceptibilities by the beautiful half-naked girls in the floor show. Meg, with her unfailing sense of consular responsibility, remarked quietly to me, 'I think that a couple of those girls are English. I am just going backstage to see that they are all right.' When she returned she said, 'I'm so glad that I saw them. There is no heating and no privacy back there, and the poor girls are pretty miserable. I shall speak to the manager tomorrow.' In the meantime I had been much enjoying the company of Gina, the lovely young blonde Italian wife of Prince Franz Josef of Liechtenstein, the most sociable Serene Highness whom I have ever met. 'My mother was a Hapsburg,' he said later on that evening, entirely without hauteur.

Much as I was enjoying this cultural sabbatical, mingling high society with academic life and consular work, my desire to escape from the benevolent (if formally correct) neutrality of Switzerland never left me.

During the last week in November, after I had done some more debriefing work for Mr Van den Heuvel, I ventured to ask him for help in getting back home. He at once offered to cable his headquarters in London to enquire whether I might be given a passage to Spain by their 'line', and suggested that I should now provide Victor Farrell with passport photographs so that he could prepare papers for me. This I did. By now I was becoming acclimatised to the secret world of espionage, counter-espionage, escape, evasion and resistance move-ments, inhabited by men and women of several nationalities, which lay below the bland surface of Swiss, and especially Genevese, life in 1943. Any information which one obtained, about anything, from any source, was just as likely to be disinformation. Furthermore, genuine information, if and when any was imparted, was on a strictly 'need to know' basis. In consequence, although I was dimly aware that representatives of more or less clandestine organisations were being provided with administrative support by the British Legation in Bern and the main consular offices in Basle, Lausanne, Zurich and Geneva, as well as certain diplomatic immunities, I had no means of knowing what these organisations actually were or who belonged to them, let alone the chain of command by which they were linked. Nor, quite rightly, was Meg Todd-Naylor prepared to tell me, even if she herself knew. Eddie Luff, I believe, knew nothing either.

On about 7 December I learnt from Mr Van den Heuvel that his London headquarters had agreed to his proposal to send me by their line through France but that all would now depend upon covering approval being obtained from the military attaché in Bern. While awaiting this I was able to arrange for Denis Laidlaw to come down from Bern to see me in Geneva. Like me, he was extremely keen to depart from Switzerland but was beginning to feel somewhat frustrated. He told me that the Dutch military attaché had offered to get him a passage to Spain the following week but that naturally his British opposite number would have to give his consent. Not only had Colonel Cartwright refused to do so, but he had reprimanded Laidlaw severely for interfering in matters which did not concern him. This did not bode well for me. About this time, also, I met Lieutenant-Commander 'Billy' Stephens RNVR, a survivor of the famous raid on St Nazaire in March 1942, who had escaped from Colditz in October of that year. Colonel Cartwright had made him sign a statement undertaking not to make any attempt to leave Switzerland on his own

The author's Christmas card to his wife, 1943.

behalf. Ironically, not long after I met him, Billy Stephens had the appallingly bad luck to break his leg while skiing, on the eve of his long-delayed departure for Spain.

Winter had now set in. I had had to buy myself an overcoat. As Christmas approached members of the British community in Geneva became increasingly hospitable. The consul and Mrs Livingstone gave a most delightful party, as also did Mr and Mrs Bloor, at whose home I met 'Joe', an American who admitted to being a member of the oss, the American Secret Service. I was still seeing Eddie Luff fairly often, and one evening he introduced me to a most attractive Swiss girl called Yolanda, with whom he had fallen deeply in love (in 1946, after a series of wartime setbacks which would have daunted less committed partners, the two were married). The three of us went to hear Ernest Ansermet and the Suisse Romande Orchestra give a fine concert, which included Beethoven's Seventh Symphony.

It was understood between Eddie and me that if I should be offered a place in the escape line by the British authorities I would take it. On 31 December it looked as though this situation had arisen. That afternoon I met Victor Farrell in the consulate. He told me that one of his men had had to opt out and that he proposed to send me in his place. I was to return to the consulate again at 6pm, ready to travel. When I arrived Victor Farrell was looking – in so far as his well-bred features ever could be said to express any emotion – glum. The military attaché had sent down from Bern a man of his own to replace Victor's non-starter – who must, I think, have been Billy Stephens.

I returned disconsolately to my digs, which I had not expected to see again. A telegram was waiting for me. It read: 'Report in person to Military Attaché Bern arriving first January.' It was unsigned and, rebelliously, I ignored it. But after a firm telephone call from Bern I went there four days later and was reprimanded by Colonel Cartwright for trying to be repatriated before my turn came.

It was now obvious that unless I could manage to repatriate myself I would be stuck in Switzerland for a very long time. The fleshpots of Geneva were beginning to erode my determination to get home and back into the fight as soon as I possibly could. I had reached a watershed. If I did not make a move shortly I would inevitably lose momentum, be relegated to the back of the queue and eventually sink without trace in the main body of evaders, few of whom could have much prospect of seeing Britain again before the war was over.

I decided to discuss with Gordon Hardy the question of our joining forces. We had an entertaining if low-key reunion – we had no wish

Maurice de Milleville.

to draw attention to ourselves – and I was able to introduce Eddie and Gordon to each other. Gordon was evidently just as keen as I was to make a move. The trouble was that, apart from being located in Zurich with no overt excuse to be transferred to Geneva, he could not speak French at all, although his German was good. If only we could obtain some false documents and if possible some addresses of 'safe houses' in France. It was agreed that as soon as we had overcome these problems we would arrange for Gordon to return to Geneva, ostensibly on a purely social visit, so that we could all set off together.

I wrote a note to Victor Farrell during the next day or two, asking yet again for help with false documents and for reliable information both about the bona fides of my American friend and contacts in France. In his reply, Victor very civilly said that the moment that he could give me an answer he would let me know. 'False papers present no difficulty but I am waiting like Micawber for "something good to turn up" before giving you the "genuine information" which you ask of me.' I decided to lie low for a bit and let the dust settle.

One day during the last week in January 1944 I met in the consulate a young Frenchman who was having a noisy altercation with Mr Bloor in a passageway. 'This young man,' said Mr Bloor, 'gives his name as Maurice de Milleville and wishes to acquire British nation-

167

ality,' adding, somewhat superflously, 'he seems to be rather worked up.' I introduced myself and, as much to disembarrass the consular staff as anything else, asked the young man to have lunch with me. I took him round the corner to a small place where I often went and we had soup and bread. Maurice never stopped talking, very fast, mostly in French, but breaking now and then into well-spoken English when he realised that I had lost the drift of what he was saying. I quickly gathered that he had just come across the frontier from occupied France. He was in an extremely nervous state and at times was almost incoherent. Aged about twenty, he was smallish, fine-featured, with pale complexion and dark hair, undernourished and clothed in a baggy suit. From time to time he looked towards the door and through the window, as if expecting to have been followed. It became obvious that we must leave the bistro. But where to go? Maurice had said that he had no papers and had entered Switzerland without permission; he was mortally afraid that he might be forced to return to France. I decided that I had better take him back to No. 14 rue de Candolle.

The essentials of Maurice's story were that his mother, the Comtesse de Milleville, was English;[1] that she had been badly injured in a motor accident; that she had resumed various activities, not specified; had been caught by the Germans and even now was probably being tortured by them to make her disclose information. He himself had also been arrested and brutally treated by the Gestapo, but he had been released; and it was only as a result of his mother's capture that he had come into Switzerland. His main purpose was to reach the United Kingdom in order to report to a certain section of military intelligence about his work in France, obtain British nationality and then join up for military service. It was for this reason that he had approached Victor Farrell for the British passport. He was completely flabbergasted at being refused this, considering what his mother and he had been doing to further the Allied cause. It was because he owed 57,000 francs on behalf of the British government to people in France who had helped British servicemen[2] that he had not gone direct to Spain and thence to the United Kingdom.

How much of all this could I safely believe? Maurice seemed to have valuable contacts in France. If only I could be sure that Maurice was genuine he, Eddie Luff and I, perhaps plus Gordon Hardy, might

[1] She was better-known as Mary Lindell, heroine of numerous escape and evasion episodes in both world wars.
[2] Colonel 'Blondie' Hasler and his companion of 'Cockleshell Heroes' fame.

168

together pass safely through France and over the Pyrenees without benefit of any repatriation organisation. I decided that I must, in the first instance, do my best to make sure that Maurice was not either interned by the Swiss or handed over to the French police at the frontier. In the event, he was able to persuade Madame Pénard – what story he told her I never knew – to allow him to stay the night, sleeping in a spare room. As usual Meg Todd-Naylor was most helpful behind the scenes, although not a little shocked by some of Maurice's turns of phrase – he was still in a highly excited state – which were in quite a different category from the genteel gallicisms which I had learned at the University of Geneva.

Next day, with Maurice's agreement, I got in touch with 'Joe', the American secret serviceman, explained that the British Consulate would not touch Maurice with a barge-pole but that he seemed to be basically OK and potentially a source of valuable information. I asked for help to find somewhere for Maurice to stay. 'Joe' duly obliged. I met Maurice every day for several days and walked with him, trying to determine whether or not he was to be trusted. Might he not have been 'turned round' by the Germans and ordered to use people like me, Gordon Hardy and Eddie Luff to bait a trap for members of the Resistance who might be harbouring us? I arranged for Eddie and Yolanda to meet Maurice. They were strongly inclined to believe him to be genuine.

It was by now mid-February and I had become very envious of the locals – young eager men with young beautiful girls who flocked to the Cornavin station at weekends with their skis. My frustration was intense. Salvation came through Eddie Luff. He had for months been cultivating various Allied repatriation organisations, Czech, Dutch, French and Polish. It was the last-named who, in the end, turned up trumps. At least, Eddie said, he was pretty sure that the Poles would give him some false papers; but he wasn't at all confident that he could persuade them to produce some for me. The only thing to do was to go together and see the individual concerned. So we found ourselves on a crisp sunny day walking across the Pont Rousseau to a majestic block of palatial flats overlooking the Lake of Geneva from the south. Eddie would not, or could not, tell me the name of the man whom we were going to see or anything about him, except that he was Polish and addressed as 'Colonel'.[1] 'I only hope that you can convince him that you are a lieutenant in the Royal Navy – that would help,' said

[1] As I discovered many years later, he was Colonel Romyko. His colleague, Major Stokatovsky, provided the false documents.

Eddie, as we rang the bell of one of the first floor flats.

The Polish colonel was wearing a silk dressing gown and smoking a cigar, with which he gestured to us courteously to be seated. He was pacing to and fro across the quite remarkably wide extent of the living room of the flat, pausing now and then as he reached the large picture window to gaze out over the calm blue waters of the lake.

Having introduced me and explained our mission, Eddie, speaking in French, said that he and I planned to cross France together if only we could obtain appropriate documents. At this point the colonel addressed me in English, saying that he had been military attaché in Rome before the war. I was able to claim acquaintance with the British naval attaché at that time. More conversation, too discursive to be called questioning, apparently satisfied the colonel as to my bona fides. It would be difficult, he said, and outside his normal activity, but yes, he would see what he could do for me. Perhaps it was the mention of two of his gallant countrymen, Commander Boris Karnicki and Lieutenant-Commander George Romanowski, submarine captains with whom I had served, that decided him. My thanks for his help were heartfelt but quite inadequate, and in any event were brushed aside by the colonel as he ushered Eddie and me politely to the door. Now our plans were beginning to take shape. Unfortunately there was no guarantee that our Polish papers would be ready for us by any particular date; all we could do to speed things up was to let the colonel have suitable passport photographs the very next day.

To avoid any unnecessary delay we decided to have a planning conference. It so happened that in one of the larger café-bars in the best part of Geneva a Parisian 'intimate review' company in exile had taken up residence. Their series of topical and political sketches, linked together by a brilliant *improvisateur*, was called *Bourrons la Pipe*, which we took to mean, roughly, 'Let's stoke up the woodstove'. Here we forgathered, Maurice, Eddie, Yolanda and me. Maurice began by saying that 'Joe', the American, wanted him to go back to Lyon and arrange some contacts for him, with the aim, he believed, of strengthening the American secret service network so that it could act independently of the British. The first proposal was for me to go with Maurice to Lyon and wait there while he doubled back to Switzerland with the information for the American, bringing also a set of papers for Gordon Hardy. He would then return to Lyon, leaving Eddie and Gordon to follow a prescribed route to Spain while he and I went on from Lyon to Spain together. The execution of this plan would depend upon the Swiss facilitating the various frontier crossings involved. This in turn would hinge upon the Americans' readiness to pass on to the Swiss some of the intelligence they had obtained. All the countries which maintained secret service agents in Switzerland provided the Swiss with a certain amount of intelligence.

It was a convivial and fruitful evening, but by the end of it I had decided that the plan which we had evolved was too complex and left us too much in the hands of the Swiss and the Americans, neither of whom could be expected to care much what happened to us so long as their own aims were achieved. I began, therefore, to formulate an alternative plan. Having acquired my false papers from the Polish colonel, I would obtain from Maurice two or three key contacts in France and particularly in Lyon. I would then set off on my own. Once arrived safely at Lyon I would send a message back to Maurice by his contacts to say that all was well and that he could come on down the line in company with Eddie Luff and Gordon Hardy. I would make every effort to cross the Swiss frontier without the knowledge of the Swiss authorities. And from Lyon onwards I would make my own way down to the Pyrenees, while welcoming any help from Maurice's contacts that I might be offered.

I confided these ideas to Meg. Her reaction was quick and practical. 'You must meet Bill and Magui Stephens,' she said. 'They have a vineyard out at Péissy-Satigny. It's right on the frontier and just opposite a little railway station. Local trains run to Bellegarde, and from there you can catch the *rapide* to Lyon.' A day or two later we went to see Bill Stephens in his office in the centre of Geneva. He was an Englishman who had married a Swiss girl, Marguerite Desbaillet. He was rather old for military service but, having retained his British nationality, he felt keenly his inability, so far, to help the Allied war effort. He now began to make up for this by entering fully into the spirit of my plan.

Two days after our call at the Desbaillet office, Meg and I were driven by Bill to the family farmhouse at Péissey. Here, after a delicious lunch accompanied by examples of the best Desbaillet wines, Bill took me up into the roof space in a huge barn, from which it was possible to look out over the frontier barbed wire towards the village of St Jean de Gonville where the railway station was. Bill had a pair of field-glasses and with these I was able to see that beyond the frontier the countryside was undulating pasturage, with here and there a clump of bushes. I could make out a village about a mile away. As I watched, fairly certain that I was unlikely to be seen, a German soldier on a bicycle pedalled into view, riding along within fifty yards or so of the frontier

The author. This photograph was taken for use on his false identity papers.

wire. As I had no intention of trying to cross into France in daylight I was not too worried about meeting a German patrol. Bill undertook to see if he could establish any pattern of these patrols. Fortunately, although it was still winter no snow had fallen. I prayed that it would not start snowing just when I was ready to go. Bill was keen to know when that would be. I said that I wished that I myself knew, but that I could not go without my false documents and it might be weeks before they were ready for me.

Partly to occupy my mind during this indefinite waiting period and partly because I knew that I would enjoy the experience, I accepted around this time an invitation from Charles Im Obersteg to travel up to Basle and stay with him for a couple of nights. He was looking forward, he said, to showing me his own works of art and the collection in the Basle Museum which he had helped to form. Charles met me at the station and I had a glimpse of the city in the dusk as we sped along to No. 45 Gelert-strasse. It was a warm, beautifully furnished, modern house. In the living room, I remember, was a finely polished table in a deep bay window with upholstered seats in a horseshoe shape almost surrounding it. Presiding over the house – Charles was a widower, whose only child, a son, was grown-up and away in the United States – was a young middle-aged, good-looking, demure woman who was introduced as Mademoiselle Denise. She had a drink with us before dinner but disappeared after we had had coffee. Charles talked with enthusiasm and expertise about modern paintings; he had been fortunate enough, he said, to have been able to buy several works from the studios of the artists themselves before the dealers had got busy.

Next day, after breakfast, Charles took me to the window so that I could look out over his lawn and behold his Maillol life-size bronze – a nubile nude of infinite grace. Indoors, Charles showed me among other paintings a superb early Picasso of a harlequin; a Fauvist still-life of a dead pheasant by Soutine; and a middle-period Chagall, fanciful, primitive and gloomy, but powerful. After lunch we visited the Basle Museum. I had expected to return to Geneva next morning but Charles insisted that while I was in Basle I must see the zoo and that Mademoiselle Denise would escort me. As we wandered round – I have never been fond of zoos and having been a POW had perhaps increased my sympathy for the unfortunate caged animals – Denise and I got on rather well. Whether or not Denise shared Charles Im Obersteg's bed I do not know. But from various throw-away comments about the years she had spent in London 'keeping house' for rich young bachelors, I shouldn't have been surprised if she had done so. She wore no make-up or scent, and was quietly, if expensively, dressed; although not flirtatious and indeed slightly 'governessy', she had a good figure and a certain air of availability which I found disturbing. Fortunately perhaps for my peace of mind, there was a train back to Geneva which I was able to catch after lunch. With my plans for leaving Switzerland rapidly taking shape, this was no time to be distracted.

At the end of February Gordon Hardy somehow managed to transfer from Zurich to Geneva, where he was allowed to stay in order to study French and International Law. Seeing Gordon again was a great bonus. Despite being somewhat of a pessimist and always openly self-critical, Gordon's contribution to any discussion was always lively, articulate and highly original. It was fortunate that both Eddie and Maurice liked Gordon and were prepared to take him along with them. My plan being therefore approved by the 'escape committee', I continued my preparations apace. I wrote to Somers in very guarded terms saying that for some reason or other, which sounded innocuous enough, she might not hear from me for a while. Next, with the highly intelligent as well as charming assistance of Yolanda, who as luck would have it was working as a secretary in the office of a firm of wine importers, I was able to establish a cover story of sorts. I was to be an employee of this firm, a *courtier en vins* sufficiently junior to have been sent to locate a large consignment of *vin rouge ordinaire* which had failed to arrive in Geneva. It had been dispatched by rail from a wine cooperative in the Roussillon area some weeks previously. My assignment was to proceed down the rail system from Geneva via Lyon and the valley of the Rhône towards Languedoc, examining all the railway sidings into which a wagon full of rough wine from the south might inadvertently have been shunted – following the dislocation of railway services by the Resistance. It seemed a good enough story at the time. Yolanda's flat was near the Cornavin and she knew a café frequented by the engine drivers. With little difficulty she found out the times of the local trains from St Jean de Gonville to Bellegarde, and of the *rapide* from there to Lyon. It was evident that I should have to cross the frontier at Péissy during the night, lie up most of the following day, catch the evening train into Bellegarde and stay the night there, going on to Lyon in the morning. Maurice said that he could give me a contact in Bellegarde.

All that now remained was to obtain my false documents, so that my *courtier en vins* story could be typed out by Yolanda on the firm's headed writing paper, using the name given to me by the Polish forger. I had not much longer to wait. During the first week in March, Eddie received his papers and mine. Maurice seemed to think that he could provide himself and Gordon with adequate documentation. I said goodbye to them all and wished them luck, as I wanted to recede totally into the background, ready to depart in my own time when the weather and the moon were both propitious. Meg had produced a pair of serviceable climbing boots and a rucksack which a Monsieur Conneaud, who was a Swiss friend of hers, had thoughtfully presented to me. I bought a shiny black valise, small enough to fit into the rucksack. I would use this when walking in the open country or mountaineering. When travelling by rail or in the city, I would roll up the rucksack and stow it in the valise, which had room also for my boots, business letters, toilet gear, spare shirts and underwear. To keep out the cold I had my overcoat, and I wore a black beret in the belief that it might help me to look less like an escaping British POW and more like a *courtier en vins* going about his business. This was a mistake and resulted from my having seen too many French films before the war. Every Frenchman from Jean Gabin downwards seemed, in my recollection, to have been wearing a dark beret and have a Gaulois depending from his lower lip as he lurked in the shadows of Montmartre, Montpellier or Marseille. I had even got Maurice to school me in a few of the *louche* phrases which the French movie star had seemed to be muttering at moments of crisis.

On 8 March, a Wednesday, Meg Todd-Naylor and I went along to

Bill Stephens's office, having alerted him by telephone the day before. As soon as I had received my documents from Eddie, who had passed on to Yolanda my fictitious name, she had completed my *courtier en vins* letters; these I now had with me, together with one more item of equipment which I thought was essential to complete my new persona. This was a brolly which I intended to carry, badly rolled, when in my businessman guise. I also had a packet of Gaulois and a book of Desbaillet's complimentary matches.

Having said goodbye to Meg with as much nonchalance as I could muster, I put my brolly and valise into the back of Bill's car and climbed into the front seat beside him. It was a good opportunity to pick up a few hints about the wine trade, although Bill himself was more interested in the production of good wine than in the importation of bad.

There was not much traffic as we sped through the western surburbs of Geneva and we were soon at Péissy. Enough of the late afternoon light remained for me to see once again the lie of the land. The approach to the house ran close by the frontier wire fence, then turned sharply into the drive. I tried to take it all in, so as to make no mistake when I had to find my way down to the fence in the dark.

The warmth, both physical and social, of my welcome by Magui Stephens and the family was unforgettable. Dinner was memorable, with *boeuf à la bourguignonne* as the *pièce de résistance*, and a sturdy Côtes du Rhône to drink. Later coffee and kirsch helped to keep our minds – mine at any rate – off the frontier crossing.

Bill looked at his watch and said, perhaps a shade too casually, 'It's half past ten. If you feel like it we might take a stroll in the garden. I think the moon should be up by now.' I agreed. The date had been chosen to ensure a reasonable degree of moonlight in which to negotiate the frontier fence, which was unlit, without the need of a torch. Although we could not be sure, it seemed probable that the German patrols were not confined to daylight hours. Nor could Swiss patrol activity be excluded.

Having put on my overcoat and beret, picked up my valise and brolly, and said goodbye and a heartfelt 'thank you' to Magui, I went to the door with Bill. 'Here, take these wire-cutters,' he suggested. 'They might come in handy.' I accepted them and said how grateful I was for all his help. We shook hands. He watched me from the hallway for a few moments as I walked away from the house – there was no domestic blackout in Switzerland – and then closed the door.

I stopped in the pitch blackness, quite unable to orientate myself. I looked at the luminous dial of the Rolex watch that Mr Wilsdorf, the manager of their plant in Geneva, had so kindly given me when he had showed me round. It was 10.45. After five minutes or so I began to be able to see dimly – very dimly – to my front. Behind me chinks of light showed where the house was. I walked towards where I felt the frontier fence should be. It was still very dark. No doubt the moon had risen (unless my information was at fault), but the sky was overcast. Quite soon, after a certain amount of groping, I came to a fence and, using the wire-cutters, eased myself through. I remember wondering what had become of the barbed wire. I tossed the wire-cutters light-heartedly away and pressed on.

I suppose it was twenty yards or so from Bill's garden fence to the frontier wire. Too far, at any rate, to go back and look for the wire-cutters with much hope of finding them in the dark. There was nothing for it but to negotiate the barbed wire as best I could. I crouched for a while, listening for any sound of an approaching vehicle or patrol. It was completely quiet. Now for it. The barbed wire was in rolls but rather high. Unhurriedly, and that was the secret, I placed my overcoat very carefully over the wire, threw my valise over and clambered gingerly after it to the other side. It was not easy to free my overcoat from the barbs without tearing it, but I managed to do so. I stood up and put the coat on. I was in occupied France.

8 · Pièce de résistance

Although not freezing it was bitterly cold. But it was not snowing, thank heavens. I remembered the miserable experience of the escapers from Campo Five at Gavi who, after months of exceptionally determined tunnelling, were frustrated by a fall of snow the very night when they were about to go. They knew that, even with a good start, their tracks in the snow would give them away. My problem would be different. Somehow I must remain unobserved for the rest of that night and the best part of the next day. The local train which I had to take would not depart, according to Yolanda's information, until 5.30pm. The railway station lay within a couple of kilometres of where I stood.

Having noted, during my reconnaissance from Bill's barn, some clumps of bushes here and there between the frontier wire and the village, I had decided to use one of them for cover. By now my eyes were fully adapted to the night and the moon, even though overcast, made it light enough to discern the lie of the land. Without too much difficulty I managed to advance in the desired direction until I found what seemed to be a suitable place of concealment. I settled down to wait, even hoping that I might doze off. An hour or two's sleep could make all the difference as I was determined to keep awake during daylight when it came. I did not wish to be prodded into consciousness by an enemy soldier once again, as had happened in Italy.

Sleep did not come readily, despite the Stephens's hospitality. Nearly six months of the good life in Geneva was not the ideal preparation for sleeping rough in winter. The ground was hard, cold and damp. Now that the intense excitement of crossing the frontier was over, I began to ask myself what the hell I was up to, abandoning the guaranteed, if wearisome, security of neutral Switzerland for the risk-ridden rigours of occupied France. It was while pondering this and reminding myself of the addresses and passwords with which Maurice de Milleville had furnished me, that I fell asleep. But not for long. I was soon awake again. I looked at my watch – it was just after midnight. It seemed to be colder and damper than ever. I must have nodded off again as the next time I awoke it was distinctly lighter. I could now distinguish a little more of my surroundings. The ground sloped gently away towards the village, which I could not yet see. There were more clumps of bushes, and as the dawn came I realised that I could find a better hiding place nearer my goal if I moved at once.

The problem was to keep awake. After gazing anxiously and intently round for another half hour or so and seeing no sign of life in any direction I gradually relaxed, and caught myself nodding off again. This would not do. I could make out the small group of buildings, complete with church spire, which was all that there was of St Jean de Gonville apart from the railway station. This, I knew, was little more than a halt on the line fom Gex to Collonges, where it connected with the main line to Bellegarde. Daylight came, though it was still overcast and inclined to drizzle. The air smelt of damp vegetation. Suddenly there were people about. No Germans yet; but presumably the unit which was guarding the frontier must be billeted in the vicinity, almost certainly in the village.

It was hours later, around midday, that I first spotted two or three figures in field-grey uniform moving about near the buildings. I began to wonder how, dressed as I was and coming from the direction of the Swiss border, I could remain sufficiently inconspicuous to reach the railway station without being noticed and questioned. By this time I was beginning to feel both hungry and thirsty. No doubt there was a café, but I could not risk going into it. I could imagine the locals putting down their glasses while they inspected the stranger. There would probably be German soldiers there as well. Eventually, at about 2.00pm, I wandered into the station, checked with the man behind the *guichet* that there would indeed be a train to Bellegarde leaving at 17.30 and bought a single ticket to that place. This was my first attempt at passing myself off as a Swiss. Did I detect, in the expression of the face peering out at me from the *guichet*, just a flicker of scepticism, the merest suggestion of a conspiratorial look?

Even on a summer afternoon in one's own country, where one might stroll into the churchyard and spend some time trying to decipher the inscriptions on the gravestones, or gaze at the hammerbeam roof in the church, or chat over the hedge to a lady in a straw hat weeding her garden, three hours seems a long wait for a train. Lurking near the frontier, in enemy-occupied territory on a raw winter's afternoon, I thought that time would never pass. Despite my feeling that the ticket clerk had guessed that I was an *évadé*, I took refuge fairly early on in the station waiting room. Shortly before 5.30pm the train arrived. By now it was nearly dark and for this I was thankful, because the station suddenly became alive with field-grey uniforms and a-buzz with German voices. I climbed into a compartment and managed to seat myself in the far corner before the Germans piled in. The seats were not upholstered but the lighting was mercifully dim, and the smoke from the cheap cigars of the soldiers did not bother me.

Twenty minutes later the train came somewhat jerkily to a halt with that hiss of released steam which has an air of terminality about it. I knew that everybody would have to change at Bellegarde, so I waited till the soldiers had got a start then alighted and followed them along the platform. What I had not realised was that Bellegarde, being the first mainline station on the line from Geneva, was a *douane*. So it was with a shock that I became aware of a long table flanking the exit. At the far end stood a *douanier*, morosely watching the gaggle of German soldiers as they filed past and out into the town, to fill the cafés with their unwelcome presence. The man turned in my direction. In a sort of reflex action I put my valise flat on the long table and gave it a mighty push in his direction, at the same time saying '*Rien à déclarer*' and walking firmly towards the exit. No doubt seeing that I was the last customer standing between him and going home he picked up a stub end of chalk and made a large X on my valise, muttering '*Ça va*' or words to that effect.

Bellegarde struck me as not so much a town with a railway junction as a junction with a town around it. But then I never saw it in daylight. Maurice had given me an address – 'just around the first corner to the right after you come out of the station and then first left'. The house where I might expect a safe haven would be facing me at the end of the street, which was a cul de sac. There it was. I rang the bell. After a long pause the door opened a crack and a man looked through it. '*Qui est-ce? Que desirez-vous?*' I could see that he was middle-aged and in shirt-sleeves. '*Je suis le Petit Jules*,' I replied, confidently, '*et je cherche ma tabatière.*' The door opened wider so that more light would shine on me. '*C'est pas possible. Vous ne pouvez pas entrer dedans*,' said the man as he looked hard at me in the illumination from the hallway. His voice carried fear. '*Il-y-a un couvre-feu*,' he went on, evidently trying to save me as well as his own household from compromise. '*Vous avez dix minutes seulement avant le couvre-feu – allez chercher l'hotel la bas,*' *tout pres de la gare, et dépêchez-vous.'* He shut the door.

The station hotel at Bellegarde looked as if its main clientele consisted of *commis voyageurs*. Not quite up to *courtier en vins* standard, but with the curfew just about due and the advice of my friend round the corner still in my ears, I was thankful to go in. The girl in reception was matter of fact. A room was available and I booked in. Having checked that the express train to Lyon did in fact leave at 8.00am, as predicted, I ordered a call at 6.30 with *petit déjeuner*. Rather than be drawn into conversation, I asked that a glass of mulled wine and some biscuits be sent up to my room, as I wished to go early to bed and fight off a cold. In due course the *glühwein* arrived. After drinking it and eating the biscuits I fell asleep easily enough.

I was awakened on time in the morning; the coffee (of sorts) and croissant were just what I needed. I should have liked, above all, to have had a hot bath, but that was not provided and I had to make do with the usual shower – first of all horribly cold and then far too hot. I paid my bill (this took a good hunk out of the 40,000 French francs with which I had started out), found the railway station and bought my ticket for Lyon with plenty of time in hand. As people gathered in the busy station I did not feel too conspicuous and when the Lyon train came in it was crowded, so that I was lucky to find a seat in the scramble. Opposite me in the compartment was a middle-aged woman, quite good-looking, whose gaze was a little too frank for my peace of mind. Unlike most of the others, she did not have a newspaper. Nor was she near enough to the window to look out of it. Then I remembered that one of my eyes had turned brown as the result of the metal splinter which had gone into it. That's what's making her stare at me, I thought, and felt relieved.

It was some time later, after we had stopped at Culoz, that I heard from along the corridor the unmistakable voice of a German security officer rasping out, *'Cartes d'identité, cartes d'identité, montrez vos cartes d'identité,'* in an execrable accent. In the most natural way (I had been drowsing) I fished about in my inside breast pocket for my wallet. Almost at once, the corridor door opened and the so-disliked and feared high-fronted peaked cap was thrust in. The nondescript face beneath it again demanded *'cartes d'identité'*, whereupon all of us in the compartment flourished our cards in the officer's direction. Satisfied, he backed into the corridor. As he moved on to the next compartment the woman opposite me looked at me again, but this time with just the faintest of smiles and a twitch of the eye muscles. Once more France had stood by me.

It was about 11.00am when the train drew into the Gare de Perrache in the middle of Lyon. My adrenalin began to work again after the comparatively relaxed journey. I had a feeling that railway stations tended to be watched by security people – railway police, civil police, secret police – and that I must not loiter about. I strode out in the hope that my inevitably worried look would be attributed to being late for a business appointment rather than total ignorance of the local topography. In my mind were the two addresses in Lyon which Maurice had given me. One was in the Place Bellecour – the equivalent of Trafalgar Square – the other in Villeurbanne, which I knew to be a district about six kilometres from the city centre, famous for its huge new housing estates for the workers. I decided, as I walked smartly past the platform barrier and gave up my ticket, to make first for the Place Bellecour. This would be a walk of about one kilometre, out of the station, across the Place Carnot and straight on.

No one seemed to notice me. When I had been going for about ten minutes I saw a trolleybus marked 'Villeurbanne'. Trusting that it was going in the right direction, I hopped on. '*Place Victor Balland, s'il vous plait.*' The conductor obliged. My problem now would be to know when we had got there. Rather than enter into conversation with him, which might quickly expose my lack of fluency in the French language and especially its Lyonnais version, I waited until the route had taken us to the vicinity of the famous (they were designed by Corbusier) workers' high-rise housing blocks and then enquired 'Victor Balland?' as if I really knew quite well where I was but was just making sure. Two stops further on and the conductor beckoned to me to alight.

I had the urge to keep on the move. Even in a workers' suburb one should not loiter about. I walked steadily along, trying to get myself orientated. Luckily the sun had come out – in fact I began to feel that my brolly was more of a liability than an asset.

One of the many good things about France is the thoroughness with which the streets, squares and so on are signposted. Victor Balland may not have been the greatest poet of the Second Empire, but as a local boy who made good his name was, quite rightly, conferred on a square and properly displayed so that a person could read it at a fair distance. Once in Victor Balland Square I was able to locate the Rue François Mole, only two blocks away.

The terraced four-storey houses here were not new. No.12 was probably typical in having an entrance hall, the door to which was open, with a lobby at the back where the concierge was installed. Flat No.1 was on the ground floor with its door in the hall. There was no name card and no bell, just the number on the door and a knocker. I knocked. There was no response. I waited and knocked again. Eventually the concierge appeared, shuffling in her slippers. 'What do you want?' she demanded, and without awaiting my reply went on, 'There's no one there. The Milice came last Friday and took them away.' Her voice seemed to be drained of all emotion, deliberately, as if to establish her non-complicity in whatever it was that the occupants of Flat 1 had been up to. This was not surprising. My actions and appearance were not such as to inspire confidence. I thanked her and departed without explanation.

By the time I was back in the city centre it was nearly 1.00pm and I was both hungry and thirsty. I was also slightly shaken. What if the next 'safe house' should turn out to be no longer safe? Rather than wander about aimlessly while pondering my situation, it seemed that the best thing to do was to go into a café and have a cup of coffee. I did so, and the coffee was vile. Even in France the coffee was made of anything but coffee beans. As I surveyed the crowded tables, I began to lose confidence in my inconspicuousness. I felt that, despite the normal buzz of conversation, the movements of the waiters and the clink of china and glass, there was an atmosphere of suspicion, of everyone being on the *qui vive*. It was time to go.

No.7 Place Bellecour was a most imposing building. I could hardly believe that I had come to the right place. I entered through huge double doors and seemed to be in the headquarters of a bank. My directions from Maurice, firmly committed to memory, were to go upstairs to the first floor and ring the bell of the first door on the left. The staircase was quite grand with a curved balustrade. When I reached the first landing I found, opening off it, three fine mahogany doors. I went to the one on the left and rang the bell. Almost at once the door was opened by a youngish man, who seemed to take me in at a glance. 'Come in,' he said, and more or less pulled me inside and shut the door. 'Now, who are you?' he asked, 'and what do you want?' I muttered something about being *le Petit Jules* looking for his *tabatière* but he seemed to be a bit overwrought and did not immediately grasp me by the hand. I explained that I was a British naval officer on his way from Geneva to Spain. From there I hoped to cross into Gibraltar and return home to England. I mentioned Maurice de Milleville. He smiled and seemed to relax a little. Then he said, 'My brother has already been questioned by the Gestapo. Luckily he was released. Only this morning they arrested my sister. But on suspicion of what? We do not know. You must not stay here. Tonight we shall take you to another house where you should be safe.'

Quite how dangerous life was for the Resistance in Lyon at that time I did not find out until much later – long after the war, in fact. The chief of the Gestapo was the notorious Klaus Barbie, known as the 'Butcher of Lyon'. No wonder my hosts were on edge. Fortunately, the sister (I never did know the names of these wonderful people) arrived home before long. It seemed that the questioning had been, on this occasion, a routine identity check.

It was already early evening and dark. Our move to another house would have to be made now, before the curfew. Lyon was, of course, blacked out. But there was no pausing for eyes to be adapted as we emerged into the Place Bellecour and hurried along. At one of the main intersections which we crossed there was a German patrol, with a motorbike and sidecar standing by. But we were not stopped and after about twenty minutes we arrived at a substantial town house with a brass plate (as I came to know many years later, it was No. 17 Avenue Félix Faure). At once we were admitted to the first floor flat and I was presented to Madame La Doctoresse Bonnier, who in turn was introduced to me as a lady dentist. She had already, it appeared, organised a party and although my host of the afternoon vanished,

17 Avenue Félix Faure, Lyon.

giving me no opportunity to thank him for hiding me at such risk, several other people soon arrived and the wine began to flow.

Two men in particular stand out in my memory. One was shortish and jolly. He told me that he was a doctor and hence found himself in a peculiarly difficult relationship with the German authorities. It had recently been decreed that every healthy male, on reaching the age of eighteen, would be subject to the '*relève*' – the call-up for service in a German labour camp. As there were no German civilian doctors available and those in military service were fully engaged elsewhere, the French medical fraternity was called upon to help by medically examining all the youths as they became due for the *relève*. This grim responsibility brought a threefold conflict of loyalties: to their medical oath was due a strictly accurate health report in each case; to the German authorities they must appear to be professional; but to France they must be loyal. Thus it came about that the number of young Lyonnais with flat feet, weak chests, softening of the bones, dicky hearts, bad lungs and rotten teeth began to overtake the quota of fit young persons and there were fears that German suspicions would be aroused. Greater care would have to be taken, however regrettably, to ensure that at least some of the palpably hundred per cent medically fit young men were indeed given a clean bill of health.

One day, according to my doctor friend, just such a fellow had gone in desperation to one of his colleagues, asking that he be registered as unfit for call-up. He had already been passed as an exceptionally fine specimen of young manhood by an elderly and perhaps somewhat timorous practitioner. Fortunately the young man, while strong and wiry, was also unusually small in stature. This had given my doctor friend's colleague an idea. It so happened that he was acquainted with the director of Lyon Zoo, from whom he had learned of the recent demise of one of the larger primates. What was proposed and immediately put into effect, was for the young Frenchman to go to ground in the zoo – at any rate during daylight hours. There he would be zipped into the skin of the deceased gorilla, whose life-style he would then counterfeit.

All went well for a week or two, with Alphonse energetically swinging from branch to branch of the great old elm tree provided by a humane zoo council as part of the habitat of its captive apes. But, alas, a white and shaken Alphonse one day reported to his keeper that he had seen and positively recognised, peering suspiciously at him through the bars of the ape enclosure, the malevolent face of a member of the Gestapo. 'Mon Dieu,' said the keeper, 'I shall tell the director first thing tomorrow. But in any event you must increase your activity. It's no good just going to sleep in a corner. You must get into that tree again and swing around properly, like poor old Susie used to do.' So Alphonse did just that. Out he went in a great swoop towards the end of a long branch – a good deal further than he had ever dared to leap before. He grabbed the end of it and as it took the full weight of his body there was an ominous cracking. Terrified, he looked down, expecting to fall many feet to the ground. Horror of horrors, he was over the stony wet Arctic environment inhabited by a group of hungry looking polar bears. '*Au secours! Au secours!*' he yelled, losing all self-control. At which one of the polar bears looked up and shouted '*Ta guele! Ta guele! Vous nous auriez tous repérés.*'

This serio-comic story could have originated in time of peace. But what I now heard from a tall saturnine man was new-minted and the reverse of fanciful, though not without an element of that grim humour with which in wartime men depreciate the great risks they may be taking in deceiving and discomfiting the enemy. This grave railway-man was responsible under German supervision for arranging train movements and stock availability so as to facilitate the military use of the railways in the region. 'Imagine,' he said, 'the danger I am in when the Resistance succeed in blowing up a train carrying German troops. How is it, I am asked, that the Resistance *réseaux* seem always to get word far enough in advance of the troop movements to place the explosives in time? How should I know?' As he said this, the tip of an index finger momentarily brushed the side of his nose and an eye narrowed slightly. 'But', he went on, 'you must tell me what you think of the war. When will the Allies land in France?'

I felt inspired by these people and honoured to be in their company. In coming together to meet me and exchange news with each other some fresh impulse may have been given to their commitment to ultimate liberation and some mitigation of the sickness of hope deferred. At the time I was aware only of the immediacy of their presence and the laughing hubbub of their talk. Quite soon the party began to disperse. It would not do, they said, for everyone to depart at once. When all the guests had gone, Madame Bonnier indicated that I should be welcome to sleep on the sofa; it had been agreed that in the morning I should be moved to yet another hiding place.

The next few days were quite extraordinary and the sequence of events, as I relate them, may not be precisely accurate. In the morning a youngish, taciturn man called for me with a motorcar and I took my leave of Madame La Dentiste. After quite a short drive we came to a halt outside an imposing three or four storey town house which, I came to know later, was No. 93 rue Tronchet. As I alighted from the car I noticed out of the corner of my eye directly across the street the entrance of a large edifice – it was obviously a public building of some sort – over which a flagpole projected into the street bearing a huge Nazi flag. I was led up a broad flight of steps, through the doorway and into a spacious entrance hall, parquet-floored but devoid of furniture. As I stood there two things struck me, adding to the sense of unreality which had begun already to displace the severely practical considerations with which I had been preoccupied since leaving Geneva. In the first place, the walls of the entrance hall were entirely covered from ceiling to floor with cinema posters. Secondly, the air was filled with the rattle of typewriters. Before I could determine where this came from, I was ushered by my guide into a small office on the right, motioned to take a chair and left alone.

A minute or two later in came my guide with an older man, stocky, with a lined, intelligent face and a warm smile. We exchanged greetings, then he asked to see the false papers which, I informed Albert (that was the name he told me to use) had satisfied the German security officer on the train. 'What on earth are these?' he muttered, as he scanned the three or four assorted coloured pasteboards with an expression of growing incredulity. He turned to his companion and said, '*Mon Dieu, Georges, regarde,*' as he took each of my treasured cards in turn and explained, across the table, that one was hopelessly out of date, another was stamped quite wrongly, a third was quite unheard of and as for the bicycle licence ... 'My friend,' said Albert, 'you are very lucky to have got away with it. These documents are quite useless. You must stay with us for a few days while we obtain for you a set of real identity papers – *les vrais vrais,*' and he smiled. 'They will be signed by the German commandant himself. You will see. And now come upstairs and meet my wife and son.'

It was not until some time after the war was over that I was able to discover what Albert's contribution had been to the Allied cause, not only in the second war but in the first. He and his wife, to whom he was evidently devoted, had come to Lyon in 1940. They had been living on the coast near Dunkirk and the German army had commandeered their bungalow when setting up the defence of the coastline. So M and Mme Dodrumez (I did not know their surname until after the war) had moved to Lyon with their only child Guy, then about fourteen years old. We chatted for a little in their comfortably furnished sitting room. I had hoped to find out why the entrance hall

Albert Dodrumez's France d'Abord membership card.

was decorated with cinema posters – perhaps even the business which kept those typewriters rattling. But, no doubt because Albert assumed that what he intended to be obvious to everyone would be so, these matters were not explained. What did become clear, however, was Albert's long-standing, deep and proven antipathy for the Germans, and in particular the German army.

Mme Dodrumez suggested that I might see the room where I was to sleep. Indeed, except for mealtimes, I would spend all my time there. Just across the street was a hospital that had been requisitioned by the German army – I said that I had noticed the flag. We went up to a large, dry and partly furnished attic. 'You see,' said Mme Dodrumez by way of explanation, 'my son Guy likes to keep his gramophone here so that he and his friends can listen to *le jazz* without disturbing us. When you are ready come downstairs. Guy should be in soon, then we'll listen to the BBC and have lunch.' Left alone, I unpacked my few bits and pieces, had a wash and joined M and Mme Dodrumez in their sitting room. This was when I met Guy. He was taller than his father, good looking, with jet black hair. We shook hands. 'Do you like jazz?' was his first question. As it happened I did. 'That's good,' he said, 'because I have plenty of records – do you know the Hot Club de France? Stephane Grapelli and Django Reinhardt? *Merveille!*'

187

I had expressed my shared delight in these heroes and was about to mention some of my own – Duke Ellington, Louis Armstrong and others – when Albert looked at his watch and said, 'Time for the BBC News.' As we went to our places in the dining room next door and I stood facing the windows, I could see opposite me, practically on a level, the dreaded Nazi flag. From the loudspeaker on a side table came the strains of 'God Save the King', whereat we all stood firmly to attention. Albert said '*bon appetit*' and we sat down to lunch, listening intently to news of the war as seen from London. Every day, while I was a guest of these wonderful, brave and hospitable people the routine was the same. In between times I remained comfortably, if somewhat impatiently, ensconced in the attic. Guy appeared quite often and we listened together to the melodious urgent beat of the Hot Club de France, with the soaring stylish improvisations of Grapelli's violin; to the exuberance of Louis Armstrong's trumpet; and to the clipped, restrained elegance and quietly insistent rhythm of a Duke Ellington arrangement.

Late one afternoon Guy appeared and flung himself down. He looked pale and exhausted. He had been to the cinema and only just escaped being caught in a *rafle*. Halfway through the main film the lights had gone on and the show was stopped by a German security officer, who ordered everyone to stay where they were and produce their identity cards. Moving at the speed of light Guy, who had very good reason not to show his card as he was now eighteen and eligible for the *relève*, had managed to nip out through an emergency exit and avoid the surrounding security cordon. Life in Lyon was not pleasant at that time, and above all for the young and healthy.

On the third day, at lunch, Albert said that he proposed to take me out to a meal that evening to meet a special friend. After dark he and I went very boldly, as it seemed to me, along the rue Tronchet, past the German hospital and into a bistro in the next street. Ignoring the two or three German soldiers present, Albert led me between the tables and past the bar into the back regions, shutting the glazed door behind him. He was greeted by two most attractive young women (one of whom, evidently, was cook and the other waitress) and in a moment we were seated at a table for four in an alcove beside the kitchen, from which were floating the most appetising smells. Through the frosted glass of the door by which we had entered could be dimly seen the shapes of the German soldiers. Albert was in good form. I suppose that these particular soldiers, not being secret police and presumably off duty, did not cause him any concern.

We were enjoying an aperitif when a couple came in to join us. The man, whom Albert called *mon colonel*, was short and swarthy, with a round head and close-cropped greying hair. He had a formidable, though courteous air, and exemplified the officer corps of the French colonial army, toughened by long years of service in Indo-China or Algeria. His companion was a young middle-aged woman of charm and breeding with that air of total freedom from the cares of family life which bespeaks the mistress. A meal of quite remarkable excellence considering the wartime shortages was put before us. As the wine flowed, the colonel described in unemotional tone and terms some of his recent activities in the continual struggle to outwit the forces of occupation. I remember him saying that for some weeks he had been able to hang about the Gestapo headquarters in Marseilles, in order to keep tabs on the comings and goings. One day, in his disguise as a vagrant-cum-road sweeper, he was set upon for no apparent reason by some Germans, who beat him up while asking him all sorts of questions which he dare not answer. After almost breaking his legs they let him go. He thought himself very lucky to have remained unknown for what he was.

I could hardly believe it when, the next day, I was presented with my new set of identity papers. I had become a French citizen named Jean Périmaux, born in 1914 in Clermont Ferrand. My mother Laura (née Herbison) was an Australian and we had spent some of my formative years in that country, which was to account for my some-times halting and oddly accented French. I was assured by Albert that my identity card had been signed by the German deputy governor and that my identity would at least stand up to a preliminary investigation because there had existed until very recently a man called Jean Pér-imaux of Clermont Ferrand. As I was not sure of my next move, I could not yet devise a story which would account for my presence wherever I might be when questioned *en route* to Spain, and provide a convincing reason for the journey upon which I was then engaged. Nor did I ever really do this before events took charge.

Without warning, just five days after my arrival under his roof, Albert told me to get ready to leave, assuring me that he would let Maurice de Milleville in Geneva know that I had passed through Lyon. It was already evening. After a quick meal I took leave of Mme Dodrumez and Guy, and left in a car with Albert and a young man called Henri. He was acting as a courier for an American espionage organisation. Owing to the blackout and the near-darkness in the railway station and the train, Henri remained, throughout the night, a shadowy figure seated diagonally opposite me in the compartment. When eventually, some five or six miserable hours after leaving the Gare de la Mouche, the dawn light enabled us to see each other, we exchanged glances of studied non-recognition. I liked the look of Henri.

As we rattled along and the sun rose I could see to my left, beyond an expanse of brush-covered sand dunes, the blueness of the Mediterranean sea. We had obviously come down the valley of the Rhône and were now heading west along the coast. When the train next stopped I could see the name on the platform. It was Sête. After another stop, at Bèziers, we came to Narbonne. Here Henri got off the train and I followed him. Across the road was a café on a corner, dignified with the sign Hotel d'Alsace. We went in, sitting down quite naturally at the same table.

At last I was able to see Henri properly. He seemed to be about the same age as myself, or a bit younger, say twenty-seven. He was tall and dark-haired, with a round somewhat reddish face. He proposed that we should have *petit déjeuner*, which was soon produced. There were some German soldiers in the café. Henri said that they were probably just waiting for a train and, sure enough, after we had been there for less than a quarter of an hour they all departed. Up to that moment Henri had been talking about nothing in particular. Now he began to explain what we were doing. From Albert he had heard who I was and where I was trying to get to. One of the problems about crossing the Pyrenees he said, was that your ordinary French identity card would not do in the 'Zone Interdite' which the Germans had established, extending thirty kilometres from the Spanish frontier. Only residents of that area were entitled to enter it and they were issued with special passes. Henri, it turned out, was a resident, although currently working in Paris in his profession of doctor of medicine. It was by virtue of his special pass that he was able to act as a courier, taking packets of intelligence reports from collecting organisations to contacts on the frontier. He proposed to use his pass to enable him to guide me to freedom – or at any rate into Spain. But in the meantime he had a job to do in Narbonne. After it was completed we would catch a train to Toulouse. There would be one at 3.35pm which should get us there before six.

It was a good half hour's walk through Narbonne to its western outskirts. Had I been on a touring holiday, looking at Romanesque antiquities in southern France, I should have been better briefed and in a more receptive frame of mind to appreciate the undoubted merits of Narbonne. As it was, lugging my valise and wearing my overcoat,

Jean-Baptiste Gadal (standing on left), Henri Bigou (standing on right),
Paulinette Gadal (bottom right).

from neither of which I dared to be parted for a moment, I was
extremely thankful when Henri, scanning the numbers on the doors
of a row of modest dwellings in a side street, said, 'Here it is,' and
knocked on the door. Using some phrase which I did not quite catch,
Henri made himself known and was asked to enter. I remained outside.
In a moment or two he had rejoined me and was walking with me
back towards the town centre. 'He wasn't there,' he said. 'Who wasn't
there?' I asked. 'The engine-driver. But he'll be back tonight and his
wife will give him the package. He's a Communist and hates the
Germans more than most people, which is saying something. So he
takes a packet from me every now and then on his run to Cerbère, on
the frontier. There he hands it over to a chum on the Spanish railway
for onward transmission. Now let's get back to the station café and
have a drink while we wait for the Toulouse train. I hope to goodness
that it's on time. We don't want to arrive after the curfew.'

In company with the now seemingly inevitable group of German
soldiers we boarded the Toulouse train. As we stopped at Carcassone,
I realised that in happier circumstances a stay would have been
rewarding. But on we went and rolled into Toulouse at about six in
the evening. It was still fully light, and sunny. The station was crowded

and Henri and I could easily have become separated. For me this would have been disastrous, because I had no idea where we were going or whom we were going to see. I never asked any questions about such matters, lest I should be recaptured and perhaps give someone away. We emerged into the station forecourt and after a short wait caught a trolleybus.

I have not been back to Toulouse since that day in March 1944 and my recollection of it is vague. But when we alighted from the bus Henri pointed out the university. We did not have far to walk before coming to a house in a terrace,[1] where he rang the bell. The door was opened by a smallish middle-aged man with a somewhat weather-beaten, tanned complexion. 'Hello, Emile,' said Henri. 'May we come in?' In the hallway, with the front door shut, I was introduced to Monsieur Villalongue.[2] His wife appeared and greeted Henri who said, 'This is the English naval officer who is trying to get to Spain.' As we were taking off our coats two smallish children appeared, to be introduced as Olivier and Claude.

Mme Villalongue produced for us all a delicious supper, during which conversation was fairly general if somewhat circumspect. Her husband, it transpired, was an enthusiastic mountaineer and in happier days had spent much time in the Pyrenees, climbing and camping in summer, and skiing in winter. I gained the impression, also, that his political views were distinctly radical – Marxist even. M Villalongue's readiness to help an ally against the Germans owed as much, I felt, to his hatred of fascism as to his love of France. The discourse having taken a philosophical turn, the professor asked me whether, as a Scot, I was well-versed in the works of David Hume. Apart from having heard of him, I was ashamed to admit that my acquaintance with his writings was non-existent. However, we found some common ground in discussing Bernard Shaw, and in general the Auld Alliance was cemented anew.

After supper when the children had gone to bed we held a council of war. Henri said that he knew of a safe house in Perpignan where I could lie up until a group of evaders had been collected, when the party would move down to Baniuls near the Spanish frontier. Here contact would be made with one or other of the brave people who guided to safety a steady stream of British and American airmen, escaped POWs and civilians obliged for one reason or another to seek sanctuary outside occupied Europe. Having a local permit, Henri felt

[1] No. 14 rue Malbec.
[2] Emile Villalongue (1909–1966), teacher of philosophy at Toulouse Lycée.

confident enough that he could escort me as far as Perpignan (which I was learning to pronounce 'Perpenyan' in the accent of the Midi). But I am afraid that I did not readily fall in with this idea. While being more than appreciative of Henri's offer, which certainly would not be without risk to himself, I demurred on the grounds that to have to lie up for an unspecified number of days or even weeks in a house in Perpignan just thirty kilometres from the frontier and then join up with a group of strangers, would diminish my control over my own movements. I should prefer, I said, to take my chance on my own. I now had a Michelin map of the region, a few thousand francs, an identity card and some ability to speak French. If I could be put on a train going in the right direction from Toulouse I would alight short of the *Zone Interdite* and continue on foot, hiding by day.

Neither M Villalongue nor Henri thought much of this. I wouldn't have much hope of passing through the zone without being asked for my permit, and if I succeeded in reaching the foothills of the Pyrenees I would almost certainly lose my way and come to grief on the mountain. After all, it was still March and there was a lot of snow about. No, said Henri firmly. He spoke rapidly to M Villalongue and I lost track of what was being said. M Villalongue seemed to be nodding agreement. 'We have a better idea,' said Henri and went on to explain that he and Emile would accompany me into the Pyrenees to the vicinity of a peak called Le Canigou, where an enclave reduced the distance to be covered to the Spanish frontier and a plateau would facilitate skiing. I protested that this would be altogether too much. But their minds were made up.

First thing next morning Henri departed. As usual I asked no questions. It was Mme Villalongue who said, when it was lunchtime, 'Henri's gone to Paris. He expects to be back tomorrow with his sister Lili. We think that it will be less risky if you and she go together to Lavelanet first. Henri's uncle and aunt will put you up.' After lunch I looked at the map. Lavelanet was about twenty kilometres south-south-east of Pamiers, the nearest railway station. In two days time Henri arrived back from Paris with Lili. Like Henri, she was tallish and dark-haired. You could see the family resemblance. I did not gather what Lili had been doing in Paris. It just seemed so incredible to me that these two, Henri and Lili, should have totally given themselves over to helping me, a very junior British officer, into Spain at considerable risk, expense and inconvenience to themselves.

What followed added to my admiration for these two families. The next evening, which was 21 March, Lili and I took a train from

Toulouse to Pamiers and a bus from there to Lavelanet, where we were warmly welcomed by M and Mme Gadal, uncle and aunt of Lili and Henri, whose surname, I now learned, was Bigou. When I revisited the Gadals about twenty years later (he had by that time retired from his post of bank manager) I was shown into the same spare bedroom, all lace curtains, lace bedspread and hair tidies on the dressing table. There was still a radio beside the bed – perhaps the same one on which I had tuned in to the BBC and heard the opening notes of Beethoven's Fifth Symphony with which 'Colonel Britain's' news programme was invariably introduced – the three short notes followed by a long one, being the morse code letter 'V', for victory. On that later visit Mme Gadal told me that the evening after my arrival in their house, in order to put the Germans off the scent, she and her husband had invited one of the less unpleasant of them to have coffee while I remained safely upstairs.

In the meantime Lili had departed. On the third night Emile Villalongue arrived with two bicycles. At 4.00am he and I set off, pedalling fast through the night. We did not have lights and keeping together

In the back row: Marie Villalongue (second from left), Lili Bigou, Oliver and Claude Villalongue, c. 1943. They are with Jewish children who had taken refuge in a Pyrenean village.

was not all that easy, especially as I had not ridden a bicycle for several years. Then I had a puncture. Fortunately we were almost in a village which Emile seemed to know. At any rate he went straight to one of the houses and awoke the inhabitants. Explaining in low urgent tones who we were and what we were about, he managed to exchange my bicycle for another one and off we sped once more. We had been going for another half hour when the first streaks of dawn appeared ahead of us. Soon we were in another village. It was Quillan, and in the square stood a single decker bus. We hoisted our bikes on to its roof rack and secured them. Having done so we climbed into the still cold and empty bus, sat down and awaited events.

It was not long before the driver appeared, grunted a greeting, started his engine and drove off. As it grew lighter people appeared here and there by the roadside, and we stopped every so often to pick up more passengers. The bus was not hurrying and took over two hours to cover the sixty or so kilometres from Quillan to Estagel, where it stopped and everyone got out. We retrieved our bikes from the roof-rack. Emile said that a friend of his who kept a chemist's shop and general store could be relied upon and would give us something to eat. Not for the first time in the course of my journey from Campo Five I found myself breakfasting off new-baked rolls and a glass or two of the local wine. That of Estagel, I recall, was full-bodied and fruity – a Roussillon in fact – and as honest as it was unpretentious.

It was mid-morning and the sun was warm on our backs as we mounted our bicycles again and set off by a minor road across the open country towards Prades, some forty kilometres to the south-west. Our route would take us into the *Zone Interdite*, and it had become all-important not to be questioned by anyone in authority because neither of us had the necessary resident's pass. It was around midday when we reached Prades, the significance of which became apparent when I saw that it had a railway station. This, Emile told me, was important to our plan of action.

Finding a secluded spot within sight of the railway, we dismounted and sat down to wait while Emile told me of his experiences in the Pyrenees. 'I suppose you can ski,' he said. As I had just spent the winter in Switzerland, that was a not unreasonable assumption. But I had to say that I had never put on skis in my life. At that he looked glum. 'Well,' he said, 'you will have to learn quickly. But as you will only have to ski along the plateau in order to reach the Spanish frontier I expect that you will be able to cope.' And he used that useful French verb *se debrouiller*, which means roughly 'to manage somehow to get yourself out of a fix'.

It was about three o'clock in the afternoon when the small local train came puffing into the station. We mounted our bikes and went to meet it. Almost the only passengers to emerge and, looking somewhat out-of-season in the sunshine, were Henri Bigou and his sister Lili. He was carrying two pairs of skis and she was carrying one, plus a large straw bag. After a suitably casual greeting we sought a café nearby, where we ordered lemonade. Lili revealed that in the straw bag was some food – mainly bread and cold sausage – which she hoped would sustain us for a day or two on the mountain. There was no need for further delay, so Emile, Henri and I said goodbye to Lili, leaving her to catch the next train back to Vinça with the bicycles, and set off up the road leading southwards out of Prades towards the Pyrenees. As we toiled along, each with a pair of skis and a knapsack over his shoulders (mine containing my valise), I was thankful that the shoes which I was wearing were comfortable and that Meg Todd-Naylor's foresight had led to my having Monsieur Conneaud's stout climbing boots, which would serve well enough for skiing.

By about six in the evening it was beginning to get dark. Looking down and back through a clearing we could see Prades and the valley of the River Tet on which it stands. Ahead, the road, now reduced to

Emile Villalongue in Chasseur Alpin uniform, 1940.

a cart track, disappeared into the trees. The scent of pinewood was strong. Suddenly, as the sun went down, we were in deep shadow and it became very chilly. Knowing that Emile was not given to imparting information which it was not necessary for me to know, I kept quiet. We were in single file now, with Emile in the lead, followed by me, with Henri bringing up the rear. So far we had not encountered a soul since leaving Prades. I was beginning to find walking in shoes in the semi-darkness rather tricky as the going was getting rougher, when mercifully we came upon a farmhouse with a large barn extending from it.[1] I suppose Emile knew it was there, but even so I thought that we were lucky to have the prospect of shelter for the night.

A minute or two later I was not so sure. We went into the barn, which was dimly lit, with bales of straw at one end and along one side. Lying or sitting on the floor were two or three men, from whom one might have expected a greeting of some sort. But no one spoke. It was quite extraordinary, until one remembered that we were within a few kilometres of the Spanish frontier, in the *Zone Interdite*, within which only Henri of us three was entitled to be. Perhaps the other men in the barn were not entitled to be there either. We kept quiet, ate some of our bread and sausage, and had a drink of lemonade from a bottle which Henri had prudently brought from the café in Prades. Then we made ourselves as comfortable as possible on the straw and slept. It had been quite a day for all of us and that, combined with the mountain air, overcame the lack of comfort and the cold.

Not long after daybreak we left the barn – the other occupants had already departed – and set off up the hill-track. The tree-line in that part of the Pyrenees is at about 6,000 feet; by mid-morning we were above it and not far below the snow-covered northern flank of the Canigou. Emile had chosen this route, he told me, because it would lead us – once over the peak – to a plateau where an enclave in the line of the frontier brought it several kilometres nearer than either further to the east or the west. Nor was it, as far as he knew, an area patrolled by the Germans.[2] A little later I understood why. By early afternoon we were climbing through snow and I was more than ever thankful for M Conneaud's boots, which I was now wearing. Our target, the sharply defined, snow-capped peak of the Canigou, was now in sight from a relatively level stretch of the ascent and was some

---

[1] It was in fact a refuge, the Chalet des Cortalets.
[2] The *Baraque des Allemands*, from which they patrolled twice daily, was about ten miles to the south west.

This certificate is awarded to

Monsieur Henri Jean Bigou

*as a token of gratitude for and appreciation
of the help given to the Sailors, Soldiers
and Airmen of the British Commonwealth
of Nations, which enabled them to escape
from, or evade capture by the enemy.*

*Air Chief Marshal,
Deputy Supreme Commander,
Allied Expeditionary Force*

1939-1945

Certificates awarded by the Allies to Henri Bigou (above) and Emile Villalongue (below).

This certificate is awarded to

Monsieur Emile Villalongue

*as a token of gratitude for and appreciation
of the help given to the Sailors, Soldiers
and Airmen of the British Commonwealth
of Nations, which enabled them to escape
from, or evade capture by the enemy.*

*Air Chief Marshal,
Deputy Supreme Commander,
Allied Expeditionary Force*

1939-1945

1,500 feet above us. Here we found, to my surprise, a shelter which must have been made quite recently as it was not covered by the snow. It consisted of many pine branches cleverly arranged in a sort of igloo, into which it was possible to crawl. After we had eaten most of what was left of our food Emile said, 'Now, Ian, put on your skis and have some practice – it is level enough here.' 'You must pretend that you are on the "nursery slopes",' added Henri, saying 'nursery slopes' in English. 'But all you will have to do tomorrow is ski along the plateau beyond the Canigou for about five kilometres *et voila!*'

After an hour or so of instruction I found that I could stand more or less upright on the skis, proceed down a gentle slope, stop, turn and climb up again. As I rested I was able to take in the fantastic view, eastwards towards the Mediterranean some sixty kilometres away, and westwards to the 11,000 foot peaks beyond Andorra. The Canigou, which the next day we must scale, being a mere 9,500 feet, could not be included in the 'first division' of Pyrenean peaks. Even so, the expedition was becoming a little more arduous than I had bargained for, a sentiment which was not dispelled as I lay awake a little later inside the shelter of pine branches. On one side of me was Emile and on the other Henri, the three of us huddled together for mutual warmth. The layer of small pine branches on which we were lying was surprisingly effective in insulating our bodies from the snow underneath. But it was not easy to find a tenable posture; only our tiredness made it possible to sleep and that only fitfully.

At daybreak we crept thankfully out of the shelter. Once again I was spellbound by the magnificence of the view, now made even more superb by the dawn light falling upon the snow-clad slopes and peaks. 'Come on,' said Emile, 'This last stretch is the hardest, and we must get you to the frontier and ourselves back here by dusk at the latest. If possible, I would rather not have to spend another night in the shelter,' – to which Henri agreed with considerable feeling. So we pressed on, with Emile skilfully leading us clear of the more unreliable-looking patches of snow. We had been climbing for about an hour and had reached an eminence within a thousand feet or so of the peak when we paused for one of our now more frequent rests. The shoulder packs and skis were beginning to feel rather heavy, as was the going through snow that was not quite firm. As we gazed upward, we noticed that flurries of snow were flying every now and then off the mountain-top in our general direction. A high wind was evidently blowing from the south, so that we ourselves were in the lee and therefore not yet fully exposed to it.

Long before we came to the summit we could hear the wind blasting and see ever more frequent snow flurries. Surprisingly there was no cloud, which would have made matters a great deal worse, and we were able to reach the top of a ridge near the peak,[1] over which we scrambled. So strong were the squalls that a gust caught one of my ski sticks, parted the leather thong looped around my wrist and tore the stick clean away. There was no question of standing upright in such a howling near-blizzard. Instinctively the three of us clambered and crawled down the south side of the ridge for perhaps two or three hundred feet, until, mercifully, we gained the false lee which you find on the windward side of a wind-battered mountain ridge.

Crouched in a slight hollow, nearly frozen but out of the worst of the gale, we held a council of war. The decision was not hard to reach. I could not hope to make enough headway over the plateau against so violent a wind – even supposing that I could avoid falling into a snowdrift – to reach the frontier at its nearest point as planned. On the other hand, if I were somehow to descend the south-east side of the Canigou until safely below the snowline I might then be able to cross the River Tech and arrive at the frontier by a longer route. On my own, if apprehended by a patrol, I could probably establish my identity as an escaping British POW and face nothing worse than reincarceration. But if the other two should be caught in company with me they would almost certainly be shot out of hand. The logic was compelling. There was no point in hanging about. I took off my skis, handed them to Henri and said farewell to those two splendid Frenchmen. Wishing me the best of luck they clambered back up the ridge and disappeared from view over the top. Both, I am glad to say, returned safely to their homes.

[1] Having by-passed the Canigou itself, we were now surmounting the Puig des Tres Vents (9,000 feet).

9 · Spanish haircut

I now considered my own situation. I knew that once I was below the false lee near the top of the ridge I would feel the full force of a wind strong enough to make it impossible to stand up. But the slopes below me, although fairly steep and snow-covered, looked reasonably even. I took off my knapsack and, holding it by the straps, began to roll over and over down the hill. My overcoat was soon encased in snow, but otherwise this somewhat unconventional mode of mountaineering paid off. I certainly could not have gone far on foot without in places sinking in the soft snow up to my waist. I must have descended a thousand feet or more in this way without too much difficulty when I sensed that the wind was far less strong than it had been near the summit. I stood up and found that I could now manage to walk or slither down the mountainside. Here and there I did sink quite deeply into the snow. The going was heavy and I floundered about a good deal. It was well after noon when I reached the bottom of the snow-line. By then the sun had come out and I could see below me the deciduous woods, fields and vineyards of the valley of the River Tech.

This seemed a good moment to take stock, so I fished out my Michelin map and began to get orientated. The church tower which I could see two or three kilometres to the south must be Prats de Mollo, right on the river, presumably with a bridge over it. A road of sorts continued south for another two or three kilometres, the contour lines showing a gentle rise up the far side of the valley; a dotted line extended towards the frontier, stopping just short of it. I felt pretty certain that if I could make it to there I would find a pathway leading right to the frontier, no doubt meeting a similar pathway from the Spanish side.

My overcoat having dried off in the continuing sunshine, I appeared, or so I told myself, reasonably respectable, though unshaven. But I had not taken account, as I should have done, of the experience in the barn two nights previously, when the deep suspicion of any strangers in the frontier zone was manifest. When, in the evening, after a not unpleasant walk down from the snowline, I went into a bar in Prats de Mollo and asked for a glass of wine, I was greeted with the stoniest silence. Not a word of welcome or even of interrogation did M le Patron utter. The few habitués present stopped talking and stared at me. Although the atmosphere was not actively hostile, I had the strongest possible presentiment that my presence, whoever I was and whatever I was doing, was unwelcome. My lack of imagination, coupled with a strong thirst and some hunger, had again led me to ignore the real danger of reprisals by the Germans against innocent people such as the citizens of Prats de Mollo, who might be thought to be harbouring the likes of me. I turned quickly from the bar, said goodnight and walked out into the street.

As usual I thought it essential to keep moving with a purposeful air, rather than be seen to loiter about. I headed for the little church, confident that in a Catholic country I should find it open. I entered. It was empty. Provided that I left early enough in the morning it was unlikely that I would be disturbed. There was an odour of somewhat musty sanctity. Before I lay down I said a prayer. I managed to sleep despite the cold hardness of the tiled floor. But I had no difficulty about waking before any Sunday worshippers arrived.

I crossed a meadow behind the church and came to a stream, a tributary of the Tech. Having had a good drink of the clear cold water, I decided to have a shave. I assumed that the local people would be dressed in their Sunday best and that to have any hope of being inconspicuous as I walked along the roads I must look as tidy as possible. I still had my shaving tackle with me in my haversack with soap and a handkerchief, although no towel. Despite the coldness of the water I managed to work up quite a decent lather and was scraping away quite happily, using my small mirror propped in a tree-nook, when I became aware of a man approaching. Possibly a farmer and the proprietor of the meadow, he greeted me civilly enough and asked me what I was doing there. Anything like a facetious reply would not have been in order. Nor would some cock-and-bull story about being on holiday from my engineering works in Clermont-Ferrand have stood much of a chance with this stern-looking fellow. So I told him that I was a British officer on the run from the Germans, and very keen to cross into Spain. The farmer said nothing, turned on his heel and went back across the meadow. As he had not seemed to be hostile, I decided to finish shaving, wash as best I could in the stream and be on my way. Before I had quite finished sprucing myself up he reappeared, bringing me half a newly-baked baguette and some salami. I thanked him warmly. He said, 'Please leave my land at once,' and departed. I stuffed the food into my knapsack, put on my overcoat and headed off down the path by the stream.

I soon found myself on the road which runs beside the River Tech. I could see on the map that there was a bridge over it at the Pas de Loup but, given the nearness of the frontier, I thought that it would probably be guarded. I decided to keep away from the vicinity until after noon and stroll across during the lunch hour, preferably just behind some locals. It was another warm, sunny day and I blessed the fact that spring comes earlier in Southern France than in England. By midday there were several people on the road, cycling or walking, some with rucksacks, and I did not feel at all conspicuous. At about 1.00 pm I crossed the bridge and followed the road southwards towards the foothills. After walking for another hour and a half or so, I was able to leave the main road and take to a mountain path. Being by this time tired, dusty and very thirsty I found a secluded spot by a stream, where I slaked my thirst and bathed and sunbathed until late afternoon. I was undisturbed. It was 26 March and my thirtieth birthday. I could not have wished for a better birthday present.

Having had plenty of time to study and memorise my map, I set off towards what could only be a hamlet, called Can Moulins. From there to the frontier was about half a mile. Although no road or track towards it was shown I was sure that once I reached Can Moulins I would find one. Just before dark I located what was probably a mule-track leading out of Can Moulins towards the frontier. The problem was to pass through its cluster of farm buildings and cottages and on to the track without alerting the inhabitants, or more probably their dogs. I muffled my boots with spare socks and walked carefully between the buildings. All was quiet. There were no lights, no voices, no barking. Luckily there was a moon and I could see just well enough to keep going in the right direction – or so I thought. But as I was skirting the last of the farmhouses along the track I put my foot on to … nothing and fell down a terraced bank about ten feet high. No serious harm was done, but I sprained an ankle and badly jarred both heels. After making sure that no bones were broken I found that I could proceed, although not without pain.

I was able to find my way back to the mule-track but in an hour or two the moon set and in the pitch darkness I could not continue. Believing that I was by then well clear of any habitation, I went a yard or two off the track, lay down in the middle of some bushes and went to sleep. Despite the hardness of the ground and the cold I managed to stay asleep until daybreak. When I awoke and found myself, fully clothed, lying in extreme discomfort with a throbbing ankle in the middle of a small wood, I could not for a moment or two think where I was or why I was there. As full consciousness returned, and I realised that I was within a few hundred metres of the Spanish frontier, I began to wonder whether I would be able to make it. There was certainly cover if I had to hide from a frontier patrol – although the thought of trained dogs was disturbing. But what about my ankle? Would I be able to cover the distance, let alone dart in behind the trees if anyone should appear?

I stood up, taking as much weight as possible off my left foot. It was painful, but as I gradually increased the weight on the foot the pain got no worse. As the initial stiffness wore off I found that I could move along fairly well. Having relocated the mule-track I set off along it in the direction of Col d'Arès. It was fortunate that the track led through wooded country because I heard voices and stopped to look and listen. Through the trees I glimpsed two or three men moving about, and a couple of carts or waggons with horses or mules. Evidently they were foresters. I kept out of sight and they moved away. But I thought it prudent to lie low for another half-hour or so. Not that I expected the local folk to give me away, but once one let oneself be seen one became a danger to people who might at any time be questioned by a German patrol.

Continuing on my painful way, I thought that I must have reached the frontier, which in so remote an area might not even be marked, when I came to the edge of the trees and saw a wooden signpost with a single arm pointing in a south-easterly (as far as I could judge) direction. The paint, if any, had long since weathered off, but somehow I felt that the arm was indicating Spain. This was the frontier. In a moment I was over it. According to my watch, I had crossed into Spain at 8.25 am.

*　　　*　　　*

The mountain track was abominable. Not only was it now quite steep in places but it was also stony. Going downhill is always harder on the legs and feet than climbing up, and my bad ankle caused me to take frequent rests. I had not covered any great distance when I met my first Spaniard. We managed to converse in French – by that time

I had an ear for the strongly-rolled 'r's of Provence. The man told me that the day before some Germans had been to his farm, well inside Spain, asking if he had seen any escapers. This news spurred me on, but even so it took me all day to drag myself down the mountainside. The first village I came to was Massenet-de-Colbranys. It was beginning to get dark; had it not been for my ankle I should have at least tried to skirt the village without being seen and carry on next day towards the Mediterranean. My plan had been to reach the railway which runs south from Perpignan, through Figueras and Gerona to Barcelona where, I felt sure, I should be safe in the care of the British Consul General. I intended to bum a ride on a goods train, rather than try to buy a railway ticket with French francs and invite arrest.

As it was, I really did not find it in me to go much further that day and so I decided to try to make telephone contact with the British Consul General and hope for the best. As I approached Massenet I descried a single telephone line on poles entering the village from the south-east side. Once in the village, I limped along to where the line disappeared into a house. I checked that I still had a couple of small gold French coins which I had brought with me from Geneva, in the belief that gold still talked in any man's language. I knocked at the door of what I took to be the telephone exchange. It was opened by a crone. My conversation earlier with the peasant on the mountainside had made me over-confident. I found it impossible to make myself understood. I was reduced to repeating, 'Consul de Inglaterra en Barcelona. Je veux lui téléphoner.'

Rather unwillingly, the old woman let me come in to the house; through a doorway I could see a small telephone exchange, dimly lit. Producing the gold coins I proffered them hopefully. There was no response. I began to have a nasty feeling that the crone was playing for time. Had there not been a small boy peeping out from behind her black skirts when she opened the door? If so, what had become of him?

As I was pondering this the door of the house was flung open and in came a Civil Guard, still doing up his uniform. Without a word he beckoned me to follow him. The guard turned out to be very civil. He took me to his guardhouse and showed me the cell in which, he explained apologetically, I should have to remain for the time being. I think that I managed to convey to him that I was a British naval officer who had been a POW in Italy and that I wished my presence to be reported to our Consul General in Barcelona. After a quarter of an hour or so, as I sat on the bed in the cell, the guard came and let me out, then brought me into the kitchen which adjoined the cell block.

I presumed that he had by now made his report to the nearest authority for, having introduced me to his wife, he said, 'Tomorrow I must take you to Figueras. But now you shall eat,' and motioned me to be seated at the table.

When one is very hungry the smell of an omelette cooking – especially a Spanish omelette – is so superbly promising that to eat it, when it is placed before you, is almost an anti-climax. Almost, but not quite. And the glass of red wine which accompanied it banished forever any tendency on my part to dismiss Spanish red as unworthy of drinking. This was ambrosia accompanied by nectar. Conversation was somewhat stilted. Apart from lack of a common language – neither the guard's French nor my Spanish were up to much – the relationship was unusual. I did not wish to appear too concerned about the possibility of a German patrol turning up. We were, after all, still within five kilometres or so of the frontier.

As soon as I had finished that delicious omelette I was invited to return to the cell and duly locked in. Sleep, on a real if not very well-sprung bed, came easily enough. In the morning, after a cup of coffee and a slice of bread, I boarded a bus, accompanied by the guard, and we set off for Figueras.

The journey of rather less than fifteen kilometres took nearly an hour, what with the terrible road and numerous stops at nowhere in particular. When eventually we arrived in the middle of the town I was handed over to the Comisaria de Policia, Frontera Zona Oriental and bundled briskly into a not very large room containing at least a dozen other people. As far as I could make out they were all French – men and women – and had just arrived in Spain by various routes.

Before I had had time to find out more about my companions I was searched, finger-printed and hauled before an interrogating officer. He was in plain clothes but he was a German, and I felt bound to give him only the minimum of information in response to his questions. It was no use, in the circumstances, trying to conceal the fact that I had just come over the frontier from occupied France, and I thought it reasonable to let him know that I had been a POW in Italy and had come from there via Switzerland. Figueras is over twenty kilometres inside Spain and it seemed to me outrageous that a German officer should be conducting interrogations in a neutral country. On rejoining the other prisoners I complained about this to a couple with whom I had been in conversation. It transpired that they were on their way from France to North Africa, having reason to believe that the Gestapo was on their trail. Fortunately they had good and sufficient documents, and were confident of being released almost at once and permitted to go on to Barcelona. With great kindness these two offered to pass the word to the British Consul General that I was in custody at Figueras.

The helpful French couple did me another good turn before they went on their way. It is (or was) the custom in Spanish prisons that the relatives of the inmates are expected to feed them. As midday approached, my French friends, aware of the local form, pointed out to one of the Civil Guards that as they had no relatives in the immediate vicinity they were liable to go hungry. The guard evidently saw the point of this and, encouraged by the sight of money, undertook to obtain some bread, salami and tomatoes. When this arrived these kind and thoughtful French people told me that they had made sure that there would be enough for me. I did not refuse my share.

The room in which I was kept for the next day and a half was extremely dirty, and the toilet arrangements were the worst which I had encountered since being in the POW transit camp at Capua. It was a relief to be taken out, handcuffed to a young Frenchman who was not lucky enough to have a passport, and marched through the streets of Figueras to the railway station – even if the natural courtesy of the Spanish people did not prevent them from gazing curiously upon us two felons. At the station our guards picked up a couple of young women, who accompanied our little party in the train to Gerona. Perhaps out of a feeling that they were out of line by entertaining women while on duty the guards took off our handcuffs.

At Gerona station I was astonished and delighted when a smiling, sober-suited man approached with outstretched hand saying, 'You must be Lieutenant Ian McGeoch. I am Rapley of the consulate in Barcelona,' adding something appropriate in Spanish to my guards. As they had put the handcuffs on again I was unable to grasp Mr Rapley's hand. However, I left him in no doubt about my thankfulness at seeing him. He regretted that he would be unable to obtain my release there and then: I would have to submit to a few more days of incarceration in Gerona while the formalities were completed.

I have a feeling that the prison at Gerona in which I soon found myself is still there. It was a forbidding building, with a look of permanence. Not all the prisoners were confined to cells, however. Indeed, in one very long room through which I passed there were scores of young men, sitting or lying about on palliasses, who were no more criminal than I was. They were, I was told, survivors from the Italian battleship *Roma* which had been sunk on 9 September 1943 by the Luftwaffe when on her way to surrender to the Allies.

COPY

COPY

Dirección General de Seguridad,
        Comisaria de Policia,
                Frontera Zona Oriental.
FIGUERAS.
                        Iltmo. Señor,

No.2865

            En cumplimiento de lo ordenado tengo
el honor de participar a V.S. que en el
dia de hoy ha sido atenido e ingresado en
la Carcel Provincial de Gerona a disposicion del Excmo. Sr. Gobernador Civil
de la Provincia por haber entrado en Espana clandestinamente, el que dijo ser y
llamarse.
            JUAN MAC GEOCH de 30 anos, casado,
marinero, hijo de Lauchlan y Margaret,
natural de Helensburgh (Inglaterra) con
domicilio en Switzerland, calle Gandolle
No.14, al cual en el momento de su
detencion le fueron intervenidos veiticinco
mil, novecientos cincuenta y cinco francos
franceses (25,955) y dos monedas de oro de
veite francos franceses, cuyas cantidades
despues de entregar el resguardo corres-
pondiente al interesado, fueron de positadas
en la Sucursal del Banco de Espana en
Gerona a disposicion del Juzgado de
Delitos Monetarios.
            Dios guarde a V.S. muchos anos
                Figueras 28 de Marzo de 1944
                    EL COMISARIO JEFE

                    (aff) Juan MARCOS

    Iltmo. Sr. Consul de Inglaterra,
                en Barcelona.

Letter from the Spanish police informing the British Consul in Barcelona of the author's arrival
in Spain, dated 28 March 1944.

208

Why they had not been repatriated I cannot imagine, except that General Franco's fascist government in Spain continued to hope that the Nazis would win. Many of those who had opposed Franco in the Spanish Civil War were still prisoners in Gerona. One of them who spoke excellent English – he had many friends, he said, in Oxford University – was most informative. It was mandatory, he told me, for the clothing of everyone who came into the prison to be taken away and fumigated. In fact as a 'trusty' it was one of his jobs to collect the clothing, and would I kindly let him have mine. By now I had been given a cell, so I started to undress. I dallied, while my new acquaintance talked. From time to time, he said in an astonishingly resigned way, one of the political prisoners would be taken away and shot without trial. Face to face with such tragedy my own immediate problem seemed so insignificant as to be hardly worth mentioning. It so happened that I had been able to buy in Geneva two wrist watches for my wife. One was a Longines and rather special; the other was more of a workaday watch, but good. Helpful as ever, Meg Todd-Naylor had sewn them into the lining of my overcoat for me. I believed that despite some rough treatment the watches were still intact. However, I did not expect that they would survive the fumigation process. What was to be done? I am afraid that I took advantage of the good nature of my new-found friend and let him think, in a conspiratorial fashion, that in the lining of my overcoat were a couple of tiny packets containing information of vital importance to Allied intelligence. Could he possibly, I asked, ensure that my overcoat was fumigated, if at all, very lightly indeed? To this he was happy to agree, and he was as good as his word. The watches were in due course found by their delighted recipient to be in perfect working order.

Disinfecting one's clothing, on entry into a prison, seemed not unreasonable. But I took grave exception to what now followed. A man approached brandishing a pair of hair-clippers and invited me to sit down and have my hair shorn. I replied that I did not intend to submit to this and asked to see someone in authority. A crowd of men quickly collected, scenting a diversion. They were mostly political detainees, I gathered. They were unsmiling although not unfriendly. Then a prison officer arrived. I asked him for an interpreter and two of the detainees stepped forward, one of whom offered his services in English, the other in French. Through both of them I expressed a firm wish to see the commandant of the prison or his deputy. I was given to understand that the prison officer was the commandant's representative. Accepting this, I caused him to be informed that I was an officer in the British Royal Navy, that if my head was to be shaved it would have to be done by force, and that I would report the matter to the British government through my ambassador in Madrid. There was a certain amount of ironic mirth at this amongst the onlookers. They did not know that I had already been in contact with our Consulate General and in any case their own experience of Franco's dictatorship was not such as to let them share my confidence that justice would prevail. In this view they were confirmed by the reaction of the prison officer, who became choleric with anger and hustled me into a small cell, assisted by one of his mates.

Helped by the interpreters I reaffirmed that if my head was to be shaved it would have to be done by force. I offered to remain isolated in the cell rather than submit to the indignity. My offer was not accepted. A box was fetched and I was forced to sit on this while the prison officer clipped away. I did not put up more than a token resistance. What concerned me particularly was this fresh evidence of the dubious character of Spanish neutrality. Thinking also, in my innocence, that the British Consul General would have me out of Gerona within a day or two, I felt it absurd that I should be treated as if I was inside for a well-merited 'stretch'.

As things turned out, the stretch I did have to do was a great deal longer than I had bargained for. As the days dragged by in that filthy gaol, and I barely subsisted on a starvation diet of the vilest food imaginable, I began to wonder if the Allies had suffered a severe reverse, so that General Franco's hopes of a Nazi victory had been revived. Admittedly, Mr Rapley of the Consulate General had said that it would be 'a few days' before I could be released. But my natural optimism had enabled me to bank on that 'few' being two or three at most. After a week had passed my euphoria at having made it into Spain had evaporated. What could have gone wrong? I never found out. When the rather bad-tempered prison officer eventually appeared at my cell door with my clothes and told me to get ready to go it was ten days since I had been put inside.

The excellent Mr Rapley had no need to apologise for the delay, although he did so. The Spanish authorities, after all, had nothing else to do but deal with cases such as mine, and why should they short-circuit their beautifully constructed bureaucratic process? I gathered from Mr Rapley during the train journey from Gerona to Barcelona, which differed in almost every possible way from that by which I had been transported from Figueras to Gerona, that ten days at General Franco's pleasure was about par for the course for those innocent of any crime, and not charged with any.

Nothing marred the bliss of being accommodated, at the expense, ultimately, I have no doubt of the British taxpayer, in a comfortable hotel in the Rambla. The next day, having had a good rest and excellent 'browsing and sluicing,' as Bertie Wooster would have said, I presented myself at the British Consulate General and was interviewed by the Consul himself. Mr Farquhar had all the hallmarks of a powerful operator. Military in appearance and bearing, with a brusque manner, which I felt to be rather uncalled for considering that I had just succeeded in coming through occupied France more or less on my own and was keen to talk about it, he took me somewhat aback. I know now that I was only the latest of an almost continual flow of British servicemen, mostly airmen who had bailed out over northern France or the Netherlands, who had been arriving unannounced and undocumented in the Consul General's parish since the middle of 1940. I was lucky and privileged to see Mr Farquhar at all. He was a very busy man. But not too busy, I found out two or three days later, to have informed the Port Admiral of Barcelona that a British submarine captain who had escaped from Italy was residing for the time being in the city.

A message from the consulate advised me to expect a call from a representative of the Spanish naval authorities. I thought that this might be the equivalent of our custom in the Royal Navy of sending an 'officer of the guard' to a foreign warship encountered in harbour in time of peace, in order to convey the compliments of the British senior officer and establish friendly liaison. What I had not expected was a visit from the admiral himself, accompanied by his flag lieutenant carrying, as a present for me, a bottle of brandy and a box of cigars. We had an interesting conversation, which reinforced a view that I had already formed in a vague way that the Spanish navy was less 'political' than the Spanish army, or for that matter the Spanish air force. Its neutrality tended, also, to be pro- rather than anti-British. Why this should be so I was not sure, but ex-King Alfonso XIII shared with our own King George V a love of the sea, of all things naval and of racing in large yachts. So much so that a near-contemporary of mine as a midshipman in the British fleet was Prince Juan, whose son was to become Spain's first constitutional – and successful – monarch on the demise of General Franco.

Once again I found myself waiting for something to happen. To begin with I filled in some time by writing a letter to the British naval attaché in Madrid, Captain Mason Scott, to complain formally about my treatment in Gerona prison. I doubt whether this went much further than the naval attaché's waste paper basket, but it gave me some satisfaction. More to the purpose was my official narrative, encompassed in ten typewritten pages, of my activities since 21 April 1943, when I was made a POW. I was able to keep a copy of this document and I have found it useful in providing dates and other key information. Unfortunately, it ends with my arrival in Spain. What follows, therefore, covering the remainder of my stay in Spain and the 'end run' back to Britain is what I can recall.

I remember that I was able to wander about Barcelona without any restriction. I had no money for shopping, just enough pocket money to pay the odd tram fare and to travel on the funicular railway to the peak above the city in order to enjoy the spectacular view. I inspected the still unfinished and almost grotesque modern baroque Church of the Sagrada Familia designed by Gaudi. In the evenings I mingled with the crowd strolling in the mild air of early spring along the Rambla, the first pedestrian precinct that I had encountered. Given the Spanish propensity for dining late – 10.00 pm and after – the Rambla seemed to be an ideal amenity. I had time, now, to wonder whether my wife had twigged, from the careful wording of my last letter posted to her in Geneva, that I had been about to cross occupied France. It seems that news of my arrival in Spain passed via the British Embassy in Madrid to London where MI9, the British secret service responsible for fostering escape and evasion, would have been the recipient of the information. At any rate, with the prospect of an imminent move from Barcelona to Madrid and from there to Gibraltar, it did not worry me too much at this stage that I could not communicate directly with home.

The official narrative of my movements was dated 24 April 1944 at Barcelona. So I reckon that it was the 25th or 26th when Mr Rapley called for me first thing in the morning at my hotel and took me, still wearing the overcoat with my two precious watches in the lining, to the main railway station. There he bought me a ticket and put me on the express train for Madrid. As we progressed, at first south-westwards along the Mediterranean coast to Tarragona, then westwards to Saragossa, the perfect aptness of Shakespeare's epithet 'tawny' Spain became evident. To my regret I did not have a map on which to keep track of our location. The more so as place names which had featured in reports of the Spanish Civil War appeared from time to time on the stations through which we passed.

When eventually our train arrived in Madrid nearly two hours

The author's safe conduct, issued in Barcelona, 24 April 1944.

late, it was quite wonderful to be met on the platform by a smiling,
uncomplaining man from the British Embassy, who bore me off in his
sleek car to his most comfortable flat in a fashionable part of Madrid.
My latest saviour – how much kind and thoughtful attention I received
from so many members of our diplomatic missions in Switzerland and
in Spain – introduced himself as Commander Gomez-Behr, Assistant
Naval Attaché. A native of Gibraltar, Gomez-Behr was singularly well
qualified to facilitate the clandestine departure from Spain of those
who had clandestinely entered it. I had to be patient for a day or two.
Security was such that plans were not talked about. Even after nearly
a month in Spain I did not appreciate that the British Embassy staff,
since the fall of France in June 1940, had been heavily engaged in
receiving in Madrid and passing on to Gibraltar an almost continual
stream of British escapers and evaders who had entered Spain and
been staged through Bilbao, San Sebastian and Barcelona. Despite the
delicacy of our relations with Spain in the early stages of the war,
when Hitler and Mussolini were in the ascendant, attachés of our
embassy such as Michael Creswell and Henry Hankey managed to

spirit individuals or groups by rail or road down to La Linea and across the few hundred metres of no man's land into Gibraltar.

Left to myself, I was able to spend a couple of days wandering about Madrid. The weather was sunny and spring-like. My recollections of this enforced tourism are twofold. First, I have an abiding impression of a great city suspended in the midst of the blue empyrean. This I derived from looking along the great, wide streets and avenues, running at right angles, each of which seemed to stretch to the horizon before falling away towards the plains below. Secondly, there was the Prado. There, in their rightful home, were the vast royal masterpieces of Velasquez, the gaunt figures of El Greco, the proud nobles of Goya – and his revolutionary horrors also – the domesticity of Murillo and so many other great paintings, not by any means all Spanish.

One evening after dark, Gomez-Behr (the only member of the embassy staff whom I had so far encountered) took me to the railway station, still wearing my precious overcoat and carrying my much travelled rucksack. There he introduced me to a shadowy figure whose name, I think, was Beaumont, and disappeared almost before I had had time to thank him for his hospitality. When I boarded the train, having been provided by Beaumont with a ticket and a sleeper reservation, I noticed three or four other figures who had that shifty look and the appearance of being dressed considerably below their means which marks out the survivor from shipwreck and the escaper or evader alike. But mingling was discouraged and I dutifully kept myself to myself.

I certainly slept well as the first thing I remember is being rousted out at a station, which must have been La Linea, very early in the morning and bundled into the back of a car. A short ride was followed by a longish halt then a rather bumpy few minutes as the car was driven smartly across no man's land and the main runway of Gibraltar's airfield to the British frontier post. The door of the car was opened. English voices. I felt a sudden sense of anti-climax. This persisted as I was whisked, now comfortably seated, along the well-known Main Street of Gib and up the hill to Thorn Cottage, where George Symonds and two of his colleagues on the staff of the Flag Officer, Gibraltar, were living. Most kindly they had arranged that I should stay with them.

I must have looked an odd character with my peculiar clothes and shaven cranium – although my hair had already started to grow again, so that it was just beginning to merit the description *en brosse* or something more lavatorial in naval officers' language. My hosts treated me exactly as I needed to be treated, namely as one of themselves. It was as if I had been away on leave for a short while between appointments. As Staff Officer (Operations) George was able to arrange a passage back for me without delay. In the ordinary course of events this would have been in the bare centre section of a bomber or the less uncomfortable but slower alternative of a Coastal Command flying-boat. But, by a happy chance, there lay alongside the South Mole what looked like a battleship of the *King George* class. This, in fact, the great ship was not. She was HMS *Centurion*, a vintage battle-wagon of the Jutland era which, between the wars, had been the world's first wireless-controlled target ship.

George, seeing me at the window as he came in to the room, said, 'Do you realise who the captain of *Centurion* is? It's Sammy Woods, and he's offered you a passage to the UK with him. He needs another watch keeper and he thinks that it won't do you any harm to get your sea legs back.'

The prospect of serving at sea again and above all under the command of Sammy Woods appeared to me infinitely preferable to hanging about awaiting transport by so unreliable, not to say risky, a means as the next warplane with a spare seat. Within two or three days I was installed in the great cabin right aft in the old *Centurion*, in which during her Grand Fleet days a succession of proud captains had lived and entertained their officers and guests while in harbour. I was duly made a member of the wardroom mess and once again began to live the normal life of a watch keeping lieutenant in a capital ship. The *Centurion* had long since been demilitarised in her role as target and, subsequently, decoy capital ship; and her navigation arrangements had remained extremely primitive by 1944 standards. The radars and the huge guns in their turrets, not to mention one of the funnels, were all dummies. All we could do was to take station meekly at the end of one of the columns in a convoy which, sweeping far out into the Atlantic, now almost free from U-boats, eventually turned north and came safely into soundings. The convoy then split up into sections, some bound for the Clyde, some for Liverpool and some, which included the *Centurion*[1], up channel, safe under the umbrella of a fighter defence which had by now gained virtually total control of the air over the United Kingdom and adjacent waters.

In due course we came to berth in Portsmouth harbour – the scene

---

[1] In June 1944 HMS *Centurion*, still under the command of Sammy Woods, was sunk off the Normandy beaches to form part of the artificial breakwater, without which the follow-up support of the Allied Expeditionary Force would have been impossible.

of so many homecomings from far-flung commissions, when wives and husbands were reunited and infants, seen for the first time, were held out for inspection. In my case, despite my unseen baby boy, whose advent had been announced on my arrival at Gibraltar in HM Submarine P228 in October 1942, the reunion and baby-viewing had to wait all of two days. Sammy Woods kindly permitted me to leave his ship almost the moment the gangway was in place. But there was the formality of reporting to MI9 in London for debriefing.[1] My dear wife, not absolutely calm at the end of the telephone, did not take too kindly to this. But what the hell? I was safely home and the two days would pass somehow. They did . . .

[1] My Resistance comrades had heard by this time on the BBC that 'Le tabac du Petit Pierre est dans la boîte à Tapioca.'

Postscript

In 1953 I had a week or two on leave between appointments. I had just completed about eighteen months as executive officer (second in command) of the cruiser HMS *Euryalus* on the Mediterranean station, and was about to become executive officer of the naval barracks at Portsmouth. We were living in a rented cottage near Danbury in Essex. One Sunday evening our friends Miles and Lalage Pitts-Tucker came to supper with us, bringing a friend who was staying with them. Her name was Marguerite de Revel and she was a most personable woman in her thirties. By the time that we had reached the coffee stage she and I had established a rapport. Suddenly my mind went back to that day in March 1944 when I had found myself sharing a rather confined space with a crowd of complete strangers in a Spanish gaol. I recalled with immense gratitude the consideration shown me by a young Frenchwoman and her companion. 'Miss de Revel,' I asked, 'were you by any chance in prison at Figueras, late in March 1944?'

'Yes,' she said. 'I wondered which of us would be the first to speak.'

Ship's crest of HM Submarine *Splendid* (formerly P228)

Appendix A

HM Submarine *Splendid*: from Admiralty records of 2 May 1943

Missing presumed killed

Bernard Boulton
Leslie Bryant
Reginald Croker
Frederick Freeman
Alexander Galloway
Leslie Gillispie
Eric Goodwin
Leslie Herbert
William Hodgson
Leslie Kempthorne
Douglas Lawrence
William Legassick
Thomas Macken
James Moody
Warren Orrom
Francis Pilton
Kenneth Savill
Leslie Smith

Prisoners of war

William Auckland
Albert Aynsley
Robert Balkwill
Kenelm Burridge
Percival Clarke
Jack Collison
Victor Davis
Harold Dinsdale
Samuel Dixon
Charles Foulkes
Leonard Frost
Frank Goodhall
Gordon Hardy
Robert Harrison
Donald Holland
John King
Frederick Knighton
Denis Laidlaw
George Marshall
Ian McGeoch
Stanley Paine
James Rae
William Ramsden
Denis Saunders
William South
Victor Strudwick
Cecil Warren
Bernard Williams
Albert Wood
Ernest Worthington

Appendix B

Seedie's Submarine List: HM Submarine *Splendid*

Built by HM Dockyard, Chatham. Launched 19 January 1942. Scuttled after being damaged by the German Destroyer *Hermes* off Capri on 21 April 1943

London Gazette – 6 April 1943 – Sank the Italian Destroyer *Aviere* off Bizerta on 17 December 1942 and one other Destroyer and three Supply Ships in the Mediterranean

Person and service if not RN	Rank/Rtg	Award	Investiture
McGEOCH, Ian Lachlan Mackay	Lt	DSO	26-3-46
BANNAR MARTIN, Rawdon	Lt	DSC	13-7-43
McMILLAN, Harold Ernest	WtEng	DSC	19-10-43
CASTLE, Harold C/J 101299	ACPO	DSM	6-11-45
DAVIS, Victor Ralph C/MX 56235	ERA4	DSM	Posted
DIXON, Samuel Hughes C/JX 125574	PO	DSM	NOK
FREEMAN, Fred D/JX 285923	AB	DSM	NOK
SOUTH, William Herbert P/SSX 22975	LSea	DSM	Posted
LOWER, Donald Horace James P/JX 147088	AB	MID	N/A
MARSHAL, GEORGE HENRY D/KX 118272	Sto	MID	N/A
SAUNDERS, Albert Denis D/MX 52852	CERA	MID	N/A
WILLIAMS, Bernard Ralph P/JX 134383	ALSea	MID	N/A

MID   Mentioned in Dispatches

London Gazette 10 October 1944 – Sunk on her sixth War Patrol

Person and service if not RN	Rank/Rtg	Award	Investiture
BALKWILL, Robert Gowan RNVR	TLt	DSC	20-7-45
McGEOCH, Ian Lachlan Mackay	Lt	DSC	26-3-46
RAMSDEN, William C/SSX 21985	ALSea	DSM	Posted
WORTHINGTON, Ernest John C/MX 66750	ERA	DSM	Posted
AUCKLAND, William R D/JX 141793	LdgSig VS3	MID	N/A
AYNSLEY, Albert Errington D/JX 237671	AB	MID	N/A
FOULKES, Charles Gordon D/JX 151153	APOTel	MID	N/A
FROST, Leonard D/KX 76235	StoPO	MID	N/A
HARDY, George Gordon RNVR	Lt	MID	N/A
CROKER, Reginald John D/KX 76748	StoI	MID(Post)	N/A
LAWRENCE, Douglas D/JX 142867	APO	MID(Post)	N/A
ORROM, Warren Stanley C/J 113100	PO	MID(Post)	N/A
PILTON, Francis John D/SSX 22220	AB	MID(Post)	N/A

Position of successful attacks:

1. 18.4.41 - tanker *Franco Martelli,* (10,535 tons) sunk by HMS *Urge*

2. 16.11.42 - A/A schooner *Sao Paolo,* sunk by gunfire by HMS *P.228*

3. 21.11.42 - destroyer *Velite* torpedoed by HMS *P.228*

4. 23.11.42 - *Luigi Favorita* (9,576 tons) sunk by gunfire by HMS *P.228*

5. 14.12.42 - *Sant' Antioca* (5,048 tons) sunk by HMS *P.228*

6. 17.12.42 - destroyer *Aviere* sunk by HMS *P.228*

7. 15.1.43 - *Emma* (7,931 tons) sunk by HMS *P.228*

8. 19.1.43 - one schooner and one armed trawler sunk by gunfire and *Commercio* (765 tons) sunk by HMS *P.228*

9. 17.2.43 - *XXI Aprile* (4,787 tons) sunk by HMS *P.228/Splendid*

10. 17.3.43 - tanker *Devoli* (3,006 tons) sunk by HMS *P.228/Splendid*

11. 21.3.43 - tanker *Giorgio* (4,887 tons) sunk by HMS *P.228/Splendid*

12. 21.4.43 - HMS *P.228/Splendid* depth-charged and sunk by German-manned destroyer *Hermes*

Active service, 1940 - 1943

Escape and evasion, April 1943 - May 1944